Fundamentals of Embedded Software with the ARM® Cortex-M3

Fundamentals of Embedded Software with the ARM® Cortex-M3

Second Edition

Daniel W. Lewis

Upper Saddle River Boston Columbus San Francisco New York
Indianapolis London Toronto Sydney Singapore Tokyo Montreal
Dubai Madrid Hong Kong Mexico City Munich Paris Amsterdam Cape Town

Vice President and Editorial Director, ECS: *Marcia J. Horton*
Executive Editor: *Andrew Gilfillan*
Vice-President, Production: *Vince O'Brien*
Executive Marketing Manager: *Tim Galligan*
Marketing Assistant: *Jon Bryant*
Permissions Project Manager: *Karen Sanatar*
Senior Managing Editor: *Scott Disanno*
Production Project Manager / Editorial Production Manager: *Pat Brown*
Creative Director: *Jayne Conte*
Cover Designer: *Bruce Kenselaar*
Cover Image: *Fotolia: Nature © Alex*
Composition: *Jouve India*
Full-Service Project Management: *Pavithra Jayapaul, Jouve India*
Printer/Binder: *Courier Westford*
Cover Printer: *Lehigh-Phoenix*
Typeface: *10/12 Times*

005 .133119 LEWIS   2013

Lewis, D. W. 1946–

Fundamentals of embedded
software with the ARM

Credits and acknowledgments borrowed from other sources and reproduced, with permission, in this textbook appear on appropriate page within text.

Many of the designations by manufacturers and seller to distinguish their products are claimed as trademarks. Where those designations appear in this book, and the publisher was aware of a trademark claim, the designations have been printed in initial caps or all caps.

ARM is a registered trademark of ARM Ltd., 110 Fulbourn Road, Cambridge, GB-CB1 9NJ, Great Britain.

MATLAB is a registered trademark of The MathWorks, Inc., 3 Apple Hill Drive, Natick, MA 01760-2098.

Pearson Education Ltd., *London*
Pearson Education Singapore, Pte. Ltd
Pearson Education Canada, Inc.
Pearson Education—Japan
Pearson Education Australia PTY, Limited
Pearson Education North Asia, Ltd., *Hong Kong*
Pearson Educación de Mexico, S.A. de C.V.
Pearson Education Malaysia, Pte. Ltd.
Pearson Education, Inc., *Upper Saddle River, New Jersey*

Library of Congress Cataloging-in-Publication Data

Lewis, D.W. (Daniel Wesley)
  Fundamentals of embedded software : with the ARM® Cortex-M3 / Daniel W. Lewis. – 2nd ed.
    p. cm.
  Includes bibliographical references and index.
  ISBN-13: 978-0-13-291654-7 (alk. paper)
  ISBN-10: 0-13-291654-1 (alk. paper)
  1. Embedded computer systems—Programming. 2. C (Computer program language)
  3. Assembler language (Computer program language) I. Title.
  TK7895.E42L49 2012
  005. 13'3–dc23

                                                        2011043104

10 9 8 7 6 5 4 3 2 1

ISBN-13: 978-0-13-291654-7

ISBN-10: 0-13-291654-1

Dedication

It may have been many more years ago than I would care to admit, but I do still remember what it was like to be an undergraduate. Like my own students, I too had to take an occasional class in which much of the material came from slides and handouts because the instructor was writing a textbook for the course. So, to all those students who have had to suffer through this same experience with me, who have unknowingly helped me organize and clarify the material, who have tactfully pointed out my mistakes, and who have fueled my inspiration—thank you. This book is for you and those that follow in your footsteps.

Contents

Preface

How many computers are in your home? Most people might answer two or three. How many *microprocessors* are in your home? Think carefully before you answer. Hint: It is a lot more than two or three! In fact, it is actually even a lot more than 10 or 20! Today microprocessors are embedded in almost every electronic appliance you can think of and many that you probably would not. They have become pervasive—not only in our home, but in our workplace, our automobiles, airplanes, stoplights, supermarkets, cell phones, and so forth—in short, in almost every aspect of our lives.

Embedded systems offer students an exciting opportunity to express their creativity. What students have not dreamed of designing the next new gadget that would capture the imagination of the public? Our challenge as educators is to capitalize on that excitement and channel the energy of those young minds to motivate mastery of a subject matter!

What Is New in This Edition

Virtually a completely rewritten edition, featuring the following significant changes:

1. Covers the architecture and instruction set of the ARM Cortex-M3 v7 processor, replacing the earlier coverage of the Intel IA32 processor. The 32-bit ARM processor was selected because (1) 75% of the embedded systems designed between 2004 and 2010 used 32-bit processors,[1] (2) the use of ARM processors is growing rapidly, from 19% of all embedded applications in 2007 to more than 35% in 2010,[2] and (3) the ARM® Cortex-M3™ is specifically designed for real-time embedded applications.

2. Covers features that make the ARM Cortex-M3 processor well suited for embedded applications, including conditional execution that avoids flushing the instruction pipeline and interrupt "tail chaining," "late arrival processing" of interrupts, and "bit-banding" for addressing individual bits in memory and I/O.

3. Covers the ARM Procedure Call Standard and the appropriate choice of registers for function parameters, return values, and temporary variables.

4. Adds a new chapter on "Implementing Arithmetic," and reorganizes and expands the coverage of assembly language programming and I/O from three to four chapters.

---

[1] Source: Jerry Krasner, Ph.D., Dolores A. Krasner, "Embedded Market Forecasters: 2010 Embedded Hardware/Software Design Preferences."

[2] Source: VDC Research Group, "Embedded Software & Tools 2010 Market Intelligence Service, Track 2: Embedded System Engineering Survey Data, Volume 1: Operating Systems."

5. Expanded coverage of binary addition and subtraction, and new material on using shifts, adds, and subtracts as alternatives to multiplication by a constant, reciprocal multiplication as alternative to division by a constant, and a fully worked example about multiplication of fixed-point real numbers.

6. Updated to reflect C99 standards for the C programming language.

7. Vastly expanded set of problems at the end of Chapters 1 to 12, including answers to selected problems.

8. The Companion Website includes 14 new laboratory programming assignments based on Texas Instruments' EKI-LM3S811 evaluation kit that includes the LM3S811 evaluation board, the source code of TI's Stellaris Peripheral Driver Library, and the Kickstart edition of IAR Systems' Embedded Workbench Integrated Development Environment. The LM3S811 evaluation board provides programmable timers, a thumbwheel-driven potentiometer, A/D converters, a graphic display, user and reset push-buttons, a user LED, parallel ports, serial UARTs, a USB port, and a JTAG connector.

9. Uses the open source Free RTOS real-time kernel to develop multithreaded laboratory assignments that investigate scheduling, processor utilization, thread starvation, unbounded priority inversion, deadlock, mutexes, semaphores, and queues.

10. Complete plans are provided on the Companion Website for an easy to assemble and inexpensive breadboard that is used in the last four laboratory assignments to develop multithreaded applications for feedback control of a small DC motor.

Objectives

The ultimate goal of this text is to lay a foundation that supports the multithreaded style of programming and high-reliability requirements of embedded software. Within this context, the following objectives were established:

1. To understand how data is represented at the machine level and to appreciate the consequences and limitations of those representations.

2. To master those language-specific features that are used most frequently in embedded systems, such as bit manipulation and variant access.

3. To obtain a programmer's view of processor architecture and how programming at the level of assembly is sometimes necessary or appropriate.

4. To learn about the various styles of I/O programming, and ultimately how an event-driven approach allows one to separate data processing into a number of independent threads of computation.

5. To learn about preemptive and non-preemptive multithreaded programming, shared resources, and critical sections, and how scheduling can be used to manage system response time.

6. To reinforce basic programming skills by revisiting such topics as scope, parameter passing, recursion, and memory allocation.

7. To learn about the problems associated with shared memory objects, how shared memory is affected by memory allocation, and what programming practices can be used to minimize the occurrence of shared memory.

Intended Audience

This text is intended to serve as the basis for a sophomore level course in a computer science, computer engineering, or electrical engineering curriculum. Such a course is envisioned as a replacement for the traditional course on computer organization and assembly language programming.

The text presents assembly the way it is most commonly used in practice—to implement small, fast, or special-purpose routines called from a main program written in a high-level language such as C. It thus covers processor organization and assembly language only from a "need-to-know" point of view rather than as a primary objective. This approach affords time within both the text and the course to cover assembly in the context of embedded software. As a result, students not only learn that assembly still has an important role to play, but their discovery of multithreaded programming, preemptive and non-preemptive systems, shared resources, and scheduling helps sustain their interest, feeds their curiosity, and strengthens their preparation for subsequent courses on operating systems, real-time systems, networking, and microprocessor-based design.

At most institutions, the introductory programming sequence (CS1 and CS2) is no longer taught in a procedural programming language such as C or Pascal; rather, the popular approach is to now use an object-oriented programming language such as C++ or Java. Despite the change, it is not uncommon to find one or more upper-division courses still using a procedural language, nor is it uncommon to find such languages still in use in industry. At the author's institution, we solved this paradox by redesigning our traditional assembly language course around the material in this text; it not only created room in an already packed curriculum to cover the procedural approach and to introduce the popular topic of embedded systems, but also offered an opportunity to strengthen student comprehension of parameter passing, scope, and memory allocation schemes that they were first introduced to in CS1 and CS2.

The text assumes that students already know how to program in C, C++, or Java, and that the similarity among the low-level syntax of those languages makes it relatively easy to move to C from either C++ or Java. Rather than covering C in excruciating detail, the text emphasizes those features of C that are employed more frequently in embedded applications and introduces the procedural style through examples and programming assignments that include large amounts of prewritten source code. In principle, the only absolute prerequisite is thus a CS1 course that uses C, C++, or Java. However, additional programming maturity such as acquired from a CS2 course on data structures is strongly recommended.

Programming Assignments and the Companion Website

The text is complemented by a collection of programming assignments described on the Companion Website at www.pearsonhighered.com/lewis. Given that the text is aimed at sophomores, the assignments are intended primarily to illustrate a topic from the text rather than as extended programming projects. As such, most of the source code for each assignment is provided and students are asked to focus only on those parts that relate directly to the topic. Some assignments address related topics not covered in the text, such as A/D conversion, feedback control, and processor utilization. The assignments are intended to be completed in order, and some do depend on work completed in earlier assignments. Assignments 6 to 10 are complete programs that are first run without modification to illustrate an issue, and then modified to explore specific solutions. Programming assignments 11 to 14 require use of the special motor breadboard described on the website.

Programming Assignment		Relevant Chapters	Comments
01	Integer Arithmetic	2, 3	No special hardware required
02	Introduction to Tools		Implements the game of Tetris
03	Time Measurement		Elapsed time, programmed delays, and PWM
04	Analog Devices		Explores A/D, PWM, and Interrupts (in C)
05	Fixed-Point Reals	3, 5, 6, 7	Coding in assembly
06	Processor Utilization		These assignments are complete programs that demonstrate topics that arise in multithreaded applications. Students modify the programs to study or correct performance issues
07	Starvation	10	
08	Mutexes, Semaphores, and Queues	9, 10	
09	Priority Inversion	10	
10	Deadlock	10	
11	Motor Speed Control—Part 1		Requires special motor breadboard
12	Motor Speed Control—Part 2	9, 10	Adds simple multitasking
13	Motor Speed Control—Part 3	9, 10	Adds mutexes, semaphores, and queues
14	Motor Speed Control—Part 4		Adds processor utilization monitoring

Choice of Platform

The processor architecture covered in Chapters 5 to 8 is the 32-bit ARM Cortex-M3. The Stellaris® LM3S811 Evaluation Board that uses this processor and incorporates a number of useful I/O devices is available separately from Texas Instruments as part of the EKI-LM3S811 evaluation kit complete with an integrated software development environment and driver library.

The EKI-LM3S811 evaluation kit.
(*Courtesy of Luminary Micro, Inc.*)

Acknowledgments

This text and the software on the Companion Website would not have been possible without the efforts of a number of people. Of them all, I owe a special thanks to the students and teaching assistants of COEN 20 at Santa Clara University over the past 10 years who witnessed the transition from the first edition to this almost completely re-written second edition, and who have helped fine-tune the text, the problems, and the laboratory assignments.

I also owe a debt of gratitude to many of my colleagues: To Qiang Li and Neil Quinn who endured the unenviable task of teaching from my materials and who graciously suggested a number of improvements to the original text. To Hal Brown and Vasu Alagar who helped me develop a mathematical representation of fixed-point multiplication of real numbers that led to an efficient straight-line implementation in assembly and an explanation of the algorithm that students find relatively easy to understand. To Darren Atkinson whose expertise in C has been invaluable. And thanks to Dana Lasher of North Carolina State University who contributed the telephone call analogy that appears in the chapter on Interrupt-Driven I/O.

I owe a debt of gratitude to Samuel Khorbotly of Ohio Northern University and others who reviewed the draft of the new edition and found my typos, misspellings, grammatical errors, omissions, oversights, and occasional outright blunder. I also would like to express appreciation to the people at Prentice-Hall and their production staff for making the creation of this text over most of 1 year as painless as possible. And finally, I thank Santa Clara University for granting me the sabbatical that made it possible to find the time to complete this revision.

C H A P T E R   1

Introduction

1.1 WHAT IS AN EMBEDDED SYSTEM?

Embedded systems are electronic devices that incorporate microprocessors within their implementations. The main purposes of the microprocessor are to simplify system design and to provide flexibility. Having a microprocessor in the device means that removing bugs, making modifications, or adding new features are only matters of rewriting the software that controls the device. Unlike PCs, however, embedded systems may not have a disk drive and so the software is often stored in a read-only memory (ROM) chip; this means that modifying the software requires either replacing or "reprogramming" the ROM.

As Table 1-1 indicates, embedded systems are found in a wide range of application areas. Originally, they were used only for expensive industrial-control applications, but as technology brought down the cost of dedicated processors, they began to appear in moderately expensive applications such as automobiles, communications and office equipment, and televisions. Today's embedded systems are so inexpensive that they are used in almost every electronic product in our life. For example, the tiny ATMEL 8-bit picoPower AVR processor in Vitality's GlowCap™ (see Figure 1-2) helps people remember to take their medication on time. It can sense when the bottle is opened, transmit that information wirelessly to a Vitality server, flash its LED, and play a ringtone.

Although the typical family may own only one or two personal computers, the number of embedded processors found within their home and cars and among their

FIGURE 1-1   NASA's 2003 Mars Exploration Rover used a BAE Systems RAD6000 32-bit RISC processor and Wind River Systems' VxWorks embedded real-time operating system. *Image credit: NASA/JPL/Cornell University.*

TABLE 1-1 Examples of Embedded Systems

Application Area	Examples
Aerospace	Navigation systems, automatic landing systems, flight altitude controls, engine controls, and space exploration.
Automotive	Fuel injection control, passenger environmental controls, antilock braking systems, air bag controls, and GPS mapping.
Gaming devices	Nintendo's DS, Nintendo Wii, Microsoft Xbox 360, and Sony Playstation 3.
Communications	Satellites; network routers, switches, and hubs.
Computer peripherals	Printers, scanners, keyboards, displays, modems, hard disk drives, and CD-ROM drives.
Home	Dishwashers, microwave ovens, DVD players, televisions, stereos, fire/security alarm systems, lawn sprinkler controls, thermostats, cameras, clock radios, and answering machines.
Industrial	Elevator controls, surveillance systems, and robots.
Instrumentation	Data collection, oscilloscopes, signal generators, signal analyzers, and power supplies.
Medical	Imaging systems (e.g., X-ray, MRI, and ultrasound), patient monitors, and heart pacers.
Office automation	FAX machines, copiers, telephones, and cash registers.
Personal	Personal digital assistants, portable media players, portable e-book readers, pagers, cell phones, and smart phones.

personal belongings is much greater. In many cases, we may not even be aware that a computer is present or do not realize just how pervasive they have become.

What is often surprising is that embedded processors account for virtually 100% of the worldwide production of microprocessors! For every microprocessor produced for use in a desktop computer, more than 100 are produced for use in embedded systems. This should not be surprising considering that the number of embedded microprocessors found in the average middle-class household in North America in 1999 was estimated to be between 40 and 50.[1] You can find them in clock radios, stereos, TVs,

FIGURE 1-2 Vitality's GlowCap™ has an embedded ATMEL 8-bit picoPower AVR processor. *Photo courtesy of Vitality, Inc.*

[1] Jim Turley, "Microprocessors for Consumer Electronics, PDAs, and Communications," Embedded Systems Conference, San Jose, CA, September 26–30, 1999.

FIGURE 1-3   The Sonicare DiamondClean toothbrush uses an 8-bit PIC microprocessor. *Photo courtesy of Philips Consumer Lifestyle.*

VCRs, DVD players, DVRs, game consoles, remote controls, washers, dryers, dishwashers, microwave ovens, refrigerators, coffee makers, thermostats, lawn sprinkler controls, garage door openers, cameras, wired and cellular phones, answering machines, fax machines, pagers, personal digital assistants (PDAs), MP3 players, watches, and even tooth brushes (Figure 1-3).

And what about your car? In 2005, the average luxury car had about 150 embedded microcontrollers and microprocessors for fuel injection systems, antilock braking systems, air bag controls, environmental controls, GPS mapping, seats and seat belts, radio, and so on, and is three times the number in 2002![2]

1.2   WHAT IS UNIQUE ABOUT THE DESIGN GOALS FOR EMBEDDED SOFTWARE?

The objective of this book is to help you learn how to design and implement software for embedded systems. Although you already have some experience writing desktop application programs in a high-level language, writing embedded application programs presents some new challenges regarding *reliability*, *performance*, and *cost*.

FIGURE 1-4   The Vue40 vending machine uses a 16-bit Hitachi H8/3007 cpu. *Photo courtesy of SandenVendo America, Inc.*

---

[2] "Embedded Systems Development Trends: Asia," EE-Time-Asia & Gartner Dataquest, February 2005.

Reliability expectations will place greater responsibility on programmers to eliminate bugs and to design software to tolerate errors and unexpected situations. Many embedded systems have to run 24 hours a day, 7 days a week, and 365 days a year. You cannot just "reboot" when something goes wrong! Hence, good coding practices and thorough testing take on a new level of importance in the realm of embedded processors.

Performance goals will force us to learn and apply new techniques such as *multithreading* and *scheduling*. The need to communicate directly with sensors, actuators, keypads, displays, and so on will require programmers to have a better understanding of how alternative methods for performing input and output provide opportunities to trade speed, complexity, and cost. Although we will usually program in a high-level language for better productivity, use of these alternatives may occasionally require that we drop to the level of the computer and program directly in *assembly language*.

Computers use *fixed precision* and *2's-complement* representation to store and process numeric values. This results in subtle differences from how humans handle numbers, and it is often an unexpected source of problems. Our software will have to live with limitations regarding the range and resolution of numbers. However, as programmers, we need to be sure that we have a comprehensive understanding of the consequence of exceeding these limitations and of how to handle such situations.

Unlike processors embedded in large, expensive systems, consumer products are designed to be mass-produced with a minimal production cost. To be competitive, they must achieve fast time to market and ideally require no modification once in production.

1.3   WHAT DOES "REAL-TIME" MEAN?

Real-time systems process events. Events occurring on system inputs cause other events to occur as system outputs. Examples of input events include such things as the detection of a telephone ring signal, the application of force to the brake pedal of a car, or the opening of a microwave oven's door. The output events produced in response to these input events might be to take the phone line "off-hook," to apply hydraulic pressure to the automobile's brake system, and to turn off the microwave oven.

One of the primary design goals of real-time systems is minimizing response time. A *soft* real-time system is one that is designed to compute the response as fast as possible but does not have an explicit deadline. If a deadline is imposed, the system is known as a *hard* real-time system. Keeping response times of hard real-time systems within the given deadlines is always important, or the entire system may fail to operate properly. For example, an antilock braking system must detect and respond to loss of traction within a few milliseconds; a delay of one or two seconds would be intolerable and potentially deadly.

1.4   WHAT DOES "MULTITHREADING" MEAN?

Embedded systems are real-time systems that have several inputs and outputs and must respond to multiple independent events. For example, the programmable thermostat that controls your furnace must continuously perform three *tasks*: (1) monitor the temperature, (2) monitor the time of day, and (3) scan the keypad for user input. There is only one computer inside the thermostat, but it may perform each of these tasks using a separate *code thread*, as shown in Figure 1-7. Although the threads communicate with each other, for the most part they run independently.

Separating code into threads simplifies software development and maintenance by allowing the programmer to concentrate on one task at a time. However, it also requires that the processor somehow continuously switch among the threads. This

```
do forever {
  measure temp ;
  if (below setting)
    start furnace ;
  else if (above setting)
    stop furnace ;
}
```

```
do forever {
  measure temp ;
  if (time == 6am)
    temp = 72° ;
  else if (time == 11pm)
    temp = 60° ;
}
```

```
do forever {
  check keypad ;
  if (raise temp)
    setting++ ;
  else if (lower temp)
    setting-- ;
}
```

FIGURE 1-7   Three concurrent code threads within a programmable thermostat.

process of *multithreading* gives the *appearance* of simultaneous execution of threads, but in reality only one thread is being executed at any one instant. The threads are said to be executing *concurrently*. To clarify, we define *task* as a job to be done and *thread* as a sequence of instructions. A task may be partitioned into one or more threads running concurrently, but a single thread may contribute to the objective of one or more tasks.

1.5 HOW POWERFUL ARE EMBEDDED PROCESSORS?

A microcontroller unit (MCU) includes a processor, memory, I/O ports, timers, and multiple peripherals all on a single chip. In the past, MCUs typically employed 8- and 16-bit processors. Today, the growing demand for intelligent devices such as smart phones, GPS devices, portable media players, and network routers for the home is pushing MCU to move to 32-bit processors that offer greater performance and functionality. As shown in Figure 1-8, 32-bit processors are rapidly replacing their predecessors in new embedded designs.

1.6 WHAT PROGRAMMING LANGUAGES ARE USED?

Although it is occasionally necessary to code some small parts of an embedded application program in assembly language, most of the code in even the simplest application is written in a high-level language. Traditionally, the choice of language has been (and

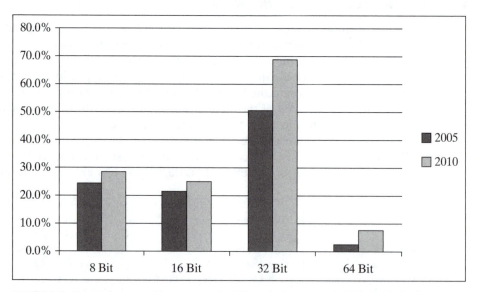

FIGURE 1-8 Instruction set architectures used within embedded systems. *Note:* Percentages sum to over 100% due to multiple responses. *Source: VDC Research Group, "The Embedded Software Strategic Market Intelligence Program 2005, Volume 1: Embedded and Real-time Operating Systems" and "Embedded Software & Tools 2010 Market Intelligence Service, Track 2: Embedded System Engineering Survey Data, Volume 1: Operating Systems".*

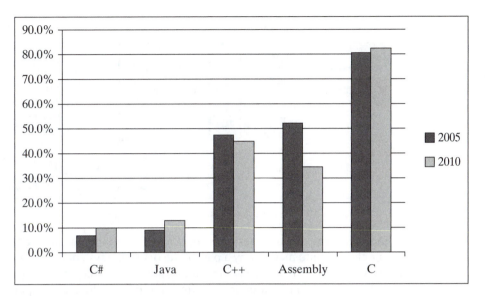

FIGURE 1-9   Programming languages used to develop embedded software. *Note*: Percentages sum to over 100% due to multiple responses. *Source: VDC Research Group, "The Embedded Software Strategic Market Intelligence Program 2005, Volume 1: Embedded and Real-time Operating Systems" and "Embedded Software & Tools 2010 Market Intelligence Service, Track 2: Embedded System Engineering Survey Data, Volume 1: Operating Systems".*

continues to be) C. Programs written in C are very portable from one compiler and/or target processor to another. C compilers are available for a number of different target processors, and they generate very efficient code.

Despite the popularity of C++ and Java for desktop application programming, they are not used extensively in embedded systems because of the large run-time overhead required to support some of their features. For example, even a relatively simple C++ program will produce about twice as much code as the same program written in C, and the situation is much worse for large programs that make extensive use of the run-time library.[3]

1.7   HOW IS BUILDING AN EMBEDDED APPLICATION DIFFERENT?

You should already be familiar with the tools and software components used to build a desktop application program and load it into memory for execution. That process is summarized in Figure 1-10. A compiler and/or an assembler are used to build one or more object files that are linked together with a run-time library to form an executable image that is stored as a file on the disk.

---

[3] P. J. Plaugher, "Embedded C++ An Overview," Embedded Systems Programming, December 1997.

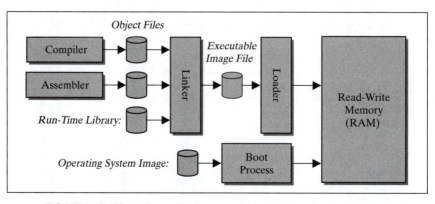

FIGURE 1-10 The build and load process for desktop application programs.

When you want to run a desktop application program, its executable image is loaded from the disk into memory by a part of the operating system known as the *loader*. The operating system itself is already in memory, put there during the boot process.[4]

The desktop system is intended to run a number of different application programs. Thus, a read/write main memory is used so that an entirely different application program can be quickly and easily loaded into memory, replacing the previous application whenever necessary.

Unlike general-purpose desktop systems, embedded systems are designed to serve a single purpose. Once the embedded software is in memory, there is usually no reason to change it. Rather than storing the program on the disk, embedded systems keep their program in a nonvolatile read-only or flash memory. Since there is no need to store the program on the disk, a significant amount of software can be eliminated that would otherwise be necessary to support a file system.

Both the embedded application's software and a real-time kernel are stored in the same memory as a single program image. With no need for a file system, the kernel is much smaller than a regular operating system and is easily linked to the program as yet another object file, as shown in Figure 1-11.

In general, the same kinds of software development tools are used to build both embedded and desktop applications. Although tool suites designed especially for embedded-application development are commonly available, in many cases it is possible to use the same compiler, assembler, and linker that you use for desktop applications. However, there are two important differences. First, the run-time library that comes with compilers for desktop applications is usually not intended for multithreaded applications and must be replaced by one that is reentrant. Second, additional software called a *locator* is required to convert the linker's output to a form suitable for storing in the program memory of the embedded system.[5] When a desktop operating system loads

---

[4] The boot process usually involves a sequence of loaders, beginning with a simple "ROM loader" in read-only memory that reads a "disk bootstrap loader" from a fixed location on the disk into read–write memory.

[5] Sometimes, the editor, compiler, linker, and locator are all transparently combined within an integrated development environment (IDE).

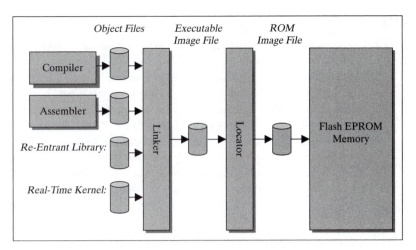

FIGURE 1-11   The build and load process for embedded application programs.

an executable program image produced by a linker into memory, it has to modify a few bytes whose values depend on the address where the program is to be loaded. Before we can use such an executable image to permanently store our embedded program in a ROM, we must first perform the same "fix-ups" using a program called a *locator*.

1.8   HOW BIG ARE TYPICAL EMBEDDED PROGRAMS?

We have grown used to desktop application programs that require several mega-bytes of memory and disk space. So, it is surprising how little memory is used in embedded products, especially when you consider that both the embedded application and its real-time kernel are stored in memory. Two typical examples appear in Table 1-2.

TABLE 1-2   Examples of Embedded Real-Time Software

Property	FAX Machine	CD Player
Microprocessor	16-bit	8-bit
Number of threads	6	9
Read-write memory (RAM)	2048 Bytes	512 Bytes
Total RAM actually used	1346 Bytes (66%)	384 Bytes (75%)
Amount used by kernel	250 Bytes (19%)	146 Bytes (38%)
Read-only memory (ROM)	32.0 KB	32.0 KB
Total ROM actually used	28.8 KB (90%)	17.8 KB (56%)
Amount used by kernel	2.5 KB (8.7%)	2.3 KB (13%)

(Adapted from H. Takada, "Designing Embedded Systems with μITRON Kernel," Embedded Systems Conference, Spring 1998.)

PROBLEMS

1. Find a photograph or an advertisement in a magazine, in a catalog, or on the Web of the *smallest* product you can that contains an embedded processor.
2. Find a photograph or an advertisement in a magazine, in a catalog, or on the Web of the *largest* product you can that contains an embedded processor.
3. Find a photograph or an advertisement in a magazine, in a catalog, or on the Web of the *least expensive* product you can that contains an embedded processor.
4. Find photographs or advertisements from magazines, catalogs, or the Web of three different *soft* real-time systems that contain embedded processors.
5. Find photographs or advertisements from magazines, catalogs, or the Web of three different *hard* real-time systems that contain embedded processors.

Short Answer

6. What is the worldwide average number of embedded microprocessors in consumer products alone per home estimated to be in the year 2000?
7. For every microprocessor produced for use in a desktop computer, how many are produced for use in embedded systems?

Multiple Choice

8. Multithreading means that:
   (a) Multiple processors are executing different threads simultaneously.
   (b) Multiple processors are executing different threads concurrently.
   (c) One processor is executing different threads simultaneously.
   (d) One processor is executing different threads concurrently.

9. The most common type of processor used in new embedded designs is:
   (a) 8-bits
   (b) 16-bits
   (c) 32-bits
   (d) 64-bits

10. The most common programming language used in new embedded designs is:
    (a) C
    (b) C++
    (c) Java
    (d) Assembly

11. The operating system used by most embedded application programs is:
    (a) MS/DOS
    (b) MS/Windows
    (c) Unix
    (d) None of these

CHAPTER 2

Data Representation

There are various types of data—numeric, text, images, audio, and so on. No matter what type we consider, if we are going to process data using a computer, then the data must first be converted into a format that the computer understands. Computers are constructed from electronic devices that use voltages to represent values. To simplify the electronics, the devices are either "on" or "off"; thus, only two voltages are used. So, it should come as no surprise that computers store information as patterns consisting of only two symbols ("0" and "1").

In the familiar *decimal* (base 10) number system, we use a *sequence* of digit symbols to represent numbers greater than 9. The same technique is used in the *binary* (base 2) system to represent numbers greater than 1. In principle, much of what you already know regarding multidigit decimal numbers (e.g., counting, adding, subtracting) remains the same with binary numbers.

2.1 FIXED-PRECISION BINARY NUMBERS

Computers store integers and real numbers differently

You probably already know that computers distinguish numbers according to whether they have a fractional part. Whole numbers with no fractional part are called *integers*, while numbers that have a fractional part are called *real* numbers. Most real numbers are stored in a computer using a *floating-point* representation. Integers and real numbers use entirely different representations because the hardware required for implementing arithmetic is much simpler and faster for integers than it is for floating-point numbers. Not only do we need to use both kinds, but because of the reliability demands on writing software for embedded systems, we also need to comprehend fully how these kinds of numbers differ from those we use in everyday math and the restrictions that are the consequence of this difference.

Computers store numbers using more binary digits than their decimal equivalent

Obviously, we must learn how to convert back and forth between decimal and binary. As we do, we will see that for any one value, more binary digits are required than decimal digits. For example, the value 1234 requires only four digits in the base 10 system, but when it is converted to a base-2 representation, the result (1011010010) requires many more digits. In general, the smaller the base, the more digits we need to represent the same value. As a result, large binary numbers are tedious and are prone to transcription errors. However, after a little practice, you will soon discover that conversion between base-2 and base-16 (hexadecimal) representations can be done almost instantly by inspection. "Hex" numbers use far fewer digits than their binary equivalent, so we'll use hex as a convenient shorthand notation when we discuss the binary numbers stored in the computer.

Computers store numbers using a fixed number of digits that limits range

With paper-and-pencil arithmetic, there is no limit to the number of digits that numbers can have. However, numbers processed by a computer use hardware that is designed to handle a limited number of binary digits ("bits"). Similar to a car's five-digit odometer that can only display values from 0 to 99,999 miles, computers store numbers using a fixed number of bits that restricts the range of values that can be represented.[1] Several *fixed precision* options are usually available: a "byte" of 8 bits, a "half-word" of 16 bits, a "word" of 32 bits, or a "double-word" of 64 bits. Numbers stored with fewer bits (such as a byte) clearly require less memory, but offer a very limited range of values. Having options allows programmers to conserve memory by choosing the smallest representation for each variable that still provides the necessary range of values. Thus, we need to fully understand these restrictions.

Computers do not store signed numbers using "sign-plus magnitude" like we do

As humans, we write the sign and magnitude of a number separately. That is, we write the magnitude as a digit sequence preceded by a minus or (optional) plus sign. This allows us to change the sign of a number without changing the digit sequence of its representation. This *sign-plus-magnitude* system is intuitive for humans, because it makes it relatively easy to comprehend the size of a number and how it relates to other numbers.

However, computers do not comprehend numbers; they simply need to process them, quickly and cheaply. Although the sign-plus-magnitude system could be used with binary numbers by allocating an extra bit to indicate the sign, it turns out that representing *signed* numbers this way unnecessarily complicates the hardware that performs arithmetic. Thus, we will need to learn another way to represent signed numbers called *2's complement*.

In summary, there are several fundamental differences regarding the storage of numbers in a computer compared with what we are used to:

1. Computers store binary numbers consisting of only 0's and 1's.
2. Computers store integers and real numbers differently.
3. Computers store numbers using more binary digits than their decimal equivalent.

---

[1] The number of digits available in modern hand-held calculators is so large that we almost never consider the consequence of exceeding its limits.

4. Computers store numbers using a fixed number of digits that limits range.

5. Computers do not store signed numbers using "sign-plus-magnitude" like we do.

Obviously, we must understand how to convert between human and computer representations and how the computer performs arithmetic when using binary numbers. We also need to understand how the above differences can have unanticipated consequences and what to do when they occur.

2.2 POSITIONAL NUMBER SYSTEMS

When we see a number written as a sequence of decimal digits, we interpret its value almost immediately without a second thought. That is because we have learned that, as we read digits from left to right, the first digits we see are more significant than those that follow and because we have memorized an ordering on the symbols that assigns more weight to "9" than to "0."

Positional number systems (such as our familiar decimal system) use sequences of symbols to represent large numbers. The *value* represented by the sequence can be expressed mathematically by a simple polynomial in which the arithmetic value of each symbol is weighted relative to its position. For example, the value of the decimal sequence 1234 is

$$1234_{10} = 1 \times 10^3 + 2 \times 10^2 + 3 \times 10^1 + 4 \times 10^0$$
$$= 1 \times 1000 + 2 \times 100 + 3 \times 10 + 4 \times 1$$

When we switch from decimal to binary, we simply use powers of 2 in the polynomial instead of powers of 10. For the more general base-R case, simply use powers of R:

$$5678_R = 5 \times R^3 + 6 \times R^2 + 7 \times R^1 + 8 \times R^0$$

This technique also handles numbers with a fractional part, as long as we remember that the *exponents* are negative on the right-hand side of the *radix*[2] point:

$$36.72_R = 3 \times R^1 + 6 \times R^0 + 7 \times R^{-1} + 2 \times R^{-2}$$

What is important about this is that we are able to use our familiar decimal arithmetic to *evaluate* this polynomial—but *only* when the target representation is decimal—that is, when we are converting from some other number base system to decimal. Going the other way would not work unless you use base-R arithmetic to evaluate the polynomial—something you really *do not* want to have to do! Thus, in what follows, we will use *polynomial evaluation* to convert *to* decimal, but an entirely different technique to convert *from* decimal.

---

[2] We are familiar with the phrase "decimal point," and you will often hear computer professionals talking about the "binary point." Decimal and binary refer to the number base (10 and 2, respectively), which is also called the "radix." Thus, the generalized version of "decimal point" and "binary point" is "radix point."

2.2.1 Binary-to-Decimal Conversion

Polynomial evaluation

With our understanding of positional number systems, we are now prepared to convert binary numbers into decimal. All that is required is to apply a polynomial evaluation with R equal to 2. For example, we convert the binary number 1011.0111_2 to decimal as follows:

$$1 \times 2^3 + 0 \times 2^2 + 1 \times 2^1 + 1 \times 2^0 + 0 \times 2^{-1} + 1 \times 2^{-2} + 1 \times 2^{-3} + 1 \times 2^{-4}$$

$$= 8 + 2 + 1 + \frac{1}{4} + \frac{1}{8} + \frac{1}{16} = 11.4375_{10}$$

Note that, since the positional weights are powers of 2 instead of 10, each binary digit contributes significantly less to the total magnitude than a digit in the equivalent decimal representation. Thus, the number of digits required to represent any particular value grows as the choice of base gets smaller.

Simplifying the arithmetic

Converting a binary number that has a fractional part may require several divisions to compute the contribution of the fractional bits. In the above example, three such divisions were necessary. Many find it easier to do the arithmetic by simply changing the problem. If we remember that 1011.0111_2 is equivalent to $10110111_2 \times 2^{-4}$, then the conversion can be evaluated with only a single division, as in:

$$(1 \times 2^7 + 0 \times 2^6 + 1 \times 2^5 + 1 \times 2^4 + 0 \times 2^3 + 1 \times 2^2 + 1 \times 2^1 + 1 \times 2^0) \div 16$$

$$= (128 + 32 + 16 + 4 + 2 + 1) \div 16 = 183 \div 16 = 11.4375_{10}$$

2.2.2 Decimal-to-Binary Conversion

We do not use polynomial evaluation to convert from decimal (base 10) to base R because doing so requires performing base R arithmetic. Although it may seem counterintuitive, it is actually easier to convert the whole and fractional parts using two different algorithms. We will use *repeated division* for the whole part and *repeated multiplication* for the fractional part. The advantage is that it allows us to use regular decimal arithmetic instead of base R arithmetic.

Repeated division

Before presenting the algorithm, first consider what happens when you divide a decimal whole number like 1234 by 10. The division yields two results—a quotient of 123 and a remainder of 4.

In effect, the operation separates the original four-digit number into two parts— it "extracts" the least significant digit as the remainder, and leaves the remaining digits as the quotient. We can then repeat the process, dividing the quotient of 123 by 10 to extract the next least significant digit, and so on until the quotient becomes zero.

If we divide by 2 instead of 10, we know that the remainder can only be 0 or 1. Just as the remainder of dividing by 10 was the least significant (right-most) digit of the

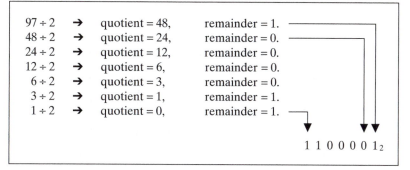

FIGURE 2-1   Using repeated division to convert 97 from decimal to binary.

original decimal representation of the value, the remainder of dividing by 2 will be the least significant digit of its binary representation. Thus, repeating the process will produce binary digits in right-to-left (least to most significant) order (Figure 2-1).

Repeated division works for any number base—that is, we can convert a decimal whole number to any other number base R simply by repeatedly dividing by R. The remainders are inherently limited to the range of 0 to R − 1, which is exactly the same as the range of digit values of a base R number. The remainder from the first division determines the least significant digit of the result, and the quotients are used to repeat the process until the quotient becomes zero.

Repeated multiplication

Repeated division works great for whole numbers, but does *not* work at all for fractional numbers. Instead, we must use a different algorithm called *repeated multiplication*.

Before presenting the algorithm, consider what happens when you multiply a fractional number like 0.1234 by 10. We can think of the product (1.234) consisting of a whole part and a fractional part. That is, the most significant digit of the original number is "extracted" as the whole part of the product, with the remaining digits left in the fractional part. Note that the whole part of the product must always be a single digit in the range of 0 to 9. We can repeat the process on the remaining fractional part to extract the rest of the digits in a left-to-right (most to least significant) order.

If we multiply by 2 instead of 10, we know that the whole part can only be 0 or 1. Just as the whole part of multiplying by 10 was the most significant (left-most) digit of the original decimal representation of the value, the whole part of multiplying by 2 will be the most significant digit of its binary representation. Thus, repeating the process will produce binary digits in left-to-right (most to least significant) order.

Repeated multiplication works for any number base—that is, we can convert a decimal fraction to any other number base R simply by repeatedly multiplying by R. The whole part of the products are inherently limited to the range of 0 to R − 1, which is exactly the same as the range of digit values of a base R number. The whole part from the first multiplication determines the most significant digit of the result, with the fractional part of the products used to repeat the process.

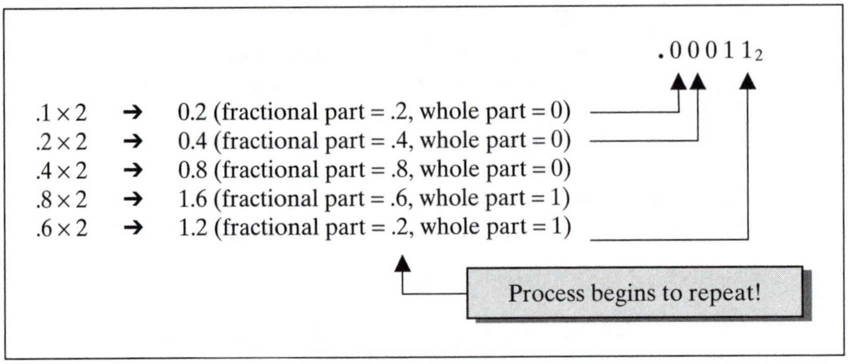

FIGURE 2-2   Using repeated multiplication to convert 0.1 from decimal to binary.

Repeated multiplication does not always terminate

Unlike repeated division, however, repeated multiplication may continue indefinitely. That is because a fractional value represented by a finite number of digits in one number base may require an infinite number of digits in a different number base. For example, everyone knows that one-third cannot be written as a decimal fraction unless you use an infinite number of digits (called a *repeating fraction*). However, writing it as a ternary (base 3) fraction requires only a single digit! (i.e., $0.333\ldots3_{10} = 0.1_3$) This also happens when we convert certain finite-length decimal fractions to a different number base representation. As shown in Figure 2-2, the decimal representation of one-tenth requires an infinite number of digits when converted to binary.

Knowing when to stop repeated multiplication

So how do we know when to stop repeated multiplication? In most cases, the fractional part of a product will become zero, and then we can simply use the whole part as the last digit of the result and stop. When the fractional part is identical to a previous fractional part, however, the result will repeat forever. No matter where we stop, we will have to discard the rest of the digits of the result, and there will be a corresponding *representation error*.

Often the decision of how many fractional digits to keep is determined not by us but by whether the result is to be stored in a byte, a half-word, a word, or a double word. If not, then a rational choice is to produce enough digits to yield the same precision as in the original decimal fraction. For example, when we write a value as the decimal fraction .123, we have expressed it to a precision of 1 part in 1,000. (Note that writing it as .1230 expresses the precision of 1 part in 10,000.) To get a precision of 1 part in 1,000 in binary requires 10 binary digits; 9 binary digits would only provide a precision of 1 part in 512 (2^9), while 10 provides a precision of 1 part in 1,024 (2^{10}).

Truncating and rounding

Simply discarding any extra digits when you terminate repeated multiplication is called *truncating* the result. To minimize error, however, we should instead *round* the result.

In decimal, rounding means adding 1 to the result when the next digit is 5 or greater; for example, rounding the decimal fraction 0.12345 to three digits yields 0.123, while rounding it to four yields 0.1235. In binary, rounding means adding 1 to the result when the next digit is 1; for example, rounding the binary fraction 0.11101 to three digits yields 0.111, while rounding it to four yields 0.1111.

In effect, rounding requires that we increment the result when what we discard is at least halfway to the next result. Rounding decimal and binary values only requires that we look at the next digit, but that is only because 10 and 2 are even numbers. When the number base is odd, "halfway" cannot always be determined by a single digit. Consider the base 3 fractional number 0.231XX...X, where "XX...X" is an arbitrary sequence of base 3 digits. If we want to round to three digits, the result will certainly be 0.231 when the left-most X is 0, and 0.232 when the left-most X is 2, but what if it is a 1? Then you have to look at the next X, and so on. Sigh....

2.2.3 Hexadecimal: A Shorthand for Binary

When we work with binary numbers by hand, the greater number of digits required increases the likelihood of a transcription error. The *hexadecimal* (base 16) number system solves this problem by essentially serving as a shorthand notation for binary numbers.

When two number bases have a power relationship, as in $R_1 = (R_2)^k$, converting a number from one number base representation to the other becomes trivial. Specifically, each digit in the base R_1 representation will be in one-to-one correspondence with k digits of the corresponding base R_2 representation. This is exactly why hexadecimal[3] (base 16) is used as a shorthand for binary. Since $16 = 2^4$, each hexadecimal digit will correspond to *four* binary digits.

Hex numbers use digit symbols with values between 0 and 15. The first 10 symbols are the same as in the decimal system ("0" through "9"); the remaining six symbols are taken from the first six letters of the alphabet ("A" through "F").

First, we have to memorize the 4-bit binary representations of the numbers 0 through 15 shown in Table 2-1. Once we have mastered that, conversion between binary and hex happens almost by inspection. To convert from hex to binary, simply replace every hex symbol by its corresponding 4-bit binary pattern. To convert from binary to hex, start at the binary point and identify groups of four bits each, filling in partial groups with 0's on the outside, and then replace each group by the corresponding hex digit (Figure 2-3).

We just saw that converting between binary and hexadecimal requires a simple table lookup. But, what if you do not have a copy of the table? Fortunately, recreating the table from scratch is also trivial once you recognize the binary counting pattern.

The principle behind counting is the same in all positional number systems. First, remember what you do in decimal: Add 1 to the least significant digit. If the result is

---

[3] Octal (base 8) has been used in the past as shorthand for binary, but has been replaced by hex as the number of bits used to represent a number has increased over time from 16 to 32 to 64.

TABLE 2-1   Binary–Hex Conversion Table

Hex Symbol	Digit Value	Binary Pattern	Hex Symbol	Digit Value	Binary Pattern
0	0	0000	8	8	1000
1	1	0001	9	9	1001
2	2	0010	A	10	1010
3	3	0011	B	11	1011
4	4	0100	C	12	1100
5	5	0101	D	13	1101
6	6	0110	E	14	1110
7	7	0111	F	15	1111

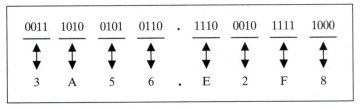

FIGURE 2-3   Converting between binary and hex by inspection.

less than 10, write it down and copy all the remaining digits on the left. Otherwise, write down zero and add 1 to the next digit position, and so on. The only difference for another choice of base is that you compare the result at each step to R (the radix) instead of to 10.

After a little practice, it is relatively easy to reproduce the binary count sequence indicated in Table 2-1. However, it becomes trivial once you notice that, starting from zero, the least significant bit changes on every count, the next least significant bit changes on every two counts, the one after that changes on every four counts, and so on. No matter how many bits are used in the representation, a value of zero is always represented by all 0's (00 ... 0). This fact, together with the previous observation, makes it trivial to reconstruct a complete binary count sequence for numbers containing an arbitrary number of bits.

Remember: Computers do not use hex. We do.

2.2.4 Fixed Precision, Rollover, and Overflow

Everyone knows that, if you drive a car long enough, eventually the odometer will "roll over" from 99,999.9 miles to 00,000.0 miles. Of course, the correct result is 100,000.0 miles, but the odometer has room for only six digits. Except for the missing digit, the rest of the representation is correct. Similarly, you can easily imagine that the odometer of a new car might roll over backwards from 00,000.0 to 99,999.9 miles if you drove it far enough in reverse.

Rollover is a consequence of fixed precision. For example, the odometer in your car uses a fixed precision of six decimal digits. A computer stores numbers by using fixed precision in multiples of 8 bits and suffers similar consequences. Counting up with 8 bits will eventually cause a rollover from 11111111 to 00000000; counting down eventually rolls over backward from 00000000 to 11111111 (and provides some insight into how negative numbers should be represented).

When binary patterns are used to represent *unsigned* values, a pattern of all 0's is assigned to the value zero and the pattern of all 1's corresponds to the maximum possible value that can be represented. Rolling over in either direction amounts to exceeding the range of representation and is known as *overflow*.

Rollover and overflow, however, are not synonymous. Rollover describes a behavior of pattern sequence, while overflow describes an *arithmetic* behavior. Whether rollover causes overflow depends on how the patterns are interpreted as numeric values. For example, when we get to 2's-complement signed numbers, we will see that a rollover occurs in the middle of the range without overflow, while overflow off either end of the range occurs without rollover.

2.3   BINARY REPRESENTATION OF INTEGERS

Integers can be either signed or unsigned. Both are stored using a fixed number of bits. If the integer is signed, one of these bits indicates whether the value is positive or negative, leaving one fewer bits available for the magnitude. Thus, the range of magnitudes that can be represented by using unsigned integers is twice that of signed integers. Sometimes, this little bit of extra range can be useful, and so some modern programming languages provide both types.

Sometimes, a programmer will declare an integer to be unsigned, not because of the greater magnitude range, but simply because the values are never expected to be negative. For many applications, such as counting or measuring distance or time, unsigned integers are more appropriate. Making the integer unsigned then becomes a kind of documentation that provides a little more insight into how the integer is used within an algorithm.

It is important to recognize, however, that whether an integer is signed or unsigned depends entirely on how you decide to interpret its bit pattern. No information is stored in the pattern that specifies how it should be interpreted. For example, if the 8-bit pattern 10100111 is interpreted as an unsigned number, then its decimal value is 167; if interpreted as a signed (2's complement) integer, then its decimal value is -89.

As we will see later in this chapter, when you program in a high-level language, the compiler selects the appropriate instruction according to how the integer was declared; when programming in assembly language, however, it becomes the programmer's responsibility to select the appropriate instruction!

As we will see, what makes the use of two interpretations reasonable is that the hardware for addition and subtraction can be identical for signed and unsigned integers. Although the hardware for comparing, multiplying, and dividing is different for signed and unsigned integers, the difference is small and inexpensive. However, it does mean that the computer must provide different instructions for these operations, depending on the type of integers used as operands.

2.3.1 Signed Integers

So far, we have only considered how to represent unsigned integers in binary. When signed integers are required, however, we must extend the simple positional representation. Although a single bit could be added to indicate sign, computers do not simply append it to an independently represented magnitude. It turns out that using such a *sign-plus-magnitude* approach would actually complicate the hardware design of the arithmetic unit, and so another method called *2's complement* is used instead.

As is seen in Figure 2-4, the 2's-complement representation of positive values is the same as for unsigned representation. The negative values can be derived by counting backwards from zero. Just as with the odometer on a new car that is driven in reverse, when we back up from zero, the binary count rolls over to all 1's and then decrements from there.

2.3.2 Positive and Negative Representations of the Same Magnitude

After studying Figure 2-4 for a while, you will quickly discover that you cannot change the sign of a 2's-complement number by simply changing a single bit in its representation. However, the good news is that the correct procedure is not very difficult. Given the representation of a positive quantity, an operation called *forming the 2's*

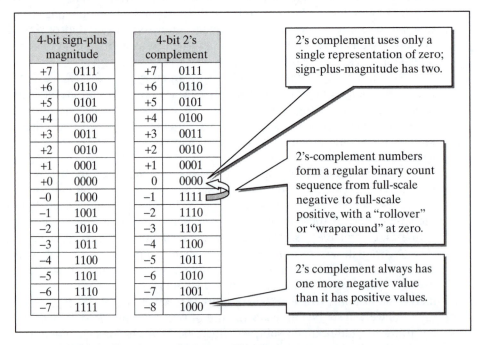

4-bit sign-plus magnitude		4-bit 2's complement	
+7	0111	+7	0111
+6	0110	+6	0110
+5	0101	+5	0101
+4	0100	+4	0100
+3	0011	+3	0011
+2	0010	+2	0010
+1	0001	+1	0001
+0	0000	0	0000
−0	1000	−1	1111
−1	1001	−2	1110
−2	1010	−3	1101
−3	1011	−4	1100
−4	1100	−5	1011
−5	1101	−6	1010
−6	1110	−7	1001
−7	1111	−8	1000

2's complement uses only a single representation of zero; sign-plus-magnitude has two.

2's-complement numbers form a regular binary count sequence from full-scale negative to full-scale positive, with a "rollover" or "wraparound" at zero.

2's complement always has one more negative value than it has positive values.

FIGURE 2-4   Sign-plus-magnitude versus 2's-complement representation.

complement of a number produces the representation of its negative counterpart, and vice versa. The simplest algorithm to do this is to invert all the bits[4] and then add 1 to the result. A second technique is to process the bits once from *right to left*, copying the bits exactly as they appear, through and including the first 1, and then copying the inverse of all the remaining bits.

First, we must know exactly how many bits are used in the representation if either algorithm is to work correctly. For example, suppose you are asked to find the 2's-complement signed representation of -27_{10}. The easiest way to do this is to first find the representation of $+27_{10}$ and then apply the 2's-complement algorithm to get the corresponding negative representation. Let us assume that you converted 27_{10} to binary and got 11011_2. Inverting these five bits and adding 1 produces 00101, which is $+5$, not -27_{10}. The problem is that we started with an unsigned representation of 27_{10} (11011_2), not a signed representation of $+27_{10}$ (011011_2). Simply adding one or more leading 0's to the original number, as in 00011011_2, causes the algorithm to produce 11100101_2 instead, which is the correct representation of -27_{10}.

Note that there is an anomaly that occurs when you try to apply the algorithm to the full-scale negative representation ($10 \ldots 0_2$). Using 4 bits as an example, if we invert 1000_2, then it becomes 0111_2, and adding 1 to this produces 1000_2 (what we started with). This should not be surprising for 2's-complement, however, because the magnitude of its full-scale negative value is always one greater than the largest positive value that can be represented.

After a little observation, you will soon realize that nonnegative quantities must begin with one or more leading 0's and that negative quantities must begin with one or more leading 1's. Hence, you can easily determine the sign of a 2's-complement number by looking only at the most significant bit. However, even though this bit is referred to as the "sign bit," do not be fooled into thinking that the sign and magnitude portions of the representation are independent.

Remember: You cannot change the sign of a 2's-complement number by simply inverting the most significant bit!

2.3.3 Interpreting the Value of a 2's-Complement Number

When given a 2's-complement number in binary and asked to convert it to decimal, most people look first at the sign bit. If it is 0, then they simply treat the number as if it were an unsigned binary number and convert using polynomial evaluation. However, if the sign bit is 1, then the value must be negative. In this case, they find the corresponding positive representation of the same magnitude by forming the 2's complement of the bit pattern, use that to determine the decimal magnitude, and then put a minus sign in front of it (Figure 2-5):

A single approach that works for both positive and negative values is to use polynomial evaluation, but with a different weight for the most significant digit. Instead of using a weight of 2^{n-1}, simply change it to -2^{n-1} as shown in Figure 2-6.

---

[4] Inverting all the bits means to change every 0 to a 1 and every 1 to a 0.

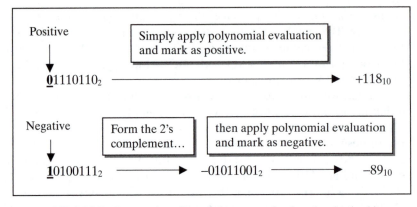

FIGURE 2-5 Interpreting a 2's-complement number based on its sign bit.

$$01110110_2 = 0\times(-2^7) + 1\times2^6 + 1\times2^5 + 1\times2^4 + 0\times2^3 + 1\times2^2 + 1\times2^1 + 0\times2^0$$
$$= 64 + 32 + 16 + 4 + 2$$
$$= 118_{10}$$

$$10100111_2 = 1\times(-2^7) + 0\times2^6 + 1\times2^5 + 0\times2^4 + 0\times2^3 + 1\times2^2 + 1\times2^1 + 1\times2^0$$
$$= -128 + 32 + 4 + 2 + 1$$
$$= -89_{10}$$

FIGURE 2-6 Modified polynomial evaluation of a 2's-complement number.

2.3.4 Changing the Sign of Numbers with Integer and Fractional Parts

When finding the 2's-complement representation of a signed decimal number, the usual approach is to first convert the positive equivalent to binary and then apply the 2's-complement algorithm to make it negative. A common mistake while converting a number that contains both integer and fractional parts is to treat the parts separately. For example, when converting the number -5.75_{10} to an 8-bit 2's-complement representation with the binary point in the middle, you might be tempted to do it as follows:

Step 1: $+5_{10} = 0101$, thus -5_{10} becomes 1011

Step 2: $.75_{10} = .1100$

Step 3: Combining yields 1011.1100_2

Unfortunately, this result corresponds to -4.25, not -5.75. The correct way of conversion is to first find the 8-bit representation of $+5.75$ and then apply the 2's-complement algorithm as if there was no binary point:

Step 1: $+5.75_{10} = 0101.1100$.

Step 2: Find the 2's complement of 01011100, which is 10100100.

Step 3: Replace the binary point, producing 1010.0100_2.

2.3.5 Binary Addition and Subtraction

Addition of two N-bit binary numbers X and Y can be broken down into a set of N identical problems of adding only two bits X_i and Y_i at a time, with carries C_i propagated from right (C_0) to left (C_N). A logic circuit called a *Full Adder* is used to combine each pair of operand bits with the carry-out from the previous digit position to produce one bit of the sum and the next carry-out:

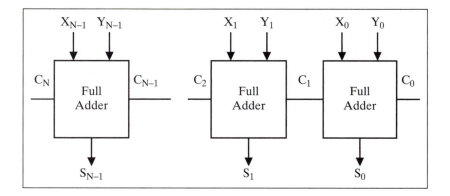

A better way to understand what a full adder does is to think of it as a circuit that adds together three 1-bit numbers, with possible sums of 0, 1, 2, or 3 as shown in the "Sum" column of the table. These four values correspond to bit patterns 00, 01, 10, and 11, where the least significant bit is S_i and the most significant bit is C_{i+1}.

C_i	X_i	Y_i	Sum	C_{i+1}	S_i
0	0	0	0	0	0
0	0	1	1	0	1
0	1	0	1	0	1
0	1	1	2	1	0
1	0	0	1	0	1
1	0	1	2	1	0
1	1	0	2	1	0
1	1	1	3	1	1

Subtraction is similar, so that X – Y calculated by a set of N "Full Subtractors" that propagate borrows (B_i) from right to left:

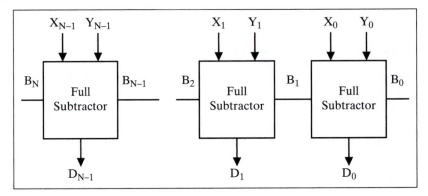

The specification of the two output functions (D_i and B_{i+1}) of the full subtractor can be derived in a manner similar to that for a full adder. The trick is to realize that the X_i input contributes either 0 or +1 to the difference, while Y_i and B_i each contribute 0 or –1 to the difference, so that the possible difference values are –2, –1, 0, or +1 and that these values are represented as a two-bit 2's-complement number. Thus, the table becomes:

B_i	X_i	Y_i	Diff	B_{i+1}	D_i
0	0	0	0	0	0
0	0	–1	–1	1	1
0	+1	0	+1	0	1
0	+1	–1	0	0	0
–1	0	0	–1	1	1
–1	0	–1	–2	1	0
–1	+1	0	0	0	0
–1	+1	–1	–1	1	1

Remember: Even though we are representing the difference using a signed representation, we already know that the same circuit that adds or subtracts 2's-complement operands works equally well to add or subtract unsigned operands.

Given the above table for the full subtractor, we can use it to do an 8-bit binary subtraction problem one bit at a time from right to left:

Borrows		B_8	B_7	B_6	B_5	B_4	B_3	B_2	B_1	B_0
		0	0	0	0	1	1	1	1	0
Minuend	$X_7...X_0$		0	1	1	1	0	0	1	0
Subtrahend	$Y_7...Y_0$		0	1	0	0	0	1	1	1
Difference	$D_7...D_0$		0	0	1	0	1	0	1	1

2.3.6 Range and Overflow

There are two possible values (0 and 1) for every bit of an n-bit binary number, so there are a total of 2^n different patterns of 0's and 1's that can be used to represent numbers consisting of n bits. When the patterns are used to represent *unsigned* integers, the range of possible values is thus 0 to $2^n - 1$. For example, an 8-bit quantity can hold an unsigned value in the range from 0 to $2^8 - 1$ (0 to 255).

When used to represent *signed* integers, half the patterns are assigned to positive values and half to negative values. Half of 2^n is 2^{n-1}, so the nonnegative half of the range covers values from 0 to $2^{n-1} - 1$. The other 2^{n-1} patterns are assigned to the negative values from -1 to -2^{n-1}. Thus, the entire range of values for a 2's-complement signed number is from -2^{n-1} to $+2^{n-1} - 1$. For example, an 8-bit quantity can hold a signed value in the range from -2^7 to $+2^7 - 1$ (-128 to $+127$).

An integer arithmetic operation that produces a value beyond the upper limit of the data type's range causes the value to "wrap around" (overflow) back into the lower portion of the range. As illustrated in Figure 2-7, adding 20 to an 8-bit unsigned number holding a value of 250 yields a result of 14. The difference (256) between the proper result of 270 (which requires 9 bits) and the actual result of 14 (the least significant 8 bits) corresponds to the weight of the 9th bit that cannot be stored in the result.

With signed numbers, overflow never occurs when adding numbers with different signs or subtracting numbers with the same sign; overflow is possible only when adding two integers of the same sign or subtracting two of different signs. For example, subtracting 17 from an 8-bit signed number holding a value of -120 will yield a result of $+119$. The difference (256) between the proper result of -137 (which requires 9 bits) and that of $+119$ (the least significant 8 bits) corresponds to the weight of the 9th bit that cannot be stored in the result.

When overflow *does* occur, it is because magnitude information has propagated into the sign bit position. For example, for a number to appear positive, the most significant bit must be 0, but as its magnitude increases, 1's begin to appear further and further to the left. Conversely, for a number to appear negative, the most significant bit must be 1, but as its magnitude increases, 0's begin to appear further and further to the left.

$$
\begin{array}{rl}
250_{10} \quad \rightarrow & 11111010_2 \ (\text{as an 8-bit } \textbf{\textit{unsigned}} \text{ number}) \\
\underline{20_{10}} & \underline{+00010100_2} \\
\text{sum:} 270_{10} & 100001110_2 \ (\text{a 9 bit result!}) \\
& 00001110_2 \ (\text{the 8 bits we keep}) \quad \rightarrow \quad 14_{10}
\end{array}
$$

$$
\begin{array}{rl}
-120_{10} \quad \rightarrow & 10001000_2 \ (\text{as an 8-bit } \textbf{\textit{signed}} \text{ number}) \\
\underline{-17_{10}} & \underline{+11101111_2} \\
\text{sum:} -137_{10} & 101110111_2 \ (\text{a 9 bit result!}) \\
& 01110111_2 \ (\text{the 8 bits we keep}) \quad \rightarrow \quad +119_{10}
\end{array}
$$

FIGURE 2-7   Overflow beyond the limits of an integer data type.

Overflow occurs *silently* during addition and subtraction of integer data types; there is no run-time checking provided by the computer. It is entirely the programmer's responsibility to anticipate the range of values possible for each variable and to allocate a data type of the appropriate size to avoid overflow.

2.4   BINARY REPRESENTATION OF REAL NUMBERS

Real numbers are those that contain a fractional part. Although *floating-point* is the usual representation used for real numbers, a *fixed-point* representation is also possible and has certain advantages that are especially important for low-cost embedded applications.

2.4.1   Floating-Point Real Numbers

Floating-point numbers are like scientific notation, that is, they consist of two pieces of information: significant digits and a scale factor. The significant digits (or *significand*) are stored as a fractional value with an implied binary point at the far left; the scale factor is a power of 2, with only the exponent stored in the representation.

Today, all desktop microprocessors include hardware to implement floating-point arithmetic, including any necessary prealignment of binary points or postnormalization of results.

Floating-point representations use a sign-plus-magnitude format and add a bias to the exponent before encoding it. The sign-plus-magnitude format is more convenient for the algorithms required by floating-point arithmetic, and the biased exponent simplifies the hardware that compares exponents for prealignment of operands.

The ANSI/IEEE standard does not impose any particular bit layout for floating-point numbers. However, the typical implementation uses the layout shown in Figure 2-8, in which the sign bit is placed in the most significant bit position of the representation, followed by the exponent and significand fields, respectively. This traditional arrangement is consistent with keeping all the information about the real number in decreasing order of significance.

An interesting characteristic of the ANSI/IEEE format is that one bit of the significand is not stored in the representation! Remember that to maintain maximum precision, we always normalize every result. This forces the most significant bit of every nonzero significand to always be 1. This bit is the integer bit of the significand, and thus

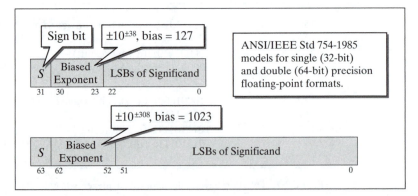

FIGURE 2-8   ANSI/IEEE floating-point representations.

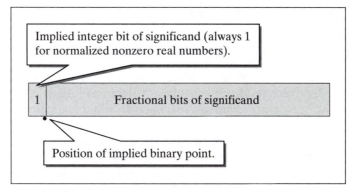

FIGURE 2-9   Construction of actual significand.

the significands of all nonzero numbers are in the range of $1.0 \le$ significand < 2.0. By not storing the integer bit, the ANSI/IEEE format is able to store an extra bit of precision in the significand (Figure 2-9).

The program shown in Example 2-1 was compiled and run on a computer that uses ANSI/IEEE floating-point with the bits arranged as shown in Figure 2-8. The output of the program illustrates the details of the 32-bit single-precision representation by printing out the binary contents of several floating-point numbers.

```c
#include <stdio.h>

int main()
    {
    static float f[] =
            {
            -2.0, -1.0, -0.75, -0.5,
            0.0, 0.5, 0.75, 1.0, 2.0
            };
    int i, j ;

    for (i = 8; i >= 0; i--)
            {
            void *p = &f[i] ;
            long bits = *((long *) p) ;
            int zero = (bits == 0L) ;
            printf("%5.2f\t",f[i]);
            for (j = 0; j < 32; j++)
                    {
                    if (j == 1 || j == 9) printf(" ") ;
                    if (j == 9) printf("(%d).", !zero) ;
                    printf("%d", bits < 0) ;
                    bits <<= 1 ;
                    }
            printf("\n");
            }

    return 0;
    }
```

```
Program output:

 2.00 0 10000000 (1).00000000000000000000000
 1.00 0 01111111 (1).00000000000000000000000
 0.75 0 01111110 (1).10000000000000000000000
 0.50 0 01111110 (1).00000000000000000000000
 0.00 0 00000000 (0).00000000000000000000000
-0.50 1 01111110 (1).00000000000000000000000
-0.75 1 01111110 (1).10000000000000000000000
-1.00 1 01111111 (1).00000000000000000000000
-2.00 1 10000000 (1).00000000000000000000000
```

EXAMPLE 2-1   Program to illustrate single-precision floating-point representation.

Regardless of how the bits are stored, the value of a floating-point number stored in the ANSI/IEEE format can be expressed as

Value of real number = $(-1)^{\text{sign bit}} \times 2^{(\text{biased exponent} - \text{bias constant})} \times$ actual significand

The *advantage* of floating-point is that errors can be minimized automatically, by *normalizing* every result. The number of significant digits is fixed, so normalization adjusts the exponent to eliminate leading zeroes in the significant digits, thus providing the greatest possible precision.

The *disadvantage* is an increase in cost and execution time. Floating-point and integer arithmetic are implemented using different parts of the processor. Thus, processors with floating-point instructions are usually a bit more expensive than those that only implement integer arithmetic. Since floating-point and integer numbers are processed separately, there is more state information inside the processor; having both means that it takes that much longer to switch from one computation to another in a multithreaded application.

2.4.2 Fixed-Point Real Numbers

Many inexpensive microprocessors do not provide instructions for floating-point arithmetic at all, or execute such instructions much more slowly than those for integer arithmetic. This speed difference and the need to change the floating-point processor state information when switching from one thread of execution to another are strong motivations to avoid real numbers in most embedded programs. Fortunately, some kinds of arithmetic can be easily performed on fixed-point real numbers by using integer operations.

In fixed-point representations, each number consists of two parts: a fixed number of bits on the left of the radix point that represent the whole part of the number and a fixed number of bits on the right that represent the fractional part of the number. The integer representations that we studied earlier are simply a special case of fixed-point in which there are no fractional bits; that is, the implied binary point is immediately to the right of the least significant bit.

Addition and subtraction of two fixed-point reals with the same implied position of the binary point can be implemented using instructions for regular integer addition and subtraction. Addition and subtraction of two fixed-point reals with different binary point positions, and multiplication and division are a bit more complicated, but very manageable as we shall see in the next chapter.

2.5   ASCII REPRESENTATION OF TEXT

One byte of memory can be used to hold any of 256 different 8-bit patterns of 1's and 0's. Besides representing small numbers, these patterns can also be used as codes. For example, we can store text in a computer by simply assigning a unique code to each of the letters (both lowercase and uppercase) of the alphabet, to each of the decimal digits, and to each of the various punctuation characters.

A standard code used for this purpose is the American Standard Code for Information Interchange (ASCII) shown in Table 2-2. The first 32 codes (and the last code) in the table are used for text formatting and control information.

TABLE 2-2   Seven-Bit ASCII Codes (in Hex)

Hex	Control/Graphic	Hex	Control/Graphic	Hex	Control/Graphic	Hex	Control/Graphic
00	NUL	20	Space	40	@	60	`
01	SOH	21	!	41	A	61	a
02	STX	22	"	42	B	62	b
03	ETX	23	#	43	C	63	c
04	EOT	24	$	44	D	64	d
05	ENQ	25	%	45	E	65	e
06	ACK	26	&	46	F	66	f
07	BEL	27	'	47	G	67	g
08	BS	28	(	48	H	68	h
09	HT	29	)	49	I	69	i
0A	LF	2A	*	4A	J	6A	j
0B	VT	2B	±	4B	K	6B	k
0C	FF	2C	,	4C	L	6C	l
0D	CR	2D	–	4D	M	6D	m
0E	SO	2E	.	4E	N	6E	n
0F	SI	2F	/	4F	O	6F	o
10	DLE	30	0	50	P	70	p
11	DC1 (X-ON)	31	1	51	Q	71	q
12	DC2	32	2	52	R	72	r
13	DC3 (X-OFF)	33	3	53	S	73	s
14	DC4	34	4	54	T	74	t
15	NAK	35	5	55	U	75	u
16	SYN	36	6	56	V	76	v
17	ETB	37	7	57	W	77	w
18	CAN	38	8	58	X	78	x
19	EM	39	9	59	Y	79	y
1A	SUB	3A	:	5A	Z	7A	z
1B	ESC	3B	;	5B	[	7B	{
1C	FS	3C	<	5C	\	7C		
1D	GS	3D	=	5D	]	7D	}
1E	RS	3E	>	5E	^	7E	~
1F	US	3F	?	5F	_	7F	DEL

The table contains a total of 128 codes, thus requiring only 7 bits of the 8 that are available in a byte of memory. Some computer manufacturers have used the 8th bit to define another 128 codes, and use them to represent Greek characters and characters that are used to compose lines or boxes, using the character cells of a display. Others have used the 8th bit as a *parity* bit to detect single-bit errors. The value of the parity bit is determined from the other 7 bits so that there is an odd number of 1's among the 8 total bits. An error is detected whenever a byte is found containing an even number of 1's.

TABLE 2-3 Character Constants Using Character Escapes in C

Constant	Hex	Character	Constant	Hex	Character
'\a'	07	alert (e.g., bell)	'\v'	0B	vertical tab
'\b'	08	backspace	'\\'	5C	Backslash
'\f'	0C	form feed	'\''	27	single quote
'\n'	0A	newline	'\"'	22	double quote
'\r'	0D	carriage return	'\?'	3F	question mark
'\t'	09	horizontal tab			

Programming languages (both high-level languages, such as C, and assembly languages) do not require the programmer to memorize the ASCII code. Rather than writing a binary or hex constant, the 7-bit pattern containing the ASCII code of a character can be produced by simply using a literal character constant. For example, suppose you want to store the ASCII code for the letter A in a byte of memory. Rather than writing the hex constant 0x41 (in C) or 41h (in assembly), both languages allow surrounding the letter by a pair of apostrophes (as in 'A') to achieve the same purpose. Some of the more frequently used of the first 32 ASCII control codes can be represented in C using *character escapes*, as shown in Table 2-3. A character escape consists of a backslash followed by a letter; surrounding the combination with apostrophes produces an ASCII code that has no corresponding graphic image. In general, the use of character literals instead of the numeric codes produces source code that is much more readable, and it helps avoid what are known as "magic constants" whose intended purpose becomes obscured over time.

Words, sentences, and paragraphs are examples of character *strings*. In addition to the string's content, somehow the *length* of the string must also be indicated. Otherwise, we would not know when to stop trying to interpret the contents of memory as ASCII codes!

The length of a character string is specified either by a character count (stored at the front of the string) or by a special *sentinel* byte that marks the end of the string. In C, a sentinel byte consisting of all zeroes (called a *NUL*) is used to mark the end of a string. Thus, a string constant such as "Hello" occupies a total of six bytes of memory; five for the letters of the word and a sixth byte for the terminating byte of all zeroes (Figure 2-10).

'H'	'e'	'l'	'l'	'o'	NUL
01001000	01100101	01101100	01101100	01101111	00000000
48	65	6C	6C	6F	00

FIGURE 2-10 Representation of the string "Hello" in C.

2.6   BINARY-CODED DECIMAL

Binary-coded decimal (BCD) is a representation in which each digit of a decimal number is encoded separately. Storing the digits separately simplifies the process of recording numeric data from a keypad or displaying results on a numeric display such as that of a cash register.

There are 10 decimal digits, thus requiring four bits to encode each digit. In packed BCD, two decimal digits are stored in a single byte of eight bits. Unpacked BCD stores only a single digit per byte to facilitate access to the individual decimal digits of a number. Examples of these two formats are shown in Figure 2-11. Packed BCD was introduced many years ago as a means to conserve memory. With the drastic decline in the price of memory, use of packed BCD is no longer as important.

The BCD format represents only the magnitude of a number; if signed numbers are required, the sign must be stored separately and the number manipulated as if it were a sign-plus-magnitude format.

Some computers provide special instructions to support BCD arithmetic and for converting between BCD and unsigned binary. Usually, however, these instructions do not provide a complete set of arithmetic operators and must be combined with other instructions within more complex algorithms to perform any really useful arithmetic.

Decimal digits can also be represented using their corresponding ASCII codes. Many display devices now use ASCII input data, and converting between a BCD digit and its ASCII representation is extremely simple. Given a byte containing a value between 0 and 9, simply OR it with 00110000 to get its ASCII representation; given the ASCII representation of a decimal digit, simply AND it with 00001111 to recover the corresponding decimal integer.

Given today's extremely fast processor speeds, any advantage that BCD instructions once offered is now relatively insignificant.

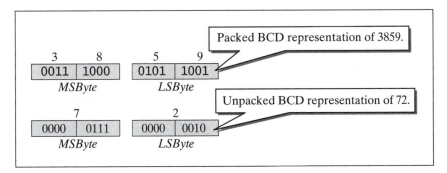

FIGURE 2-11   Packed and unpacked BCD representations.

PROBLEMS

1. Give the entire count sequence of binary patterns for 3-bit unsigned integers.
2. What is the decimal value represented by the 8-bit binary number 11001001.0101_2 when interpreted as:
   (a) An unsigned number?
   (b) A 2's-complement number?

3. What is the decimal value represented by the binary number 10001101_2 when interpreted as:
   (a) A sign + magnitude number?
   (b) A 2's-complement number?

4. Use polynomial evaluation to:
   (a) Convert 101101_2 to base 10.
   (b) Convert $DEAF_{16}$ to base 10.
   (c) Convert 0.324_7 to base 10.

5. Use repeated division to:
   (a) Convert 150_{10} to base 2.
   (b) Convert 1500_{10} to base 16.
   (c) Convert 400_{10} to base 7.

6. Use repeated multiplication to[5]:
   (a) Convert 0.9_{10} to base 2.
   (b) Convert 0.9_{10} to base 16.
   (c) Convert 0.9_{10} to base 3.

7. Use shortcuts based on power relationships to:
   (a) Convert $ACE5_{16}$ to base 2.
   (b) Convert $FACE_{16}$ to base 8.
   (c) Convert 1011.0111_2 to base 8.
   (d) Convert 232.1_4 to base 8.
   (e) Convert 17.6_9 to base 3.

8. Perform the indicated conversions:
   (a) Convert $FA.CE_{16}$ to base 2 (binary).
   (b) Convert 101011.01101_2 to base 16 (hexadecimal).
   (c) Convert 56.23_{10} to base 2 (binary).
   (d) Convert 11011.01101_2 to base 10 (decimal).
   (e) Convert 12.34_5 to base 7.

9. Convert the decimal number -37.1_{10} to 16-bit 2's-complement binary, with 8 bits of integer part and 8 bits of fractional part.

---

[5] If the process repeats indefinitely, calculate as few digits as necessary to provide same or better resolution.

10. What is the 2's-complement 8-bit representation of -100_{10}?

11. Give the 2's-complement 8-bit representation of -7.7_{10}, with the binary point in the middle (e.g., bbbb.bbbb).

12. For each of the following 2's-complement numbers, give the corresponding 8-bit representation of the negative of its value:
   (a) 01010101.
   (b) 10101010.
   (c) 1000.0001
   (d) 0111.1110

13. Consider a 2's-complement number represented by n bits, with the binary point placed between the two most significant bits (e.g., b.bb. . . . b).
   (a) Give an algebraic expression in terms of n for the *positive* value that has the smallest nonzero magnitude.
   (b) Give the binary representation of (a), where n is 8.
   (c) Give an algebraic expression in terms of n for the *negative* value that has the smallest nonzero magnitude.
   (d) Give the binary representation of (c), where n is 8.

14. Give the 32-bit binary representation of the floating-point value -25.1:

31	30	23	22	0

15. The ASCII code for the symbol "0" is 30_{16}. Use this fact to determine the hex constants that would be stored in memory, starting at address N, for the C character string "12345":

Address N	N+1	N+2	N+3	N+4	N+5	N+6	. . .

16. Perform the indicated addition on the following 4-bit operands, filling in all the indicated fields:

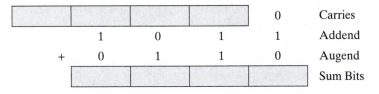

				0	Carries
	1	0	1	1	Addend
+	0	1	1	0	Augend
					Sum Bits

17. Perform the indicated subtraction on the following 4-bit operands, filling in all the indicated fields:

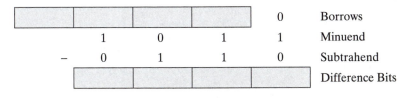

				0	Borrows
	1	0	1	1	Minuend
−	0	1	1	0	Subtrahend
					Difference Bits

18. If the operands are unsigned, then does an overflow occur:
    (a) In problem 16?
    (b) In problem 17?

19. If the operands are signed, then does an overflow occur:
    (a) In problem 16?
    (b) In problem 17?

20. Find the indicated *sum* of the following signed 8-bit 2's-complement numbers and indicate which cause an arithmetic overflow to occur:

    (a)   00111110   (b)   01011011   (c)   11101011
         +01101100   + 10110101   + 11110100

21. Find the indicated *difference* of the following signed 8-bit 2's-complement numbers and indicate which cause an arithmetic overflow to occur:

    (a)   00101100   (b)   00101110   (c)   11000100
         +01011010   +11101011   +10101101

22. Assume that the C assignment statement "s = a + b" has just been executed, where all variables are declared as signed ints. Write a C expression that is true if and only if the addition results in an overflow.

23. Repeat problem 22 for the C assignment statement "s = a – b".

24. What is the most positive decimal value of a 6-bit 2's-complement number?

25. What is the most negative decimal value of a 6-bit 2's-complement number?

26. What is the minimum decimal value of a 6-bit unsigned number?

27. What is the maximum decimal value of a 6-bit unsigned number?

28. The exact binary representation of one-sixth (1/6) requires an infinite number of digits. Truncating it (discarding extra bits) to make it fit within a fixed-precision representation creates a representational error. What is the absolute error that results from storing one-sixth without rounding using 8 fractional bits?

True/False:

29. Overflow is impossible when subtracting one unsigned number from another.

30. Overflow is impossible when subtracting two signed operands of the same sign.

31. There are two representations of zero in 2's complement.

32. If rollover occurs when incrementing an integer, there is an overflow.

33. In 2's complement, the absolute values of full-scale negative and full-scale positive are identical.

CHAPTER 3

Implementing Arithmetic

3.1 2'S-COMPLEMENT AND HARDWARE COMPLEXITY

Computers manipulate bit patterns. *How* those patterns are assigned to the values they represent has a big effect on hardware complexity. For example, both the sign-plus-magnitude and the 2's-complement representation allow us to recognize whether a number is positive or negative simply by looking at the most significant bit. However, wouldn't it be great if patterns were assigned to values in such a way that the same hardware could be used to perform integer arithmetic regardless of whether the operands were signed or unsigned? That is exactly what the 2's-complement representation is intended to do!

For example, suppose we were to add the two *unsigned* decimal values 9 and 3. The computer would be given their binary equivalents, 1001 and 0011. The correct decimal result is 12, so the hardware that performs addition is designed to produce the binary equivalent, 1100. But what happens if those same binary patterns are interpreted instead as *signed* numbers according to the 2's-complement scheme shown in Figure 3-1? Then, the operands would be −7 and +3, and the same binary result of 1100 produced by the hardware would correctly be interpreted as −4.

The fundamental characteristic of 2's-complement representation that makes this work is that it follows a count sequence[1] from full-scale negative to full-scale positive (with a rollover at zero), in much the same way that the representation of unsigned numbers follows a count sequence from the smallest magnitude (zero) to the largest. The sign-plus-magnitude representation does not share this characteristic.

In a similar manner, using the 2's-complement representation permits one hardware subtractor for both signed and unsigned integers. However, it also turns out that we do not even need separate hardware for addition and subtraction! All we need to do in order to compute the difference A − B is to *add* the negative of B to A, as in A + (−B). In other words, we simply need to add some hardware to form the 2's complement of B.

All hardware adders accept an initial "carry-in" that can be used to add a constant of 0 or 1 to the sum. Normally, this input is set to 0. However, if we set it to 1 and invert all the bits of B, the net effect will be the same as adding −B instead of B. We can

---

[1] The sequence of numeric values represented by the sequence of patterns is monotonically increasing, meaning that it increases by one at each step.

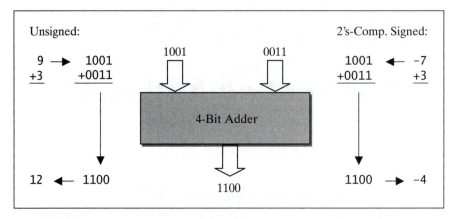

FIGURE 3-1   One adder for both unsigned and 2's-complement signed numbers.

then implement a single circuit with one control input that will compute either A + B or A − B by simply using a set of exclusive-OR gates as a controlled inverter that passes either B or its inverse to the adder, as shown in Figure 3-2.

There are minor differences, however, in how other operations are implemented. Suppose, for example, that we need to compare two integers X and Y. Knowing their bit patterns is not sufficient to determine which represents the greater value. For example, 1001 is not always greater than 0011. That is true only if these patterns represent unsigned integers. If they represent signed integers, then 0011 represents the greater value.

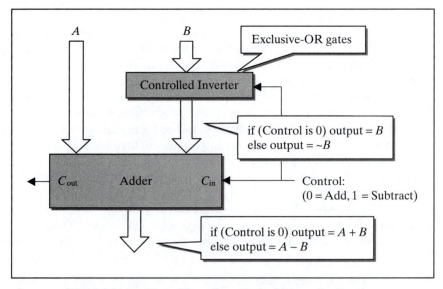

FIGURE 3-2   Modified adder performs both addition and subtraction.

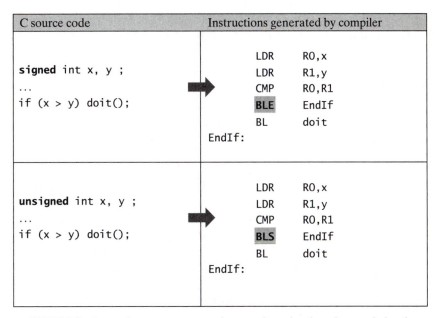

C source code	Instructions generated by compiler

signed int x, y ;
 	
...
 	
if (x > y) doit();
	LDR R0,x
	LDR R1,y
	CMP R0,R1
	BLE EndIf
	BL doit
	EndIf:

unsigned int x, y ;
 	
...
 	
if (x > y) doit();
	LDR R0,x
	LDR R1,y
	CMP R0,R1
	BLS EndIf
	BL doit
	EndIf:

FIGURE 3-3   Instructions to compare two integers depend on how they are declared.

The approach is to compute their difference without regard to whether the operands are signed or unsigned, and then examine the characteristics of the difference — the borrow-out and (in the case of signed integers) the sign of the result and whether an overflow occurred. The borrow-out determines which is the greater of two unsigned operands, but, for signed operands, we must look at the sign of the difference and whether an overflow occurred.

Although a single subtractor can be used to compute the difference, to determine which of the two values is greater, the computer must examine the characteristics of the result. In Figure 3-3, the compiler generates code that uses a compare (CMP) instruction to compute the difference $X - Y$. It actually *discards* this difference, saving only the characteristics of the difference and then uses that information in a conditional branch instruction that follows the comparison. As you can see, the code generated by the compiler to compare two integers uses different conditional jump instructions for signed and unsigned operands (Figure 3-3).

Unsigned Operands		Signed Operands		
Borrow Out	Relationship	Sign of $X - Y$	Overflow	Relationship
0	$X \geq Y$	Positive	No	$X \geq Y$
1	$X < Y$	Negative	Yes	
		Positive	Yes	$X < Y$
		Negative	No	

FIGURE 3-4   Comparing signed and unsigned integers.

Differences in how multiplication and division work for signed versus unsigned integers will require us to use different machine instructions for those operations as well.

3.2 MULTIPLICATION AND DIVISION

Compared to addition or subtraction, multiplication and division are inherently more complex operations that involve a number of intermediate calculations. Some of the least expensive and older processors do not even provide multiply or divide instructions, requiring that these operations be implemented in software. Designing a processor with multiply and divide instructions involves a design trade-off between chip real estate and execution time. One solution is to implement the intermediate steps as a sequential process that requires only a small amount of digital circuitry but results in a significantly longer execution time. On the other hand, the execution time can be made faster, but only by calculating the intermediate steps in parallel by using more digital circuitry. These issues have led programmers to look for situations in which there are faster and more efficient ways to multiply and divide.

3.2.1 Signed Versus Unsigned Multiplication

Computers often have two different multiply instructions: one for unsigned operands and the other for signed (2's-complement) operands. What is interesting is that the difference between the two only appears in the most-significant half of their double-length product.

Consider two 4-bit operands whose bit patterns are 1100 and 0110. As unsigned numbers, their decimal equivalents are 12 and 6 whose product is 72, represented as the double-length product $0100\ 1000_2$. However, if interpreted as signed 2's-complement numbers, their decimal equivalents are -4 and $+6$ whose product is -24, represented as $1110\ 1000_2$.

In a high-level programming language like C, when you multiply two numbers of the same type, the product is also the same type. In other words, the product of two n-bit integers will also be an n-bit integer. This means that the code generated by the compiler actually discards the most significant half of the product, and thus the compiler could use either a signed or an unsigned multiply instruction.

On some processors, a signed multiply may take slightly longer to execute than an unsigned multiply. So, if you are programming in assembly and store a product in a variable the same size as the operands used to produce it, then always use an unsigned multiply!

3.2.2 Shifting Instead of Multiplying or Dividing by Powers of 2

The least expensive microprocessors sometimes do not provide integer multiply or divide instructions, or execute such instructions much more slowly than the instructions for integer addition or subtraction. Multiplying by a power of 2, however, is easily implemented as a left-shift that will often execute in very few clock cycles:

$$2^k \times A = A << k\,(A \text{ is shifted left by k bits})$$

This works for both positive and negative values of A.

Positive operands can be divided by a power of 2 by right shifting, as in:

$$A \div 2^k = A >> k \,(A \text{ is shifted right by k bits})$$

However, negative operands are more problematic. First, we must use an "arithmetic" right shift that *preserves* the sign bit. Rather than entering a 0 into the most significant bit position as in a regular ("logical") right shift, an arithmetic right shift fills the most significant bit position with a copy of its previous value. For example, dividing the 8-bit 2's-complement number -80_{10} (10110000_2) by 2^1 should produce -40_{10} (11011000_2). Repeating the process divides by higher powers of 2. That is, arithmetically shifting -80_{10} right twice produces 11101100_2 (-20_{10}).

Another issue is the difference between an arithmetic right shift and an integer division that occurs when the dividend is both negative and odd. For example, -1 divided by 2 is 0, but if you shift it right arithmetically, the result will be -1. The problem is the different way in which the two operations handle the fractional part of the quotient. Dividing -15 by 2 should ideally produce a quotient of -7.5, but of course integer division discards the fractional part of the result leaving only the integer -7. While division always truncates toward 0, an arithmetic right shift always truncates toward negative infinity. This difference only shows up with negative odd numbers:

Operand	Operation	True Quotient	Integer Quotient	Arithmetic Right Shift
Positive & even	$+10 \div 2$	$+5.0$	$+5$	$+5$
Positive & odd	$+11 \div 2$	$+5.5$	$+5$	$+5$
Negative & even	$-10 \div 2$	-5.0	-5	-5
Negative & odd	$-11 \div 2$	-5.5	-5	-6

The error introduced for negative odd dividends can be corrected if we always reduce the magnitude of a negative dividend by one before shifting:

Operand	Original Operation	Adjusted Dividend	Arithmetic Right Shift
Positive & even	$+10 \div 2$	$+10$	$+5$
Positive & odd	$+11 \div 2$	$+11$	$+5$
Negative & even	$-10 \div 2$	-9	-5
Negative & odd	$-11 \div 2$	-10	-5

The pre-shift adjustment can be implemented as an "if" statement that only adds $+1$ to the dividend if it is negative. Processors, however, are designed to optimize the execution of instructions fetched sequentially from memory because the vast majority of code is a "straight-line" that does not branch. Any deviation from sequential execution (as inherent in an "if" statement) disrupts the sequential flow and causes a small delay that we prefer to avoid when possible. Fortunately, there is a better way to do the pre-shift adjustment.

Many processors can extend the sign of an integer using a single instruction, effectively doubling the number of bits in its representation:

$$11101010 \rightarrow 11111111\ 11101010, \text{ or}$$

$$00101011 \rightarrow 00000000\ 00101011$$

When interpreted as an integer, the sign extension (the most significant half of the result) will be 0 for positive operands and −1 for negative operands. This can be used to correct the result of an arithmetic right shift by subtracting the sign extension from the operand before the shift is applied.

3.2.3 Multiplying by an Arbitrary Constant

Multiplication by constants other than powers of 2 can sometimes be implemented more efficiently using a sequence of shifts, additions, and subtractions. Depending on the processor, these instructions can execute as much as 50 times faster than a multiplication and thus can be an effective alternative. There is, however, usually more than one possible sequence for any particular constant and the optimal choice depends on the constant's binary bit pattern. In general, constants whose representation contains isolated 1's are best implemented using addition, while those containing a sequence of 1's are best implemented using subtraction:

Decimal Constant	8-bit Binary Representation	Optimal Decomposition	Number of Instructions[2]
+9	01001010	$2^6A + 2^3A + 2^1A$	3 shifts and 2 additions
+30	00111110	$2^6A - 2^1A$	2 shifts and 1 subtraction
−14	11110010	$-2^4A + 2^1A$	2 shifts and 1 subtraction
−17	11101111	$-2^4A - 2^0A$	1 shift and 2 subtractions

Rearranging the decomposition can make implementation a little easier to envision. For example, the decomposition of +9 can be rewritten as $2^1 \times (A + 2^2 \times (A + 2^3A))$. By processing the expression from right to left, the sequence of instructions becomes:

1. Get a copy of A: → A
2. Shift left 3 bits: → 2^3A
3. Add A: → $A + 2^3A$
4. Shift left 2 bits: → $2^2(A + 2^3A)$
5. Add A: → $A + 2^2(A + 2^3A)$
6. Shift left 1 bit: → $2^1(A + 2^2(A + 2^3A))$

---

[2] A single shift instruction can typically shift an operand multiple bit positions.

Many modern reduced instruction set computer (RISC) microprocessors (such as the ARM family of processor chips) are able to pre-shift the operand of any instruction, allowing an even more efficient implementation:

1. Get a copy of A, left-shifted 6 bits: $\rightarrow 2^6A$
2. Add A, left-shifted 3 bits: $\rightarrow 2^6A + 2^3A$
3. Add A, left-shifted 1 bit: $\rightarrow 2^6A + 2^3A + 2^1A$

3.2.4 Dividing by an Arbitrary Constant

If your divisor is a constant but no divide instruction is available, it is still possible to divide if your processor has a multiply instruction using the principal of reciprocal multiplication. In principal, we simply multiply by $1/B$ instead of dividing by B:

$$A \div B = A \times (1/B)$$

The problem of course is that $1/B$ is zero for any B greater than 1. To solve this, use $2^k/B$ instead of $1/B$ and divide the result by 2^k by simply shifting it right (arithmetically) by k bits.

$$A \times (1/B) = [A \times (2^k/B)] \div 2^k$$
$$= [A \times (2^k/B)] >> k$$

Since a multiply instruction produces a double-length product P, the most and least significant halves will always be left in a pair of single-length storage locations, P_{hi} and P_{lo}. If we choose k to be the same as the fundamental word size of the processor, then rather than shifting P to the right by k bits, we can simply take the quotient from the more significant half, P_{hi}.

Reciprocal multiplication can introduce an error in the quotient. When $2^k/B$ is not a whole number, discarding the fractional part provides a multiplier whose value is a little too small.[3] If the difference is large enough, the resulting quotient will also be too small. This can be corrected, however, by computing the remainder as the dividend A minus the product of B times the quotient. If the remainder is greater than the divisor, then you must add 1 to the quotient.

3.3   ARITHMETIC FOR FIXED-POINT REALS

Many embedded application have little or no need for real numbers. When they are needed, fixed-point reals are more likely to be found than floating-point for a variety of reasons. The processor may not have floating-point instructions, a processor with floating-point may add too much cost, or using floating-point may cause an unacceptable performance penalty.

---

[3] More correctly, discarding the fractional part of a positive multiplier will make the values of the multiplier and resulting product smaller, but doing the same for a negative multiplier will actually make them larger.

Scaling provides a way to process real numbers with the same hardware that is used for integers. For example, the 8-bit number 01011110 has a decimal value of 94 when interpreted as an integer. However, if we assume that 3 bits are on the right of an implied binary point as in 01011.110, then the decimal interpretation becomes 11.75. In effect, the integer has been scaled by dividing it by 2^3, where the exponent is determined by the number of bits on the right of the binary point.

As shown in Table 3-1, if you add or subtract two fixed-point real numbers that share a common scale factor, the result will also have the same scale factor.

Operands with different scale factors must be aligned before adding or subtracting. To do this, shift one operand until the binary points of both line up and their scale factors become equal. If you shift the operand that has fewer fractional bits (as shown in Table 3-2), then you must be careful that the required left-shift does not cause overflow. If, instead, you shift the operand that has more fractional bits, then you must be careful that the required right-shift does not cause a loss of precision (as shown in Table 3-3). Either approach could be used, but the scale factor of the resulting sum or difference will be quite different.

TABLE 3-1   Adding and Subtracting Scaled Fixed-Point Real Numbers

Operand/Result	Bit Pattern	Integer	÷Scale Factor	=Value
A	00011.110	+30	2^3	+3.750
B	00110.011	+51	2^3	+6.375
A + B	01010.001	+81	2^3	+10.125
A − B	11101.011	−21	2^3	−2.625

TABLE 3-2   Aligning Operands by Shifting Left

Operand/Result	Bit Pattern	Integer	÷Scale Factor	=Value
A	0001001.1	19	2^1	+9.500
B	00011.110	30	2^3	+3.750
$2^2 \times A$	01001.100	76	2^3	+9.500
$2^2 \times A + B$	01101.010	106	2^3	+13.250

TABLE 3-3   Aligning Operands by Shifting Right

Operand/Result	Bit Pattern	Integer	÷Scale Factor	=Value
A	0001001.1	19	2^1	+9.500
B	00011.110	30	2^3	+3.750
$B \div 2^2$	0000011.1	7	2^1	+3.500
$A + B \div 2^2$	0001101.0	26	2^1	+13.000

As with any fixed-precision scheme, we have to be careful about overflow. Addition and subtraction with fixed-point real numbers can overflow just as easily as with integers. If necessary, we can avoid the overflow by pre-shifting both operands to the right by 1-bit position, that is, by preadjusting their scale factors to trade a bit of precision for one more bit of range.

Multiplication and division do not require that the binary points of their operands be aligned. The number of fractional bits in the product $A \times B$, for example, is simply the sum of the number of fractional bits in A plus the number in B (Table 3-4). Dividing two fixed-point real numbers is similar to reversing the multiplication: the number of fractional bits in the quotient $A \div B$ is the number of fractional bits in A minus the number in B (Table 3-5).

You may have noticed that the quotient in Table 3-5 is not exactly accurate[4] because integer division truncates the result to the largest whole number less than or equal to the exact quotient. We can improve the accuracy of our result by pre-shifting the dividend to the left as much as possible before dividing, as is shown in Table 3-6. Of course, this changes the scale factor of the dividend (and thus that of the quotient), but it provides more fractional bits in the result, for a more accurate result.

TABLE 3-4   Multiplying Fixed-Point Real Numbers

Operand / Result	Bit Pattern	Integer	÷Scale Factor	=Value
A	0000000000011.110	30	2^3	+3.7500
B	00000000001100.11	×51	2^2	+12.7500
$A \times B$	00000101111.11010	=1530	2^5	+47.8125

TABLE 3-5   Dividing Fixed-Point Real Numbers

Operand / Result	Bit Pattern	Integer	÷Scale Factor	=Value
A	00000101111.11010	1530	2^5	+47.8125
B	0000000001110.011	÷115	2^3	+14.3750
$A \div B$	00000000000011.01	=13	2^2	+3.2500

TABLE 3-6   Shifting Before Dividing Fixed-Point Real Numbers

Operand / Result	Bit Pattern	Integer	÷Scale Factor	=Value
$2^3 \times A$	00101111.11010000	12240	2^8	+47.8125
B	0000000001110.011	÷115	2^3	+14.3750
$2^3 \times A \div B$	00000000011.01010	=106	2^5	+3.3125

---

[4] The true quotient (correct to 10 decimal digits) is ±3.326086957.

Moving our imaginary binary point to the left as much as possible allows fixed-point values to be expressed with greater precision. For any given variable, therefore, we should always choose the scale factor with the largest possible negative exponent that still leaves enough integer bits for a reasonable range of values.

3.3.1 Fixed-Point Using a Universal 16.16 Format

Finding the optimum choice of scale factor for a fixed-point variable requires knowing what range of values it will have during execution. When range and resolution requirements are modest, however, a simple approach is to use 32 bits for all fixed-point numbers, with 16 bits in both the whole and the fractional parts (Figure 3-5).

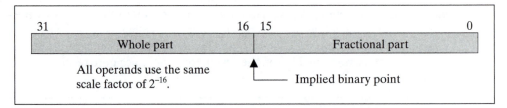

FIGURE 3-5   The 16.16 fixed-point representation.

With all operands using the same scale factor, addition and subtraction no longer require pre-alignment of operands. Multiplication and division, however, still require *some* adjustments or else the result will not have the same scale factor as the operands. Remember that when you multiply two fixed-point operands together, their scale factors are multiplied as well:

$$\text{Product} = (A \div 2^{16}) \times (B \div 2^{16})$$
$$= (A \times B) \div 2^{32}$$

What we need is a product in 16.16 format (i.e., a result with a scale factor of 2^{16}). In other words, the integer product needs to be right-shifted by 16 bits. Multiplying the two 32-bit integers produces a 64-bit product, with an implied binary point in the middle. Right-shifting this product by 16 bits and then putting the result back into a 32-bit location means that we are discarding 16 bits from each end of the integer product. Discarding the least significant 16 bits simply causes some loss of precision; discarding the most significant 16 bits requires imposing a maximum magnitude restriction on the operands to avoid overflow (Figure 3-6).

When you *divide* one 16.16 fixed-point operand by another, their scale factors cancel:

$$\text{Quotient} = (A \div 2^{16}) \div (B \div 2^{16})$$
$$= (A \div B) \div 2^{0}$$
$$= A \div B$$

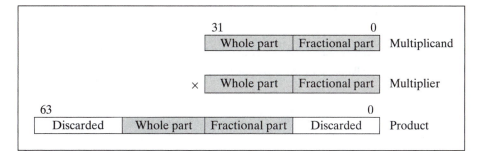

FIGURE 3-6   Using integer multiplication to produce a fixed-point product.

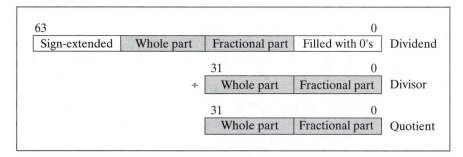

FIGURE 3-7   Using integer division to produce a fixed-point quotient.

Again, what is needed is a result with a scale factor of 2^{16} (not 2^0)! Rather than shifting the quotient left by 16 bits, however, it is better to left-shift the dividend because division with a 64-bit dividend and a 32-bit divisor produces a 32-bit quotient. Given the extra dividend bits, it is better to pre-shift the sign-extended dividend left by 16 bits, as shown in Figure 3-7.

Fixed-point multiplication and division are typically implemented as functions written in assembly language, to take advantage of the double-length products and dividends available with the integer instruction set of most processors. This makes implementation of multiplication and division of fixed-point numbers in 16.16 format rather straightforward in assembler on a 32-bit processor. Implementation in a high-level language (such as C), however, is problematic, because a single data type (and thus word size) is used for both the operands and the result.

3.3.2 Fixed-Point Using a Universal 32.32 Format

The range of the 16.16 format is limited to approximately ±32767 with a precision of about five decimal digits to the right of the radix point. When memory space is not an issue, a significant improvement in range and precision can be obtained by using 64 bits

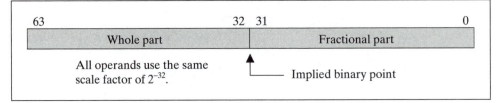

FIGURE 3-8   The 32.32 fixed-point representation.

for all fixed-point numbers, with 32 bits in both the whole and the fractional parts (Figure 3-8).[5]

3.3.3 Multiplication of 32.32 Fixed-Point Reals

By now, you can guess that the 32.32 format would be most easily implemented on a 64-bit processor. Unfortunately, 64-bit processors are generally considered too expensive for almost all embedded applications. As an example of how 32.32 fixed-point arithmetic can be implemented on a 32-bit processor, let us consider multiplication. Since multiplication is such a fundamental operation, our objective will be to maximize performance by devising an algorithm that can be coded in assembler, using regular 32-bit integer operations, and without using any loops or branching.

Our strategy will be to consider first how to compute the 128-bit product of two 64-bit *unsigned* integers and then to modify that result to handle *signed* integers. Next, we use our 32.32 scaling to select which 64 bits of the 128-bit product to keep, and note how discarding the rest simplifies the computation.

Consider a 64-bit integer A, with the bits numbered in little endian format $(A_{63}A_{62}...A_0)$. The *unsigned* value of A can be expressed, via polynomial evaluation, as:

$$A_u = 2^{63} A_{63} + 2^{62}A_{62} + \cdots + 2^0A_0$$

Separating the first term from the rest, we have

$$A_u = 2^{63}A_{63} + (2^{62}A_{62} + \cdots + 2^0A_0)$$
$$= 2^{63}A_{63} + A_{62...0} \text{ (where } A_{62...0} = 2^{62}A_{62} + \cdots + 2^0A_0)$$

Thus, the 128-bit product of two 64-bit unsigned integers is

$$A_uB_u = (2^{63}A_{63} + A_{62...0}) \times (2^{63}B_{63} + B_{62...0})$$
$$= 2^{126}A_{63}B_{63} + 2^{63}A_{63}B_{62...0} + 2^{63}B_{63}A_{62...0} + A_{62...0}B_{62...0}$$

---

[5] This approach was used in the Sony PlayStation, whose MIPS processor has no floating-point unit.

Now, consider what happens when the bits are interpreted as a 64-bit *signed* integer. First, note that the signed value of A can be expressed as

$$A_s = -2^{63}A_{63} + (2^{62}A_{62} + \cdots + 2^0 A_0)$$
$$= -2^{63}A_{63} + A_{62\ldots0}$$

Thus, the 128-bit product of two 64-bit signed integers is

$$A_s B_s = (-2^{63}A_{63} + A_{62\ldots0}) \times (-2^{63}B_{63} + B_{62\ldots0})$$
$$= 2^{126}A_{63}B_{63} - 2^{63}(A_{63}B_{62\ldots0} + B_{63}A_{62\ldots0}) + A_{62\ldots0}B_{62\ldots0}$$

This differs from $A_u B_u$ only in the sign of the middle term, so we can simply compute $A_s B_s$ as:

$$A_s B_s = A_u B_u - 2 \times 2^{63}(A_{63}B_{62\ldots0} + B_{63}A_{62\ldots0})$$
$$= A_u B_u - 2^{64}A_{63}B_{62\ldots0} - 2^{64}B_{63}A_{62\ldots0}$$

Graphically, the product $A_s B_s$ is computed as shown in Figure 3-9.

Remember that the 0's shown in the most significant bits of the last two partial products in Figure 3-9 occur because $A_{62\ldots0}$ and $B_{62\ldots0}$ are 63-bit (not 64-bit) unsigned values.

A and B hold fixed-point real numbers in a 32.32 format; given that $A_s B_s$ is to be stored in the same format, then, we must discard 32 bits from both ends of the partial products, to preserve the proper 32.32 scaling, as is shown in Figure 3-10.

Computing the middle 64 bits of the product $A_u B_u$ (the first of the three terms shown above) using integer multiplication on a 32-bit processor is accomplished by breaking each 64-bit operand into two 32-bit halves (i.e., $A_u = 2^{32}A_{hi} + A_{lo}$ and $B_u = 2^{32}B_{hi} + B_{lo}$) and then combining the cross-products:

$$A_u B_u = (2^{32}A_{hi} + A_{lo}) \times (B_u = 2^{32}B_{hi} + B_{lo})$$
$$= 2^{64}A_{hi}B_{hi} + 2^{32}(A_{hi}B_{lo} + A_{lo}B_{hi}) + A_{lo}B_{lo}$$

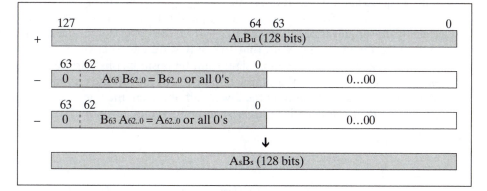

FIGURE 3-9   Computing a signed fixed-point product from an unsigned product.

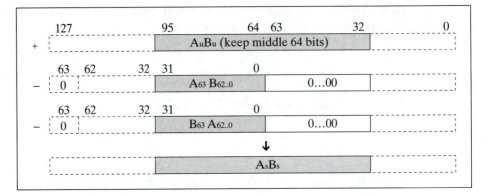

FIGURE 3-10   Converting from 64.64 to 32.32 fixed-point format.

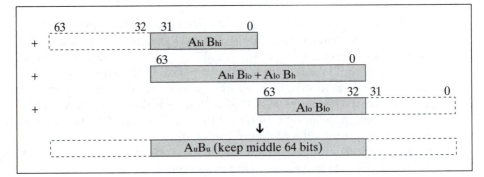

FIGURE 3-11   Computing the 32.32 unsigned fixed-point product.

We are going to keep only the middle 64 bits, so we can discard the 32-bit upper half of $A_{hi}B_{hi}$ and the 32-bit lower half of $A_{lo}B_{lo}$ as shown in Figure 3-11.

All that remains (to compute the signed product A_sB_s) is to conditionally subtract the lower halves of $A_{62...0}$ and $B_{62...0}$ from the upper half of the unsigned product A_uB_u (see Figure 3-11). Note that the only difference between A and $A_{62...0}$ and between B and $B_{62...0}$ is the most significant bit position; this is irrelevant since we use only their lower halves in the subtractions. Thus, to convert the unsigned product into a signed product, simply subtract the lower half of B from the upper half of the unsigned product A_uB_u if A is negative ($A_{63} = 1$) and subtract the lower half of A if B is negative ($B_{63} = 1$).[6]

---

[6] Note that changing the unsigned product to a signed product by adjusting the upper half is related to the earlier discussion about the difference between signed and unsigned multiplication.

3.3.4 Example: Multiplying Two 4.4 Fixed-Point Reals

To illustrate the total algorithm, consider the problem of multiplying two numbers A and B, each represented as a 2's-complement 4.4 fixed-point real. To simplify the example, let us assume that this is to be implemented on a 4-bit microprocessor whose unsigned multiply instruction produces an 8-bit product from two 4-bit operands.

$$\text{Let A} = -1.50_{10} = 1110.1000_2 \quad \text{Note: As an unsigned integer, } A_u$$
$$= 11101000_2 = 232_{10}$$
$$\text{Let B} = +2.75_{10} = 0010.1100_2 \quad \text{Note: As an unsigned integer, } B_u$$
$$= 00101100_2 = 44_{10}$$

The 16-bit product $A_u B_u$ should be $232 \times 44 = 10208_{10}$. The following expression shows how it would be calculated on a 4-bit CPU:

$$A_u B_u = 2^8 A_{hi} B_{hi} + 2^4 (A_{hi} B_{lo} + A_{lo} B_{hi}) + A_{lo} B_{lo}$$
$$= 2^8 (1110 \times 0010) + 2^4 (1110 \times 1100 + 1000 \times 0010) + (1000 \times 1100)$$
$$= 2^8 (00011100) + 2^4 (10101000 + 00010000) + 01100000$$

The powers of 2 simply determine how the various 8-bit partial products should be aligned:

```
0001   1100
       1010   1000
       0001   0000
              0110   0000
-----------------------------
0010   0111   1110   0000   = 10208₁₀
```

Remember that of this, we really only need the middle 8 bits (01111110_2). All that is left is to conditionally subtract the lower halves of A and B, depending (respectively) on the signs of B and A. Since only A is negative, we simply subtract the lower half of B from the upper half of the 8-bits calculated above:

```
0111   1110
-1100
-----------
1011   1110
```

Inserting the binary point and converting to decimal to check, we get:

$$1011.1110_2 = -0100.0010_2 = -4.125_{10} (\text{which is correct!})$$

With a little ingenuity, this algorithm for multiplication of two signed 32.32 fixed-point real numbers can be implemented as straight-line code (without any loops or branching). Unfortunately, the algorithm for signed division is much more difficult. In practice, however, most divisions use a constant divisor, and so may be rewritten as an equivalent multiplication by the inverse of the constant. True division of fixed-point reals is only required when the divisor is a variable.

PROBLEMS

1. What shift direction and number of one-bit shifts will divide an unsigned value by 8?

2. What is the shortest sequence of shift, add, and subtract operations applied to x that will produce:
   (a) 21 times x?
   (b) 57 times x?
   (c) 100 times x?
   (d) 188 times x

3. Consider a 12-bit fixed-point real number in 6.6 format. What is:
   (a) The largest positive value in decimal? In binary?
   (b) The largest negative value in decimal? In binary?
   (c) The smallest (nonzero) positive value in decimal? In binary?
   (d) The smallest negative value in decimal? In binary?

4. Give both the 8-bit binary product and its decimal equivalent produced by multiplying the two 4-bit numbers 0110_2 and 1011_2 using:
   (a) Unsigned multiplication?
   (b) Signed multiplication?

5. Overflow during multiplication of two n-bit integers is often defined as a product that exceeds the range of representation available with n bits. Suppose n is 8 and one operand has the value of 100. Give two values for the other operand that differs by 1, such that one product overflows and the other does not.

6. Multiply the following two 16-bit fixed-point signed real numbers together and convert the result into another 16-bit fixed-point signed real number:

	15	14	13	12	11	10	9	8	7	6	5	4	3	2	1	0
−25 1/3	1	0	0	1	1	0	1	0	1	0	1	0	1	0	1	0

	15	14	13	12	11	10	9	8	7	6	5	4	3	2	1	0
+2.5625	0	1	0	1	0	0	1	0	0	0	0	0	0	0	0	0

   Determine what scale factor is required to maximize the fractional precision of the result while making sure that no portion of the whole part is lost in the process.

7. Suppose you need to divide a 32-bit 2's-complement integer variable by a constant, but your CPU has no divide instruction.
   (a) What kind of divisor values allows you to use an arithmetic right shift?
   (b) How do you determine how many bit positions to shift the dividend?
   (c) If shifted, what kind of dividend values causes the answer be off by one?

8. Assume that a divisor is such that division cannot be done by a simple arithmetic right shift so that you must use reciprocal multiplication instead.
   (a) Does this method always produce the same quotients as an integer divide instruction?
   (b) How do you determine the integer value of the constant multiplier?

(c) Multiplying two 32-bit numbers produces a 64-bit product. What subset of these bits holds the integer quotient?

(d) Reciprocal multiplication sometimes produces a result that is not as accurate as that of a true division. When will reciprocal multiplication produce the *correct* integer quotient?

9. Suppose you multiply two 32-bit numbers using an integer multiply instruction that produces a 64-bit double-length product. Assume that one number is a 32-bit integer, and the other is a 16.16 fixed-point real.

(a) How many bits hold the integer portion of the product?

(b) How many bits hold the fractional portion of the product?

10. Reproduce all the steps in the example of Section 3.3.4 using the values -2.5_{10} and -1.75_{10}.

CHAPTER 4

Getting the Most out of C

This chapter assumes that you have already had an introduction to programming in C, C++, or Java. Knowledge of any one is sufficient to program in C, since all three languages share a common syntax for data types, declarations, expressions, and control statements.

Few students manage to master a programming language in their first programming course. This chapter is not a complete treatment of C, nor is it intended to be. However, it does provide several examples of complete C programs to help reinforce the basics. If your only experience has been in C++, or Java, do not be surprised if it takes a while to make the paradigm shift from the object-oriented style of programming to the procedural style used in C.

Every programming language has its own variety of syntactic and semantic features. Some of these have more significance in software written for real-time embedded systems than in normal desktop applications. Writing software for embedded systems demands a careful understanding of integer data types and of facilities for manipulating bits and bytes. This chapter describes in detail how these facilities are implemented, using features of C that are either omitted or only touched on briefly in most introductory courses and usually only mastered after years of experience.

4.1 INTEGER DATA TYPES

In 1989, the International Organization for Standardization published the C89 standard (often referred to as ANSI C), which defined an extensive set of integer data types as shown in Table 4-1. The reserved words char and int are the names of fundamental data types, with unsigned, signed, short, long, and long long modifiers. If one or more modifiers appear in a declaration, the reserved word int is usually understood and may be omitted. If neither signed nor unsigned is used, signed is assumed by default.

The sizes and ranges given in Table 4-1 are typical, but are not required by C89. In fact, the 1989 standard allowed three possible signed representations: sign-plus-magnitude, 1's-complement, and 2's-complement. When used to hold an integer, the fundamental data type char may default to either signed or unsigned, and the primitive data type int may have a size anywhere between that of a short or a long int.

In embedded applications, it is often imperative to know the exact number of bits and range of variables. Several new data types that resolve the data type size and range ambiguities were introduced in the 1999 ISO C99 standard, are documented in the new stdint.h header file introduced by C99, and are now widely implemented by most C compilers (Table 4-2).

TABLE 4-1   Fundamental Integer Data Types in ISO C89 (ANSIC)

Signed Types	Typical Size	Typical Range
signed char	8 bits	−128 to +127
signed short int	16 bits	−32,768 to + 32,767
signed long int	32 bits	−2,147,483,648 to +2,147,483,647
signed long long int	64 bits	-2^{63} to $+(2^{63}-1)$
Unsigned Types	Typical Size	Typical Range
unsigned char	8 bits	0 to 255
unsigned short int	16 bits	0 to 65,535
unsigned long int	32 bits	0 to 4,294,967,295
unsigned long long int	64 bits	0 to 18,446,744,073,709,551,615

Note: ANSIC does not specify the size or range of values for these integer types, but does require that their size be at least as large as listed above. When used without a modifier, the primitive data type int must not be smaller than a short int, nor larger than a long int. The long long integer types are common, but were not formally part of the C language until the ISO C99 standard of 1999.

TABLE 4-2   Additional Integer Data Types in the ISO C99 Standard

Signed Types	Specified Size	Specified Range (2's-complement)
int8_t	8 bits	−128 to +127
int16_t	16 bits	−32,768 to + 32,767
int32_t	32 bits	−2,147,483,648 to +2,147,483,647
int64_t	64 bits	−9,223,372,036,854,775,808 to +9,223,372,036,854,775,807
Unsigned Types	Specified Size	Specified Range
uint8_t	8 bits	0 to 255
uint16_t	16 bits	0 to 65,535
uint32_t	32 bits	0 to 4,294,967,295
uint64_t	64 bits	0 to 18,446,744,073,709,551,615

Although the new C99 integer data types are an important addition for embedded applications, there are some compilers that still do not support them.[1] In most situations, a simple workaround is to create your own header file containing typedef declarations of the new type names. As shown, the C99 pre-defined macro (__STDC_VERSION__) can be used to hide these declarations from a C99-compliant compiler.

```
#ifndef __STDC_VERSION__
typedef signed            char          int8_t  ;
typedef signed            short int     int16_t ;
```

----

[1] C99 is not supported by the Microsoft Visual Studio 2010 C compiler.

```
typedef signed        long  int       int32_t ;
typedef signed        long  long int int64_t ;

typedef unsigned      char            uint8_t ;
typedef unsigned      short int       uint16_t ;
typedef unsigned      long  int       uint32_t ;
typedef unsigned      long  long int uint64_t ;

#endif
```

4.1.1 Integer Range and the Standard Header File LIMITS.H

Before defining your own data types for a compiler that does not support the C99 standard, you should verify that the size and range of the fundamental integer data types are the same as shown in Table 4-1. Most compilers provide a standard header file called limits.h that specifies the range of integer types implemented by the compiler. The minimum and maximum values supported by each type are specified by macros as given in Table 4-3.

TABLE 4-3   Minimum and Maximum Integer Values Defined in LIMITS.H

Data Type	Minimum	Maximum
signed char	SCHAR_MIN	SCHAR_MAX
signed short int	SHRT_MIN	SHRT_MAX
signed long int	LONG_MIN	LONG_MAX
signed long long int	LLONG_MIN	LLONG_MAX
unsigned char	0	UCHAR_MAX
unsigned short int	0	USHRT_MAX
unsigned long int	0	ULONG_MAX
unsigned long long int	0	ULLONG_MAX

You can also compile and run the program in Example 4-1 to check the size and range of integer data types for any C compiler (Figure 4-1). The program measures the size of each data type by counting how many 1-bit shifts are needed to empty all the 1's out of an operand.

The program then determines if the data type is unsigned by comparing an operand that has a 1 in its most-significant bit against zero. The operand's value will be interpreted as less than zero only if the data type is signed.

If the data type is signed, the program then determines whether the representation is 2's-complement, 1's-complement, or sign-plus-magnitude by checking how it represents the value of −1. The maximum (most positive) value will always be the same for all three representations. The minimum (most negative) value is determined by the appropriate bit patterns for that representation.

The program does not attempt to compute the range of either signed or unsigned long long int simply because some of the older compilers that are not C99 compliant (and for which this code is most useful) do not support those data types.

```c
#include <stdio.h>

#define LSB1(type, bits)    (1)
#define MSB1(type, bits)    (((type) 1) << (bits-1))
#define BOTH(type, bits)    (LSB1(type, bits) | MSB1(type, bits))
#define ALL1(type, bits)    (~((type) 0))

#define UNSIGNED(type, bits)    ((type) MSB1(type, bits) > 0)
#define TWOSCOMP(type, bits)    (ALL1(type, bits) == -1)
#define ONESCOMP(type, bits)    (~LSB1(type, bits) == -1)
#define SIGNPLUS(type, bits)    (BOTH(type, bits) == -1)

#define RANGE(type, name)                                       \
        {                                                       \
        type minval, maxval, bit ;                              \
        unsigned bits ;                                         \
        char *format ;                                          \
                                                                \
        /* Measure size of data type in bits */                \
        bits = 1 ; bit = 1 ; while ((bit <<= 1) != 0) bits++ ;  \
                                                                \
        if (UNSIGNED(type, bits))                               \
                {                                               \
                format = "%12lu" ;                              \
                maxval = ALL1(type, bits) ;                     \
                minval = (type) 0 ;                             \
                }                                               \
        else                                                    \
                {                                               \
                format = "%12ld" ;                              \
                maxval = (type) ~MSB1(type, bits) ;             \
                                                                \
                if (TWOSCOMP(type, bits))                       \
                        minval = MSB1(type, bits) ;             \
                                                                \
                else if (ONESCOMP(type, bits))                  \
                        minval = MSB1(type, bits) ;             \
                                                                \
                else if (SIGNPLUS(type, bits))                  \
                        minval = ALL1(type, bits) ;             \
                }                                               \
        printf("%20s (%2u bits): ", name, bits) ;               \
        printf(format, (long) minval) ;                         \
        printf(" to ") ;                                        \
        printf(format, (long) maxval) ;                         \
        printf("\n") ;                                          \
        }
```

EXAMPLE 4-1   Displaying the size and range of C integer types (Part I).

```
void main()
  {
  printf("\nTesting range of UNSIGNED ints ...\n\n"      } ;
  RANGE(unsigned char,          "unsigned char"          } ;
  RANGE(unsigned short int,     "unsigned short int"     } ;
  RANGE(unsigned int,           "unsigned int"           } ;
  RANGE(unsigned long int,      "unsigned long int"      } ;

  printf("\nTesting range of SIGNED ints …\n\n"          } ;
  RANGE(signed char,            "signed char"            } ;
  RANGE(signed short int,       "signed short int"       } ;
  RANGE(signed int,             "signed int"             } ;
  RANGE(signed long int,        "signed long int"        } ;
  }
```

EXAMPLE 4-1   Displaying the size and range of C integer types (Part II).

```
Testing range of UNSIGNED ints ...

                    unsigned char ( 8 bits):        0 to           255
              unsigned short int (16 bits):         0 to         65535
               unsigned long int (32 bits):         0 to    4294967295



Testing range of SIGNED ints ...

                      signed char ( 8 bits):      -128 to           127
                signed short int (16 bits):     -32768 to         32767
                 signed long int (32 bits): -2147483648 to    2147483647
```

FIGURE 4-1   Typical results of running the program of Example 4-1.

4.2 BOOLEAN DATA TYPES

The original C language also did not include a Boolean data type, and it was not added until the 1999 C99 standard. Traditionally, C used integer data types to hold Boolean values.[2] For backward compatibility, C99 created both a new primitive integer data type _Bool that can only hold values of 0 and 1 and a new standard header file called stdbool.h containing the following macro definitions:

```
#define bool    _Bool
#define false   ((_Bool) 0)
#define true    ((_Bool) 1)
```

---

[2] A value of zero is interpreted as Boolean false, and any other value (even a negative value) is interpreted as true. Boolean operators are guaranteed to produce a result of either 0 (false) or 1 (true).

The lack of a Boolean data type and constants in older C compilers impairs readability. There are several possible remedies to create your own "pseudo" Boolean data type. For example, a popular solution is to simply map Booleans onto bytes using macros, as in:

```
#ifndef __STDC_VERSION__
#define bool unsigned char
#define false 0
#define true 1
#endif
```

Or with a typedef declaration, as in:

```
#ifndef __STDC_VERSION__
typedef unsigned char bool ;
const unsigned char false = 0 ;
const unsigned char true = 1 ;
#endif
```

A third alternative is possible by defining bool as an enumerated type:

```
#ifndef __STDC_VERSION__
typedef enum {false = 0, true = 1} bool ;
#endif
```

Although this definition may seem more intuitively appropriate, there is no strict enforcement of what values may be assigned to enumerated types. Most C compilers use an int as the underlying implementation of an enumerated type, and thus will allow any integer constant to be assigned to such a variable.

4.3 MIXING DATA TYPES

Sometimes a little knowledge can be dangerous. Understanding when to declare an integer variable as signed and when to use unsigned ultimately results in programs that use both. However, this level of detail carries with it a responsibility that goes beyond just specifying the appropriate data type.

When an operator combines signed and unsigned integers, C *converts* the data type of the signed integer to match that of the unsigned integer before evaluating the expression. In this particular case, no corresponding change in the underlying bit pattern occurs, which can cause unanticipated effects, as in the following code[3]:

```
unsigned int u ;
...
if (u > -1) ...
```

The condition in the if statement above may at first appear to always be true since unsigned integers are always greater than or equal to zero. In fact, however, the condition is always false! The reason is that the signed integer constant −1 (a word of all 1's) is converted to *unsigned* and is thus interpreted as a full-scale value.

---

[3] Harbison and Steele, *C—A Reference Manual* (3rd ed.), Prentice Hall, 1991, p. 102.

This example should not be used as an argument against the use of unsigned integers. Rather, consider it as part of the challenge of using integers *properly*!

Some data-type conversions, however, require a corresponding change in the bit pattern used to represent the value. For example, although the signed and unsigned integer representations of 4 are identical, the floating-point representation of 4 is entirely different.

Conversions are considered to be either data-type *promotions* or data-type *demotions*. A conversion is called a "promotion" when there is no potential loss of accuracy, as when assigning an integer value to a floating-point variable. Conversely, a demotion occurs when the conversion can cause a loss of accuracy, as when a floating-point value is assigned to an integer variable, or when a 32-bit integer value is assigned to an 8-bit char. Demotions usually cause the compiler to issue a warning.

Some conversions occur implicitly, for example, when assigning an integer value to a floating-point variable:

```
double gpa = 4 ;
```

An implicit conversion can always be made explicit by the use of a *cast*, as in

```
double gpa = (double) 4 ;
```

The parentheses and the data type name between them form a *cast operator*, which is applied to a single operand on the immediate right. Using a cast

to make the conversion explicit also indicates that it was intentional and thus eliminates the warning message caused by an implicit demotion.

4.4 MANIPULATING BITS IN MEMORY

Programmers often pack a number of operands with distinct but related meanings into a single memory location. An example is the following packed representation that the old operating system MS/DOS used to store the current date and time into a single 32-bit location (Figure 4-2):

31	25 24	21 20	16 15	11 10	5 4	0
Year 1980	Month	Day	Hours	Minutes	Secs ÷ 2	

FIGURE 4-2   Packed 32-bit representation of date and time used in MS/DOS.

Small embedded systems also pack data to reduce the amount (and thus the cost) of read–write memory. For example, a large array of Boolean values would most efficiently be stored by packing eight 1-bit Boolean variables into each byte rather than using an entire integer to hold a value that can be only 0 or 1:

```
uint8_t flags[10] ; /* 80 1-bit Boolean flags, 8 per byte */
```

Manipulation of these bits is usually implemented using a set of macros or functions that rely on C's bitwise operators. As shown in Table 4-4, both the bitwise and Boolean operators provide the basic operations of AND, OR, exclusive-OR (XOR), and NOT. However, Boolean operators are used to form conditional expressions (as in an *if* statement) while the corresponding set of bitwise operators are used to manipulate bits.

TABLE 4-4   Boolean Versus Bitwise Operators

Operation	Boolean Operator	Bitwise Operator
AND	&&	&
OR	||	|
XOR	*unsupported*	^
NOT	!	~

The older C compilers did not provide a Boolean data type, and programmers had to use integer variables to hold Boolean values. The Boolean operators were designed to yield results of type *int*, with true and false represented by 1 and 0, respectively. When interpreting integer values as Boolean values, a value of zero is treated as false, and *any* nonzero value is considered true.

Bitwise operators work on individual bit positions within the operands; that is, the result in any single bit position is entirely independent of all the other bit positions. As shown below, applying the bitwise AND operator (&) to operands A and B produces a result in which bit 5 depends only on the value of bit 5 of A and bit 5 of B.

As Figure 4-3 demonstrates, bitwise operators treat each operand as an ordered bit vector and produce bit vector results. Boolean operators, however, treat each multibit operand as a single value to be interpreted as either true or false. Figure 4-4 illustrates how this difference can produce very different results for identical operands.

FIGURE 4-3   Bitwise operators
work on individual bits.

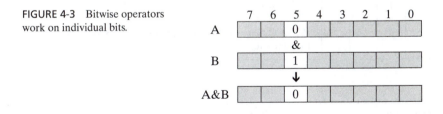

It is usually easier to envision how the bitwise operators are used to manipulate packed operands by thinking of one of the bits of one operands as controlling what happens to the corresponding bit of the other operand as it propagates through to the result. As illustrated in Tables 4-5 to 4-7, the value of the control bit (*a*) determines whether the corresponding bit (*b*) of the packed operand propagates into the result unchanged or inverted, or whether that bit of the result is cleared to 0 or set to 1.

Boolean: (5 || !3) && 6 ⇒ (true OR (NOT true)) AND true
                         ⇒ (true OR false) AND true
                         ⇒ (true) AND true
                         ⇒ true
                         ⇒ 1

Bitwise: (5 | ~3) & 6   ⇒ (00..0101 OR ~00..0011) AND 00..0110
                         ⇒ (00..0101 OR 11..1100) AND 00..0110
                         ⇒ (11..1101) AND 00..0110
                         ⇒ 00..0100
                         ⇒ 4

FIGURE 4-4   Boolean versus bitwise operators.

TABLE 4-5   Interpreting the Bitwise-AND

a	b	a AND b	Interpretation
0	0 1	0 0 } 0	If control bit a is 0, bit b is ignored and a 0 is propagated through to the result.
1	0 1	0 1 } b	If control bit a is 1, bit b propagates through to the result unchanged.

TABLE 4-6   Interpreting the Bitwise-OR

a	b	a OR b	Interpretation
0	0 1	0 1 } b	If control bit a is 0, bit b propagates through to the result unchanged.
1	0 1	1 1 } 1	If control bit a is 1, bit b is ignored and a 1 is propagated through to the result.

TABLE 4-7   Interpreting the Bitwise-XOR

a	b	a XOR b	Interpretation
0	0 1	0 1 } b	If control bit a is 0, bit b propagates through to the result unchanged.
1	0 1	0 1 } b'	If control bit a is 1, bit b propagates through to the result inverted.

4.4.1 Testing Bits

The bitwise AND operator is often used to test the value of a single bit. A "mask" consisting of a single 1 in the bit position of interest is AND'ed with the packed operand containing the bit to be tested. Thus, the result will be nonzero if and only if the bit of interest was 1. For example, consider

```
if ((bits & 64) != 0)      /* check to see if bit 6 is set */
```

Since any nonzero value is interpreted as *true*, some programmers omit the redundant comparison to zero, thinking (perhaps) that it may reduce the amount of assembly language code. However, the comparison creates no additional code and improves readability.

```
if ((bits & 0x0040) != 0)      /* check to see if bit 6 is set */
```

As shown, the mask (64) is often written in hex (0×0040) to make it somewhat easier to identify which bit is being tested. An even better solution is to use a shift expression as shown below.

```
if ((bits & (1 << 6)) != 0)    /* check to see if bit 6 is set */
```

Again, there is no increase in the number of assembly language instructions. Since both operands of the shift operator are constants, the compiler will replace the shift expression with an equivalent constant.

4.4.2 Setting, Clearing, and Inverting Bits

Setting a bit to 1 is easily accomplished with the bitwise-OR operator:

```
bits = bits | (1 << 7) ;       /* sets bit 7 */
```

This would usually be written more succinctly as

```
bits |= (1 << 7) ;             /* sets bit 7 */
```

Note that we do not *add* (+) the bit to the operand! That only works if the current value of the target bit in the operand is known to be 0. Otherwise, *adding* a 1 would leave a 0 in the target bit and propagate a carry that modifies bits in more significant bit positions. Although the phrase "set a bit to 1" suggests that the bit was originally 0, most of the time the current value of the bit is actually unknown. ORing a 1 ensures that the result will be 1 regardless of the current value, and that no other bits of the operand are affected in the process.

Clearing a bit to 0 is similarly accomplished with the bitwise-AND operator:

```
bits &= ~(1 << 7) ;            /* clears bit 7 */
```

Note that for reasons similar to those described above, we do not *subtract* the bit from the operand!

The right-hand side of the above assignment is a constant used as a bitmask containing all 1's except for a 0 in bit 7. The AND operator uses that 0 to force a 0 into the corresponding bit position of the result, while all other bits of the other operand pass through unchanged.

When clearing bits in variables whose size (width in bits) is greater than that of integer constants (which default to type int), you must be careful that constants used to define the mask are as wide as the operand. For example, if the variable 'bits' is of type uint64_t, the 1 in the right-hand side of the assignment must also be promoted to the same width before the shift, as in

```
bits &= ~(((uint64_t) 1) << 7) ; /* clears bit 7 */
```

Otherwise, the compiler will first evaluate the constant expression on the right-hand side as a default int (normally 32 bits wide), and then pre-pend leading 0's to the resulting constant to match the width of variable bits. These extra 0's will then clear unintended bit positions in the result.

Inverting (or toggling) a bit is accomplished with the bitwise-XOR operator:

```
bits ^= (1 << 6) ;              /* flips bit 6 */
```

Although *adding* 1 instead of using the bitwise-XOR would invert the target bit, it may also propagate a carry that would modify more significant bits in the operand.

4.4.3 Extracting Bits

A *bit field* is a contiguous subset of bits stored within a larger variable, such as the individual components of date and time stored in a single 32-bit location. Extracting the value of a bit field is accomplished by shifting right to remove unwanted bits to the right of the field and ANDing with a mask to remove unwanted bits on the left (Figure 4-5):

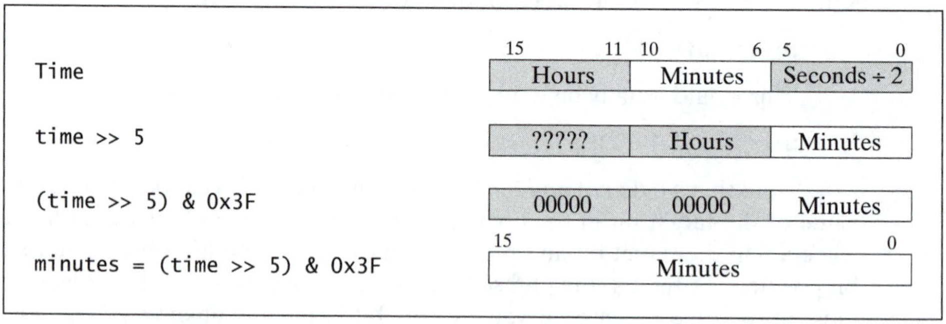

FIGURE 4-5   Extracting minutes from a packed representation of time.

4.4.4 Inserting Bits

Storing a new value into a bit field requires that we first clear it to all 0's, align the new value with the bit field by left shifting, and then OR'ing that value into the packed operand. If there is any chance that the inserted value could exceed the width of the destination bit field, it is always a good idea to AND the new value with a mask before OR'ing it into the packed operand (Figure 4-6).

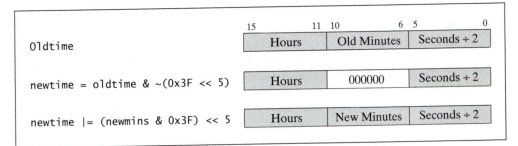

FIGURE 4-6   Inserting minutes into a packed representation of time.

4.5   MANIPULATING BITS IN INPUT/OUTPUT PORTS

Input and output devices hold information in locations referred to as I/O ports. I/O devices usually have ports for data, for status information, and for control or command information.

It is a common hardware-design practice for the command and status ports to contain packed information, as shown in Figures 4-7 and 4-8.

Bit 7	Bit 6	Bit 5	Bit 4	Bit 3	Bit 2	Bit 1	Bit 0
Carrier Detect	Ring Indicator	Data Set Ready	Clear To Send	Δ Carrier Detect	Ring Indicator	Δ Data Set Ready	Δ Clear To Send

FIGURE 4-7   UART modem status port (read-only).

Bit 7	Bit 6	Bit 5	Bit 4	Bit 3	Bit 2	Bit 1	Bit 0
Reserved	Reserved	Reserved	Enable IRQ	Select Printer	Initialize Printer	Auto LineFeed	Data Strobe

FIGURE 4-8   Parallel printer control port (write-only).

Some computers use separate address spaces for memory and I/O devices. In this case, I/O ports can only be accessed using special processor instructions for I/O operations. There is no direct support for this in the syntax of the C language. In such cases, you must use special compiler-specific library functions (or write your own) to access I/O data.

In many situations (and common in embedded applications) the address space for read–write memory is far greater than what is required. For example, a 32-bit processor will usually have a 32-bit memory address bus that can support a memory containing more than 4 gigabytes of data, yet most embedded applications will never require anything close to this limit. As a result, embedded applications that use 32-bit processors often employ hardware that decodes a portion of the memory address space for I/O devices instead of memory. Data held in an I/O device may then be accessed via a pointer whose value has been initialized to its address using the techniques described in Section 4.6.

Unfortunately, the situation is usually somewhat more complex: I/O hardware is often designed so that the data is either read-only or write-only. Sometimes multiple I/O devices are assigned to a single address, requiring other techniques to access the specific data of interest. The following sections discuss common strategies for solving these situations.

4.5.1 Write-Only I/O Devices

The read-modify-write techniques presented earlier for manipulating bits within variables stored in read–write memory cannot be used with write-only I/O ports such as the parallel printer-control port of a PC (see Figure 4-8). The solution is to keep a copy of the last bit pattern written to the port in a variable. To modify one or more bits in the port without affecting the other bits, apply the read-modify-write techniques (described earlier in this chapter) to the variable, and then copy the resulting value of the variable to the I/O port.

Synchronization between the value in the variable and that in the actual I/O port is critical. The initial value of the variable must match the hardware reset condition of the port, and *every* modification of the value in the port must be accompanied by a corresponding update of the variable. An effective technique to insure synchronization is to encase all access to the write-only port in a function that also updates the value of the associated variable. Figure 4-9 illustrates one such function and its usage.

```
void LPT1Control(uint8_t bits2set, uint8_t bits2clr)
    {
    static uint8_t bits = 0x00 ; // should match hardware reset condition

    if (bits2set != 0 || bits2clr != 0)
        {
        bits |= bits2set ;              // Insert 1's as needed
        bits &= ~bits2clr ;             // Insert 0's as needed
        Byte2Port(bits, 0x3BE) ;        // Copy bits to the printer port
        }
    else bits = 0x00 ;                  // Reinitialize to hardware reset condition
    }

void PulseLPT1DataStrobe(int msec)
    {
    LPT1Control(0x01, 0x00) ;           // Set data strobe line to 1
    DelayMilliseconds(msec) ;           // Keep at 1 for a short time
    LPT1Control(0x00, 0x01) ;           // Clear data strobe line to 0
    }
```

FIGURE 4-9   Manipulating bits in a write-only I/O port.

4.5.2 I/O Devices Differentiated by Reads Versus Writes

Sometimes two (or more) different I/O ports share a single address. This usually occurs when one port is write-only (such as a command port) and another is read-only (such as a status port). Data written to the command port cannot be read from the status port. Writes to the address access the write-only port, while reads access the read-only port.

For example, consider the set of eight port addresses assigned to one of the serial UART devices on a PC, as shown in Table 4-8. Bit 7 of I/O address 02FB is called the Divisor Latch Access Bit (DLAB). When DLAB is 1, I/O address 02F8 is connected to the least-significant byte of the current baud rate divisor, which can be read or written; when DLAB is 0, *writes* to 02F8 send characters out on the serial line, but *reads* from 02F8 retrieve characters that have arrived.

TABLE 4-8   I/O Addresses Used by One of the PC Serial Ports

I/O Address	DLAB	Restriction	Description
02F8	0 0 1	Write-Only Read-Only	Transmitter holding register (holds character to be sent) Receiver buffer register (contains the received character) Least-significant byte of baud rate divisor latch
02F9	1 0		Most-significant byte of baud rate divisor latch Interrupt enable register
02FA 02FB 02FC	n/a n/a n/a	Read-Only	Interrupt ID register Line control register (*Bit 7 is the DLAB bit*) Modem control register
02FD 02FE 02FF	n/a n/a n/a	Read-Only Read-Only	Line status register Modem status register Reserved

4.5.3 I/O Devices Differentiated by Sequential Access

Sometimes multiple read-only ports are assigned to a single address; in this case, they are usually distinguished by the *order* in which the data is read. Of course, an access counter must exist somewhere in the hardware of the I/O device, and there must be a separate means of initializing it. Multiple write-only ports assigned to a single I/O address can also be distinguished by order, or by the value of specific bits in the data that is written.

Consider the 8259 programmable interrupt controller used in the PC. As indicated in Table 4-9, it contains six registers, accessed via only two I/O addresses. For example, registers OCW1, ICW2, ICW3, and ICW4 share the same I/O address. Access to ICW2, ICW3, and ICW4 is sequential, and can only occur immediately after writing to ICW1.[4] At all other times, writes to this address go to register OCW1. Figure 4-10 illustrates a function that initializes the four ICW values.

---

[4] The sequence of instructions that write data into these registers must be executed with interrupts disabled. Otherwise, the code sequence might be invalidated by an interrupt routine that executes code that happens to write to these same registers.

TABLE 4-9   I/O Ports of the 8259 Programmable Interrupt Controller in the PC

Addr.	Data	Restriction	Description
0020		Read-Only	Interrupt request or in-service register
	xxx1xxxx	Write-Only	Initialization command word 1 (ICW1)
	xxx00xxx	Write-Only	Operation Control Word 2
	xxx01xxx	Write-Only	Operation Control Word 3
0021			Operation Control Word 1 (Interrupt mask register)
		Write-Only	ICW2, ICW3, ICW4 (in order, only just after writing ICW1)
0022-003F			Reserved

```
void InitializeICWs(uint8_t icw[])
    {
    bool was_enabled ; // Used to save the current interrupt enable state

    icw[0] |= (1 << 4) ;                     // Bit 4 must be 1 to write ICW1
    was_enabled = GetInterruptEnable() ;     // Get current interrupt enable state
    DisableInterrupts() ;                    // Sequence must not be interrupted!
    Byte2Port(icw[0], 0x20) ;                // Output ICW1 and reset ICW counter
    Byte2Port(icw[1], 0x21) ;                // Output ICW2
    Byte2Port(icw[2], 0x21) ;                // Output ICW3
    Byte2Port(icw[3], 0x21) ;                // Output ICW4
    if (was_enabled) EnableInterrupts() ; // Restore interrupt enable state
    }
```

FIGURE 4-10   Function to initialize the four ICW values of the 8259 chip.

4.5.4 I/O Devices Differentiated by Bits in the Written Data

Table 4-9 shows that reads from I/O address 0020 access the read-only interrupt request/in-service register, while writes to the same address select one of the write-only registers ICW1, OCW2, and OCW3, according to the value of bits 3 and 4 in the data that is written. For example, writing 01010111 to port 0020 sends the data to ICW1, while writing 01000111 to the same port sends the data to OCW2.

4.6   ACCESSING MEMORY-MAPPED I/O DEVICES

Modern microprocessors are capable of addressing gigabytes of memory, yet embedded systems typically need significantly less than a megabyte. If the hardware is designed to assign some of the unused addresses to I/O devices, we can then manipulate their "memory-mapped" I/O ports as if they were memory locations. For example, the hardware could be designed so that data written to a specific memory address is sent instead as a command to a particular I/O device, while data read from that same address might provide information about the current status of the device.

A typical example of a memory-mapped I/O device is a display buffer in which each character position on the screen is assigned one or more unique memory addresses. In the PC, for example, the color-display buffer is mapped to memory starting at address $B8000_{16}$. Each character position is assigned two bytes; the first contains an ASCII character code followed by a second byte that specifies the foreground and background colors of the character. The address of the first byte assigned to a specific row and column is thus calculated as

$$B8000_{16} + 2 \times (80 \times \text{row} + \text{col})$$

4.6.1 Accessing Data Using a Pointer

When using variables in C, you normally never worry about where in memory they are located. You merely create the variable (i.e., allocate memory for it) by declaring it, and then manipulate its content by referring to its identifier. To display text on the screen, however, we have to use a *pointer*.

A pointer in C is a variable that contains an address. There is no pointer data type name. Instead, we declare that a variable is a pointer by placing an asterisk ("*") in front of its identifier in the declaration:

```
uint8_t *p ; /* "p" is a pointer to a byte */
```

Note that the declaration makes explicit the type (and thus the size) of the object that is pointed to. Although the declaration allocates memory to hold the pointer, it must still be initialized before it can be used, as in

```
p = (uint8_t *) (0xB8000 + 2 * (80 * row + col)) ;
```

Of course, the initial value may be specified in the declaration if desired, as in

```
uint8_t *p = (uint8_t *) (0xB8000 + 2 * (80 * row + col)) ;
```

Without the cast, the last example represents an attempt to store data of type int in a variable intended to hold an address. Although an address and an int may use the same number of bits, if we do not use a cast the compiler will still issue a warning that we were mixing "apples and oranges."

Once a pointer has been initialized, we can access the data that it points to by using the asterisk as a *de-reference* operator:

```
*p = 'A' ; /* Display 'A' on the screen. */
```

The result of declaring and initializing such a pointer and then using it to store a character into the display buffer is depicted graphically in Figure 4-11.

Note that since p was declared as a pointer to a byte, the de-referenced pointer (*p) can be used in any context where you would normally use a variable of type uint8_t — that is, on either side of an assignment operator.

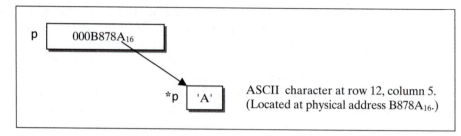

FIGURE 4-11   Relationship between a pointer and what it points to.

4.6.2 Arrays, Pointers, and the "Address of" Operator

When we declare an array of bytes called "a", a corresponding sequence of bytes is allocated in memory. The element a[0] is stored in the first byte, and its address is known as the *base address* of the array. We can obtain this address by applying the "*address of*" operator to a[0], as in &a[0]. Since &a[0] is the address of data of type uint8_t, we think of it as an expression whose value is of type "pointer to uint8_t" (Figure 4-12).

uint8_ta[10];   /* an array of 10 bytes */

a[0]	a[1]	a[2]	a[3]	a[4]	a[5]	a[6]	a[7]	a[8]	a[9]
127	128	129	130	131	132	133	134	135	136

&a[0] (the "base address" of array "a")

FIGURE 4-12   An array of chars and their corresponding memory addresses.

In C, the name of an array by itself with no subscript (e.g., "a") is strictly equivalent to the address of its first element (e.g., &a[0]). Thus, the data type of a is also "pointer to uint8_t," which means that we may substitute a pointer in place of the name of an array when subscripting (e.g., p[k]). This fact can be used to access our display buffer as an array by initializing a pointer to the base address of the display buffer and then applying subscripting:

```
uint8_t *color_display_buffer = (uint8_t *) 0xB8000 ;
...
color_display_buffer[2*(80*row+col)] = 'A' ;
```

Of course, it would be nicer to use one subscript to select the row, a second subscript to select the column, and a third to differentiate between the ASCII and attribute bytes of the character cell. To do so requires that we first describe a row of 80 two-byte cells using a pair of typedefs:

```
typedef uint8_t        ONE_CELL[2] ; // 1 cell of 2 bytes
typedef ONE_CELL       ONE_ROW[80] ; // 1 row of 80 cells
```

Then, we can declare a pointer to an object of the latter type and initialize it to the base address of the display buffer:

```
ONE_ROW *color_display_buffer = (ONE_ROW *) 0xB8000 ;
```

Then, the expression "color_display_buffer[i]" is a reference to the ith row of cells. Since each row is an array of cells, a second subscript may be applied to this expression ("color_display_buffer[i][j]") to select the jth cell of that row. Finally, since each cell is an array of two bytes, we can store the character code to be displayed into the first of these using the following assignment statement:

```
color_display_buffer[row][col][0] = 'A' ;
```

4.7 STRUCTURES

Like an array, a structure is an *aggregate* data type composed of several distinct members. Although the members of an array share a common data type, there is no such requirement for a structure. A single structure variable can therefore contain member elements that represent a mix of chars, ints, doubles, and so on—even members that are themselves structures.

The C declaration statement

```
struct   PERSON
      {
      int    age ;
      char   gender ;
      };
```

is a structure *description* that can be referred to using the identifier "PERSON," known as a *structure tag*. This declaration does not allocate any memory nor create an instance of a structure; it merely describes how the structure data is organized. We can create a structure variable named "sue" using this tag in a declaration statement:

```
struct   PERSON sue ;
```

Some programmers prefer to use a typedef instead of a structure tag, as in

```
typedef struct
      {
      int    age ;
      char   gender ;
      } PERSON;
```

This allows an instance of the structure named "sue" to be declared simply as

```
PERSON sue ;
```

Initial values for the member elements may be specified in the declaration. For example, the declaration

```
PERSON sue = { 30, 'F'} ;
```

would initialize the "age" member of "sue" to 30 and the "gender" member to 'F'.

Structure members may be used like regular variables and are referenced using one of the two member selection operators. With "sue" declared as just shown, "sue.age" and "sue.gender" are used to reference the two member elements of "sue," as in

```
sue.age = 25 ;
```

By default, function parameters are passed by value, which means that the function is given a copy of the parameter. Rather than taking execution time to copy the structure, we usually prefer to pass only its address. The function prototype might then look like this:

```
void foo(PERSON *p) ;
```

Inside the function, we have only a pointer to the structure. In such a case, we must use different syntax so that a reference to the "age" member of the structure pointed to by "p" becomes

```
p->age = 21 ;
```

4.7.1 Packed Structures

Structures are stored in memory with their member components in the same order as they appear in the structure description. However, there is no requirement that the components be contiguous. This freedom allows the compiler to align members on word boundaries in order to trade memory space in return for faster access time (Figure 4-13).[5]

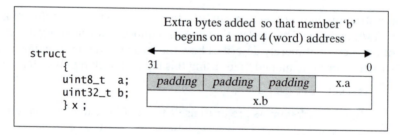

FIGURE 4-13   Structure padding used for address alignment.

Sometimes, however, we need to use structures to describe a layout in which all the data are contiguous. In such cases, we must disable our compiler's structure padding to accurately describe the organization of the data. The way this is done sometimes varies from one compiler to another, but with a Microsoft, Borland, or GNU (gcc) C/C++ compiler, this can be accomplished with pragma directives as demonstrated by the program shown in Figure 4-14.

---

[5] Memory alignment is discussed in more detail in the next chapter.

```
#include <stdio.h>
#include <stdint.h>

#pragma pack(1) // Turn off structure padding...

typedef struct  // This struct occupies 6 bytes
        {
        int8_t          a ;
        int32_t b ;
        int8_t          c ;
        } PACKED ;

#pragma pack()  // Turn on structure padding...

typedef struct  // This struct typically occupies 12 bytes
        {
        int8_t          a ;
        int32_t b ;
        int8_t          c ;
        } PADDED ;

int main()
        {
        printf("size packed = %d bytes\n", sizeof(PACKED)) ;
        printf("size padded = %d bytes\n", sizeof(PADDED)) ;
        return 0 ;
        }
```

FIGURE 4-14 Comparing packed and padded structures.

Structures can often improve the readability of code used to access memory-mapped I/O devices. In Section 4.6.2, we described a character cell on the PC display as an array of two bytes:

```
typedef uint8_t ONE_CELL[2] ;
```

Most programmers prefer to refer to the cell's ASCII and attribute bytes using something more suggestive of their content than simply a third subscript. This can be accomplished by describing the cell as a packed structure:

```
#pragma pack(1)
typedef struct
        {
        uint8_t ascii ;
        uint8_t attr ;
        } ONE_CELL ;
#pragma pack()
```

Displaying a character on the screen can then be more effectively written as

```
color_display_buffer[row][col].ascii = 'A' ;
```

4.7.2 Bit Fields

In Sections 4.4.3 and 4.4.4, we used the bitwise-AND, bitwise-OR, and shift operators to extract and modify the "minutes" field within a packed representation of time. Structure bit fields allow us to access this data using a cleaner syntax that hides all the necessary bit manipulation. We begin by describing the time as a structure in which the hours, minutes, and seconds are declared as structure bit fields (Figure 4-15):

```
typedef struct
    {
    uint16_t    seconds    :6,    /* actually, half seconds! */
                minutes    :5,
                hours      :5 ;
    } TIME ;
```

FIGURE 4-15   Using bit fields to describe the packed representation of time.

Note that bit fields are only available within structures and must be declared using an integral data type.[6] The width of each field is specified by a constant that is separated from the field name by a colon.

Warning! *The ISO standards do not specify the order in which compilers must assign bit fields to the bits of the corresponding memory location(s). While some may assign bit fields from least- to most-significant bit positions, others may do exactly the reverse.*

If we use type TIME (instead of uint16_t) to declare our time variable, as in

```
TIME time ;
```

then the three bit fields can be referenced as regular structure members, leaving the extraction and insertion problems to the compiler! For example, storing the time 13:34:18 in our packed representation is now easily accomplished with three simple assignments:

```
time.hours = 13 ;
time.minutes = 34 ;
time.seconds  = 18 / 2 ;
```

In many cases, one or more bit positions in a packed operand are not used or are reserved, as in the case of the processor status register in the ARM processor. One or more unnamed bit fields may then be included in the corresponding structure to skip over these bit positions, as shown in Figure 4-16.

---

[6] Pre-ANSIC (C89) compilers typically did not support signed bit fields.

```
struct PSR        // Assumes bitfields are allocated from LSB to MSB
    {
    uint32_t    exception    :9,    // Current exception number
                             :1,    // (reserved)
                ici_it1      :6,    // (see technical reference manual)
                             :8,    // (reserved)
                T            :1,    // Always 1
                ici_it2      :2,    // (see technical reference manual)
                Q            :1,    // Saturation flag
                V            :1,    // Signed overflow flag
                Z            :1,    // Zero or equal flag
                C            :1,    // Unsigned carry flag
                N            :1 ;   // Negative flag
    } ;
```

FIGURE 4-16   The Program Status Register of the ARM processor.

4.8   VARIANT ACCESS

Sometimes it is useful to be able to think of the same data in memory as being available in a variety of different organizations. For example, rather than treating a 32.32 fixed-point real as a single 64-bit quantity, on occasion it may be more convenient to treat it as a pair of 32-bit locations containing the whole and fractional parts, respectively.

First we will see how to use pointers, casts, and subscripting to access different views of an object. However, then we will use unions to accomplish the same thing with a cleaner syntax, just as structure bit fields provided a cleaner syntax for manipulating bits than did the bitwise-AND, bitwise-OR, and shift operators.

In Section 4.6.2, we learned that subscripting could be applied to a pointer variable as if it were an array. Then in Section 4.7, we learned that a pointer to a structure could be used to reference its member elements. In both cases, the pointer's value and its declaration provide the information required for properly constructing the reference—that is, the base address and data type of the object to which it points. Now, instead of having a pointer to an object, we have the object itself, but we can apply operators to that object and produce an equally useful pointer-valued expression.

4.8.1 Casting the Address of an Object

Given any object, we can obtain its address by applying the "address of" operator ("&"), and we can then cast that address as a pointer to data of any desired type. For example, the expression

```
(uint8_t *) &x
```

is treated as a pointer to data of type uint8_t, regardless of how "x" may have been declared. There are several ways to put this expression to work. Simply adding the regular de-reference operator on the left-hand side of the expression, as in

```
*((uint8_t *) &x)
```

or a subscript of zero on the right-hand side, as in

```
((uint8_t *) &x)[0]
```

yields a reference to the *first* 8-bit byte stored in x. Of course, we can just as easily access *any* byte of x with a different choice of subscript.

With an appropriate choice of data type in the cast, we can de-reference the pointer to access the bits held within x in any manner we choose. For example, to access the whole part of a 32.32 fixed-point real called "result," we simply write

```
((uint32_t *) &result)[1]
```

You can just as easily cast the address as a pointer to a structure. If we create a structure that names the whole and fractional parts of a 32.32 fixed-point real, as in

```
typedef struct
    {
    uint32_t        fract ;
    uint32_t        whole ;
    } FIXED64PARTS ;
```

then we can use a member name instead of a nonintuitive subscript to access the whole part:

```
((FIXED64PARTS *) &result)->whole
```

Of course, one may legitimately object to this syntax as being less than elegant. If you need to make several such references, you can improve the appearance of your code by creating a pointer to the desired type and initializing it to the address of the object:

```
FIXED64PARTS *f64 = (FIXED64PARTS *) &result ;
```

Then simply reference the member elements via the pointer:

```
f64->whole
```

If you object to allocating memory for the pointer and the associated run-time overhead that using it introduces, then create a macro, as in

```
#define F64(object) ((FIXED64PARTS *) &(object))
```

and use it to disguise the messy details of the reference:

```
F64(result)->whole
```

Note that when the size of the desired data component does not correspond to that of one of the standard data types, we can still arrange our structure declaration to describe the data in terms of structure bit fields.

4.8.2 Using Unions

Variant access can also be accomplished using a *union*. The syntax of a union declaration is identical[7] to that of structures except for the corresponding change of keyword.

---

[7] Unlike structures, unions cannot specify bit fields.

Semantically, however, there is a big difference. All of the members of a structure occupy separate locations in memory, whereas all of the members of a union occupy the same memory (i.e., they *overlay* one another). Thus, the size of a structure is the sum of the sizes of its members, but the size of a union is the same as the size of its largest member.

For example, consider the following:

```
typedef union
    {
    uint64_t          real ;
    FIXED64PARTS      part ;
    } FIXED64REAL ;
```

This declaration defines a data type for a single 64-bit object that can be accessed either as a single 32.32 fixed-point real number or as its separate component parts—the whole and the fractional parts. If we create a union of this type named "result," then we can refer to the entire object or its parts using the identifiers shown in Figure 4-17.

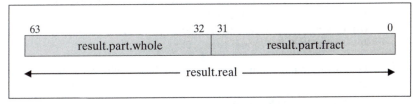

FIGURE 4-17   The component parts of the FIXED64REAL union.

Use of a union to accomplish variant access eliminates the need to create a macro to hide the messy details of using a cast and the "address of" operator. Whether or not you use a union probably depends on the number of variant accesses required and (of course) your own choice of programming style.

PROBLEMS

1. True/False:
   (a) Compilers generate more instructions to evaluate x & (1 << 5) than for x & 32.
   (b) The C expression &a[5] is a constant.
   (c) The ANSIC standard requires signed integers to use the 2's-complement representation.
   (d) Incrementing a pointer to a long changes the number it holds by 1.
   (e) In C, the value of 'A'+3 is 'D'.
   (f) In C, the value produced by a Boolean operator is 0 if false and 1 if true.
   (g) The value of !x is 0 if and only if the value of x is 1.
   (h) If "x" is an unsigned int, then the expression X > −1 is always true.
   (i) The statement c = a + b has overflowed if and only if:

   ```
   (c<0 && a>0 && b>0) || (c>0 && a<0 && b<0) is true.
   ```

2. Give the number of bytes contained in each of the following data types:
   (a) `char`
   (b) `short`
   (c) `long`
   (d) `long long`

3. Give the maximum values (expressed as decimal integers, not as powers of 2) that can be held in each of the following data types.
   (a) `unsigned char`
   (b) `unsigned short int`
   (c) `unsigned long int`

4. Give the range of 2's-complement values (expressed as decimal integers, not as powers of 2) that can be held in each of the following data types.
   (a) `signed char`
   (b) `signed short int`
   (c) `signed long int`

5. What is the hex (base 16) value of each of the following expressions:
   (a) `(unsigned char) 0x12345678`
   (b) `(short) ((signed char) 0xFF)`
   (c) `(short) ((unsigned char) 0xFF)`

6. Given the macro defined below, show how each of the following usages would be expanded:

   ```
   #define REM(a, b) a % b
   ```

   (a) `REM(5, 2)`
   (b) `REM(5 + 2, X)`
   (c) `REM(5, X -2)`

7. Define a macro called BIT(x, n) that expands into an expression whose value is exactly 0 or 1, corresponding to the value of the bit n of x.

8. Define a C macro named "SQUARE" that will produce the proper result in all four of the following possible situations:

   ```
   x = SQUARE(y) ;
   x = SQUARE(SQUARE(y - 2)) ;
   x = SQUARE(y - 2) ;
   x = SQUARE(5 + SQUARE(y - 2)) ;
   ```

9. Define a macro called "SHL" with two operands. The macro should expand into an expression that reliably computes a value corresponding to a left shift of its first operand by the number of bit positions specified by its second operand. The content of the operands must not be modified.

10. What values are left in the variables after executing the following C code:

    ```
    unsigned char u ;
    signed char s ;
    u = (unsigned char) -128 ;
    s = (signed char) +128 ;
    ```

11. Give the decimal value of each of the following expressions:
   (a) ~!5
   (b) !~5
   (c) ~6+1
   (d) 6 && 2
   (e) 6 & 2
   (f) 6 && −2
   (g) 6 & −2
   (h) 3 | 5
   (i) 3 || 5
   (j) !−3
   (k) ~−3
   (l) !0(1)
   (m) ~0
   (n) !!13
   (o) 3 << 4
   (p) 60 >> 2
   (q) ~~13
   (r) 3 ^ 5
   (s) 3 & ~5

12. What is the hexadecimal (base 16) value of each of the following expressions:
   (a) 0x7D | 0x4E
   (b) 0x7D & 0x4E
   (c) 0x7D ^ 0x4E
   (d) 0x7D & −0x4E
   (e) 0x7D & ~0x4E

13. Give the 8-bit binary value that remains in the unsigned char "x" after executing the indicated line of code:

Initial Value of "x"	Line of Code
(a) 11100101_2	x |= (1 << 4) ;
(b) 11011001_2	x &= ~(1 << 6) ;
(c) 01111010_2	x ^= (1 << 5) ;
(d) 10101010_2	x = (x >> 3) & 0x0F ;
(e) 00001111_2	x = ~x ;
(f) 00001111_2	x = !x ;
(g) 00000000_2	x ||= 0x20 ;
(h) 11111111_2	x &&= 0xF0 ;

14. Give the integer value of each of the following C expressions as a decimal constant. If the value cannot be determined, enter "NEI" (Not Enough Information):
   (a) x && !x
   (b) x & ~x
   (c) x || !x

(d) x | ~x
(e) x ^ ~x

15. Write an expression in C that is true if and only if bit 5 of the integer variable "x" is a 1.

16. Assume that individual bits are numbered right to left starting at 0. For each of the following, write a single line of C code that:

    ```
    unsigned int n ;
    unsigned char x ;
    ```

    (a) Sets bit n of x to a 1 without modifying other bits.
    (b) Inverts bit 5 of x without modifying other bits.
    (c) Clears bits 6, 3, and 2 of x to a 0 without modifying other bits.
    (d) Shifts x left by n + 2 bits.
    (e) Replaces n by the value of the 4-bit number held in bits 5-2 (the middle 4-bit "nibble") of x.

17. Assume that a variable "x" has been declared as data type char. The values of the individual bits within "x" are represented as:

    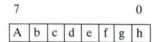

    For each of the following, assume that the initial value of "x" is as shown above. Give the contents of "x" that remains after the indicated assignment statement has been executed.
    (a) x |= (1 << 3) ;
    (b) x &= ~(1 << 4) ;
    (c) x ^= (1 << 5) ;

18. For each case below, give the hex value of the right-shift expression or enter the phrase "compiler dependent."
    (a) unsigned char x = 0x80 ; x >> 1 ;
    (b) signed char x = 0x80 ; x >> 1 ;

19. What hexadecimal values might different compilers produce for the following expression?

    ```
    ((signed char) 0xFF) >> 1
    ```

20. Describe the following 16-bit packed operand using structure bit fields:

14	13		11	9		7		0
	Gender		Hair color			Age		

21. Write code to increment only the third byte (bits 16 to 23) of a 32-bit operand called "x" using:
    (a) ANDing, ORing, and Shifting
    (b) Casts and subscripting

22. The first printf statement below prints "1C3F." What is printed by the second printf?

```
union {
      short w ;
      char b[2] ;
} x ;
x.w = 0x1C3F ;
printf("%04X\n", x.w) ;
x.b[1] = 0xA6 ;
printf("%04X\n", x.w) ;
```

23. Write a C function that sets a specified bit within an array of bits that are packed eight per byte into an array of bytes. The function must have exactly two parameters: The first is the name of the array of bytes and the second is the index (starting at zero) of the bit to be set. The function prototype should be.

```
void SetBit(BYTE8 bits[ ], int index) ;
```

24. Enter "YES" or "NO" in each cell of the table below as appropriate to compare the various techniques for manipulating packed operands.

Characteristic	Bitwise Operators	Structure Bit Fields	Variant Access	Unions
Messy syntax?				
Ambiguous semantics?				
Bit-field assignment restrictions?				
More efficient code generation?				

25. Consider the problem of extracting a value from bits 8 to 15 of a 32-bit variable.

1 16	15 8	7 0
Ignore these bits	*Extract this value*	*Ignore these bits*

   (a) Assume that the variable is declared as an unsigned long named "packed." Write code using only shift and bitwise operators to copy the extracted value to a variable called "value."
   (b) Declare the variable as a union named "packed" with the appropriate member elements so that its content can be accessed as a single 32-bit long called "l," an array of two 16-bit shorts called "s," or an array of four 8-bit chars called "c." Then write code using only the union member selection operator to copy the extracted value to a variable called "value."

CHAPTER 5

Programming in Assembly
Part 1: Computer Organization

Application software for today's embedded systems is written almost exclusively in a high-level language such as C, yet there will always be situations that require portions of the code be written in the low-level instructions of the processor. Writing in assembly language is a tedious and error-prone exercise that should be avoided unless absolutely necessary. There are, however, a couple of situations in which programming in assembly is appropriate or necessary:

1. There may be parts of a program where absolute speed is critical.
   Programming in assembly can result in more effective use of the central processing unit (CPU)'s registers and instruction set, thus producing code that runs faster than that produced by a compiler.

2. There may be no other way to access a particular feature of the hardware.
   For example, the C compiler may not provide library functions to access I/O ports or to disable or enable the interrupt system. Or the compiler may generate code that does not take advantage of some of the more specialized instructions of the CPU, such as those that implement bit and byte reversal, bit-field extraction and insertion, binary–ASCII conversion, table lookups, or high-speed copying of entire blocks of data.

For most of the code, however, it is better to write it in a high-level language. Using a high-level language is less tedious, more reliable, and inherently more productive. The speed penalty is usually not an issue at the upper organizational levels of a program, and the algorithms are more easily expressed and comprehended in this context.

Mastering assembly language programming takes time and involves becoming familiar with a lot of new and detailed information covered in the pages that follow. Once mastered, however, you will have a vastly stronger understanding of how computers work, how the code you write in C is translated into machine language, and thus a better understanding of how to write effective and efficient programs in C.

Writing code in assembly is tedious and error-prone. Thus, our approach will be to avoid assembly whenever possible, writing the vast majority of our code in C. When assembly is necessary or desirable, it will be used only to create small subroutines (functions) called from C. Our application programs will be a mix of C and assembly, and will demand a thorough understanding of the function call/return interface.

First, we must learn about the internal organization of a simple computer—its internal components and how calculations are performed as data is manipulated and moved from one part to another.

Every computer consists of three major components: (1) a *CPU*, where operations are performed, (2) a *memory*, where data is stored, and (3) an *input/output (I/O) system*, to gather input data or to output results. The three units are interconnected by groups of wires called buses.

Desktop processors use one set of buses to connect the CPU and memory, and another to connect the CPU and I/O. Data transferred between memory and I/O devices normally goes through and is coordinated by the CPU. When greater data transfer rates are required, a Direct Memory Access (DMA) controller can be added to let perform these transfers. Data is transferred faster because the CPU is no longer required to execute instructions to transfer the data, and the CPU is free to perform its own calculations concurrent with the data transfers (Figure 5-1).

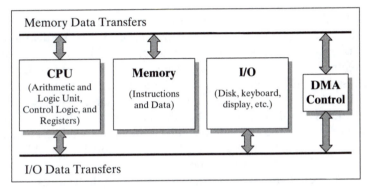

FIGURE 5-1   Configuration of a typical desktop processor.

Most modern embedded processors use a single interconnection path in a configuration known as *memory-mapped I/O*. The 32-bit address of today's processors is capable of referencing 4 GB (2^{32} bytes) of information. Since this is far more than would ever be required for an embedded application, a portion of the address space is reserved for and decoded by the I/O devices. This eliminates the need for separate I/O instructions since all of the regular instructions for accessing memory can then be used to access I/O devices. Most embedded applications do not require the higher data transfer rates and omit the DMA controller entirely. If a DMA controller is added, performance would be a little slower anyway because each transfer would require a read cycle followed by a write cycle, whereas two interconnection paths would allow the cycles to occur simultaneously (Figure 5-2).

Within the computer, the CPU retrieves data from memory, operates on it, and stores the results back in memory. Information flows between the CPU and memory over three sets of wires called the *address bus*, the *data bus*, and the *control and status bus*. The CPU places information on the address bus to tell the memory which data to access and uses the control and status bus to determine the direction of information transfer and to coordinate timing. The data itself is transferred over the data bus.

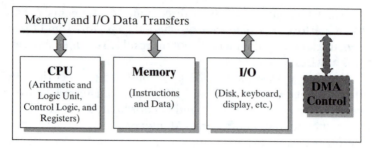

FIGURE 5-2   Configuration of a typical embedded processor.

5.1   MEMORY

We already know that computers store data using bits of 1's and 0's. For convenience, these bits are usually organized into *bytes* of 8 bits. To distinguish one byte from another, each byte is assigned a unique *address*. Whenever we want to examine the contents of a byte in memory, or to replace its contents, we must specify its address. An address is simply a binary number. The number of bits used to specify an address is fixed and limits the maximum number of bytes that the memory can hold. For example, if an address consists of 20 bits, then the maximum number of different addresses is 2^{20}. This number is close to 1 million, and so the corresponding memory capacity is often referred to as 1 megabyte. Today's 32-bit processors have a 32-bit address bus that can address 4 GB (2^{32} bytes) of memory (Figure 5-3).

Adjacent bytes are combined to form 16-bit half words, 32-bit words, and 64-bit double words. By convention, the address of these larger operands is always specified as the address of their least significant byte. For example, the 16-bit half word whose

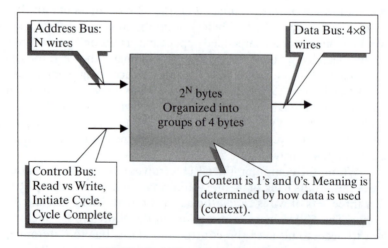

FIGURE 5-3   Main memory of a computer.

32-bit address is 104 consists of 2 bytes located at addresses 104 and 105. There are two possible byte orderings: "little endian" and "big endian." The popular Intel processors use little-endian format, in which the least significant byte of information is stored at the lowest address. In this format, the address of a 32-bit quantity is the same as the address of its least significant byte. Little-endian format is illustrated in Figure 5-4. Motorola processors and all data transmitted over the Internet use big-endian format, in which the order is reversed. ARM processors are essentially little-endian architectures, although they do provide limited support for accessing big-endian data.

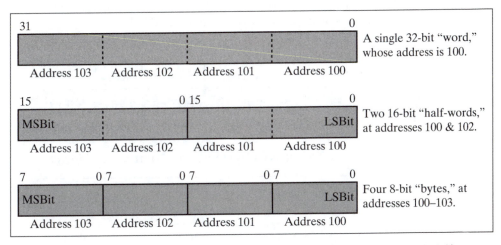

FIGURE 5-4   Little-endian byte and bit ordering (most significant bits and bytes at far left).

There are two fundamental operations that memory can perform: *reads* and *writes*. When data is written into memory, it *replaces* the previous contents of that location, which are discarded. A memory-read operation is nondestructive, and retrieves a *copy* of the contents of a memory location. Physically, however, memory uses a 32-bit data bus so that it can transfer as many as 4 bytes in a single read or write cycle.[1] Sometimes, less than 4 bytes are actually used, either because the operand is a byte or a half word or because the operand is misaligned—that is, split across two adjacent 32-bit memory words. Misaligned or double-word operands require more than one memory cycle.

5.1.1 Data Alignment

To understand why alignment is important, consider a byte-addressable memory with a data bus that is 32 bits (4 bytes) wide. Every memory read delivers 32 bits (4 bytes) of information. The first 16 bytes of memory (addresses 0 to 15) are arranged as physical

---

[1] Physically, the memory is organized as 2^{30} 32-bit words. The most significant 30 bits of the 32-bit address select the word, while the remaining bits are used to select the appropriate byte(s) within that word.

32-bit words of 4 bytes each, with each word beginning on a mod-4 address as shown below.

Address 15	Address 14	Address 13	Address 12
Address 11	Address 10	Address 9	Address 8
Address 7	Address 6	Address 5	Address 4
Address 3	Address 2	Address 1	Address 0

A 32-bit word of data can be stored within *any* contiguous set of 4 bytes. For example, the word starting at address 4 is highlighted below:

Address 15	Address 14	Address 13	Address 12
Address 11	Address 10	Address 9	Address 8
Address 7 (MSbyte)	Address 6	Address 5	Address 4 (LSbyte)
Address 3	Address 2	Address 1	Address 0

However, we could just as easily store a word starting at address 6:

Address 15	Address 14	Address 13	Address 12
Address 11	Address 10	Address 9 (MSbyte)	Address 8
Address 7	Address 6 (LSbyte)	Address 5	Address 4
Address 3	Address 2	Address 1	Address 0

The difference is that the word at address 4 can be read from memory in a single memory cycle, but because the word at address 6 is split between two "physical" words, two memory read cycles are required to retrieve all 32 bits. The first read cycle would retrieve 4 bytes from addresses 4 through 7; of these, the bytes from addresses 4 and 5 are discarded, and those from addresses 6 and 7 are moved to the far right:

		Address 7	Address 6 (LSbyte)

The second read cycle retrieves 4 bytes from addresses 8 through 11; the bytes from addresses 10 and 11 are discarded, and those from addresses 8 and 9 are moved to the far left:

Address 9 (MSbyte)	Address 8		

Finally, the two halves are combined to form the desired 32-bit operand:

Address 9 (MSbyte)	Address 8	Address 7	Address 6 (LSbyte)

The positioning and combining of bytes is done in hardware much faster than the time required for a single memory cycle. However, each memory cycle time is usually significantly slower than the basic clock cycle of a processor, and represents the primary performance bottleneck. Hence, compilers intentionally allocate memory for 32-bit operands so that they start on an address that is divisible by 4, and allocate memory for 16-bit half words so that they start on an address that is divisible by 2.

5.2 THE CENTRAL PROCESSING UNIT

The CPU of a computer is where the computation occurs. It consists of several components, including the *arithmetic and logic unit (ALU)*, a set of *registers,* and a *control unit*. One or more data and control buses interconnect these components.

Within the CPU, the *ALU* performs arithmetic operations (e.g., addition, subtraction), bit manipulation operations (e.g., bitwise AND, OR, XOR, and shifting), and is where conditional branch decisions are made. Such low-level operations are characterized by their simplicity, requiring only one or two input operands and producing a single output result. Since only a single operand can reside on the memory data bus at any one time, the ALU needs one or more *registers* to hold the other operands and the result. In the simplest configuration, a single register called the *accumulator (ACC)* is used, as shown in Figure 5-5.

The ALU can transfer one input through to the accumulator unmodified; this allows preloading the accumulator with one of the two operands. One input of the ALU is always connected to the accumulator; this allows the ALU to combine the current contents of the accumulator with a copy of the contents of some memory location

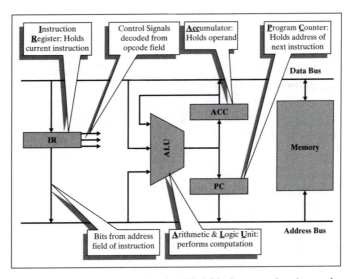

FIGURE 5-5 Components of a simplified (single accumulator) central processing unit.

and to store the result back in the accumulator. This result can then be stored in memory via the return path from the accumulator back to the memory data bus. Using this structure to add two numbers together and to store the results in memory requires three steps:

```
ACC ← MEM[adrs_of_op1]          ;Copy 1st operand from memory into ACC
ACC ← ACC + MEM[adrs_of_op2]    ;Replace contents of ACC by sum
MEM[adrs_of_result] ← ACC       ;Store contents of ACC into memory
```

Most CPUs have more than one register that can serve as an accumulator. In addition to specifying the address of the memory operand, instructions for such machines must also specify which of these registers to use:

```
REG[r] ← MEM[adrs_of_op1]        ;Copy 1st operand from memory into register 'r'
REG[r] ← REG[r] + MEM[adrs_of_op2] ;Replace contents of register 'r' by sum
MEM[adrs_of_result] ← REG[r]     ;Store contents of register 'r' into memory
```

The number of registers varies from one computer to another, but is typically around 16.

Processors that use what is known as a "*Load/Store*" architecture require that *all* operands reside in registers—that is, that the only operations that may access memory are those that merely load (read) data from memory into a register or store (write) the contents of a register into memory:

```
REG[r1] ← MEM[adrs_of_op1]     ;Copy 1st operand from memory into register 'r1'
REG[r2] ← MEM[adrs_of_op2]     ;Copy 1st operand from memory into register 'r2'
REG[r3] ← REG[r1] + REG[r2]    ;Perform the addition, leaving the result in a
                                3rd register
MEM[adrs_of_result] ← REG[r3]  ;Store contents of register 'r3' into memory
```

5.2.1 Other Registers

There are a number of other registers inside the CPU. Each of these has a dedicated purpose. For example, every CPU has an instruction register that holds the current instruction, a program counter (PC) to specify the address of the next instruction to be executed, and a status register to hold information about the most recent result produced by the ALU. Other common special-purpose registers include a stack pointer (SP), used to emulate a stack in memory, and index registers, for subscripting arrays.

5.2.2 The Fetch-Execute Cycle

The control unit of the CPU is responsible for fetching instructions from memory, decoding them, and then executing the instructions by directing the appropriate sequence of data transfers and operations among the various parts of the computer. This sequence repeats ad infinitum as the basic *fetch-execute cycle* of the computer (Figure 5-6).

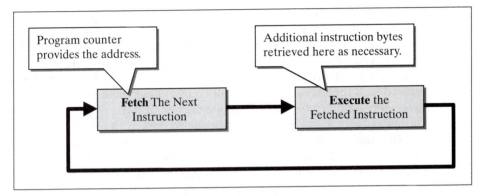

FIGURE 5-6   The fetch-execute cycle of the control unit.

During the fetch phase, the control unit places the current contents of the PC on the memory address bus and initiates a memory read operation to retrieve the first byte of an instruction from memory. While waiting for the memory read to complete, the control unit increments the PC in preparation for the retrieval of the next instruction byte. When the memory has completed its read, the control unit copies the data from the memory data bus into the instruction register (Figure 5-7).

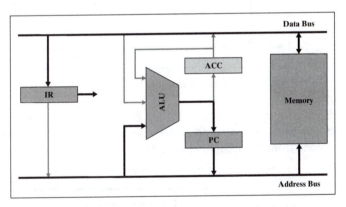

FIGURE 5-7   CPU components used during the fetch phase.

The detailed sequence of events in the fetch phase is as follows:

1. Memory Address Bus ← Program Counter
2. Start Memory Read Operation
3. Increment Program Counter
4. Wait for Memory Read to Complete
5. Instruction Register ← Memory Data Bus
6. Go to execute phase

The first byte of an instruction contains the operation code (or simply "opcode") and an indication of whether there are additional bytes in the instruction that need to be retrieved. The opcode bits are decoded by the control unit, which then causes the appropriate sequence of control signals to occur in a specific order to carry out the execute phase of the instruction. Any additional bytes of the instruction will be retrieved (and the PC incremented) during this phase; these bytes may be required to provide a constant to be used as an operand, or to retrieve information about what registers to use or about how to compute the address of an operand in memory.

The specific details of what happens during the execute phase depend on the particular instruction that is being executed. For example, an instruction that loads data from memory into the accumulator (Figure 5-8) takes the address of the memory operand from the instruction register, places it on the memory address bus, initiates a memory read operation, and then transfers the memory data through the ALU to the accumulator.

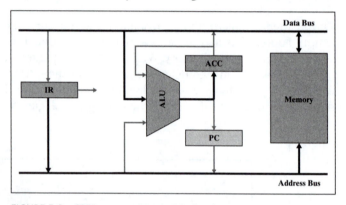

FIGURE 5-8   CPU components used during the execute phase to load a register from memory.

Once an operand has been loaded into the accumulator, a subsequent instruction can perform an addition between it and a second operand, taking one operand from memory, a second from the accumulator, and replacing its content with the result (Figure 5-9).

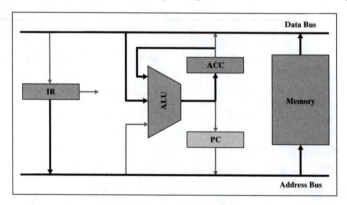

FIGURE 5-9   CPU components used during the execute phase of an ADD instruction.

The fetch-execute cycle inherently provides sequential (i.e., "straight-line") execution of instructions. Loops and decisions require that we branch and begin fetching instructions from some location other than the one immediately following the current instruction. Branch instructions accomplish this by loading an entirely new address into the PC during the execute phase. This address may have been stored as a constant embedded within the instruction, as a value retrieved from a register or read from memory, or as the result of some calculation performed during the execute phase of the branch instruction (Figure 5-10).

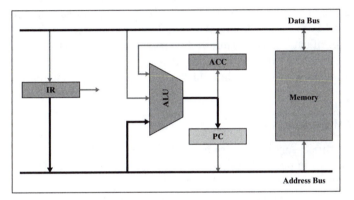

FIGURE 5-10   CPU components used during the execute phase of a branch instruction.

5.3 INPUT/OUTPUT

The I/O system of a computer includes everything other than the CPU and memory. This includes not only devices designed to interface with humans, such as keyboards and displays, but also other kinds of devices, such as disk drives, network interfaces, sensors, and actuators.

Every I/O device is connected to the computer through some sort of interface. The interface may exist as a plug-in adapter card, as additional circuitry that resides on the same printed circuit board as the CPU, or may even be built into the processor chip itself.

Connecting external devices to a computer is primarily a problem of synchronization. I/O devices usually operate at speeds that are unrelated to and much slower than the processor—typically orders of magnitude slower. Some form of handshaking to coordinate transfers between the two is always necessary so that the computer will not output data faster than an output device can accept it and not try to process input data that has not yet become available.

There are a number of different hardware and software strategies for I/O. These are considered in more detail in a later chapter. Choosing the most effective combination for a particular kind of device is a system-level design decision that is almost always a compromise between performance and cost.

5.4   INTRODUCTION TO THE ARM® CORTEX™-M3 v7M ARCHITECTURE

Any practical discussion of computer organization must ultimately focus on a particular CPU. Although the information presented here is for a single processor among the ARM family of microprocessors, this section is not intended to be a comprehensive description of that processor or others in the ARM family. Our objective here is to understand how the algorithms we implement in a higher-level language like C are brought to life within the architecture of a specific microprocessor, and to be able to code at either level when appropriate or necessary.

Here, we present only a first introduction to the ARM® Cortex-M3 v7M architecture, which was specifically designed for small-footprint embedded applications. The Cortex-M3 processor implements the Thumb-2 instruction subset of the ARM architecture specification. Most Thumb-2 instructions are 16 bits wide, expanded internally to a full 32-bit ARM instruction. The next few chapters provide a number of examples of assembly language code that illustrate the more commonly used Thumb-2 instructions.

5.4.1 Internal Organization

ARM processors have a sophisticated CPU capable of performing multiple low-level operations in parallel. As operands are read from memory and placed on the data bus, a hardware sign extender converts 8-bit and 16-bit operands to a full 32-bit representation so that all data inside the CPU are always 32 bits wide.

The ARM processor uses a "load-store" architecture. This means that any computation must first use *load* instructions to read the operands from memory into registers and a *store* instruction must be used to write the result back to memory. In other words, instructions such as add, subtract, bitwise-and, and so on can only operate on the contents of registers; they cannot operate directly on the contents of memory locations. Such instructions take their operands from registers (referred to as R_m and R_n) and leave a result in a register referred to as R_d.

A barrel shifter allows operand R_m to be shifted left or right arithmetically, logically, or rotated any number of bit positions before being combined with operand R_n in the ALU. Among other advantages, the barrel shifter allows calculations of the form $R_n \pm 2^k R_m$. When the same register is specified for both R_n and R_m, the barrel shifter simplifies the calculation of certain multiples of a value, such as $5X = X + 2^2 X$ or $-7X = X - 2^3 X$ (Figure 5-11).

A separate memory address calculator (MAC) prepares subscripted and relative address references for memory access, and a special incrementer can adjust the memory address on subsequent instructions without having to entirely recalculate the address, which can be useful in repetitive operations such as initializing the contents of an array to a constant value.

The CPU contains a set of 13 general-purpose registers (R0 through R12) and three special-purpose registers (R13, R14, and R15). The general-purpose registers are divided into the "low" registers (R0 through R7) and the "high" registers (R8 through R12), with minor restrictions regarding which instructions can use the latter. R15 is used as the PC, R13 as the SP, and R14 as the "link" register (LR) that holds the return address when a subroutine is called.

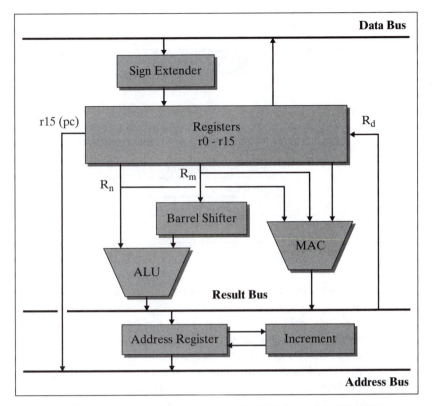

FIGURE 5-11   Internal organization of the ARM Cortex-M3 v7M CPU.

A collection of 1-bit status flags and other information is held in a single 32-bit program status register (PSR) (Figure 5-12). The PSR is divided into three bit fields: the Application Program Status Register (APSR), the Interrupt Program Status Register (IPSR), and the Execution Program Status Register (EPSR). Most important for application programs are the four most significant bits of the PSR that hold information used to make conditional branch decisions. The Q bit is the sticky saturation bit and supports two rarely used instructions (SSAT and USAT). The EPSR holds the exception number during exception processing. The ICI/IT bits hold state information for IT block instructions and instructions that are suspended during interrupt processing and continued on return. The T bit is always 1 to indicate Thumb state.

5.4.2 Instruction Pipelining

Since most instructions are fetched from sequential address locations, the ARM processor uses a technique called "pipelining" to speed up the fetch-execute process. Pipelining allows three instructions to be in progress simultaneously during any one processor clock cycle. While one instruction is fetched, another is decoded, and a third is executed. Thumb instructions are 16 or 32 bits wide, with the majority being 16 bits. Thus, while the address held in PC is being used to read one 16-bit instruction from memory, the previous instruction (from address PC-2) is decoded, and the one before

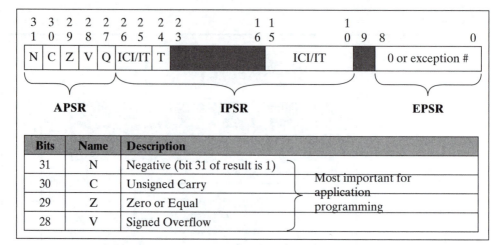

FIGURE 5-12 Bit fields within the Program Status Register.

that (from address PC-4) is executed. Note that the PC holds the address of the instruction currently being fetched, not the one being executed. By overlapping these operations, instructions can be executed at the rate of one every clock cycle rather than one every three clock cycles (Figures 5-13 and 5-14).

When a branch instruction is executed, the other two instructions in the pipeline must be discarded and the pipeline refilled. To accelerate the process, the processor fetches the destination instruction during the decode stage. For conditional branch instructions, the branch decision is determined during the execute stage. If the branch decision fails, then the next sequential instruction already in the pipeline is executed. Otherwise, the destination instruction fetched during the decode stage can be decoded and executed with only a one-cycle delay. To further reduce these "pipeline stalls," some Cortex-M3 instructions can be selectively enabled or disabled based on the status of the flags rather than using a conditional branch instruction to avoid them.

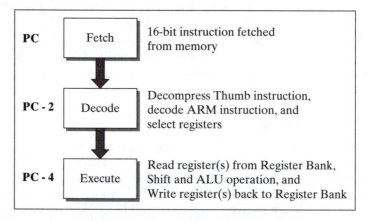

FIGURE 5-13 Cortex-M3 instruction pipeline.

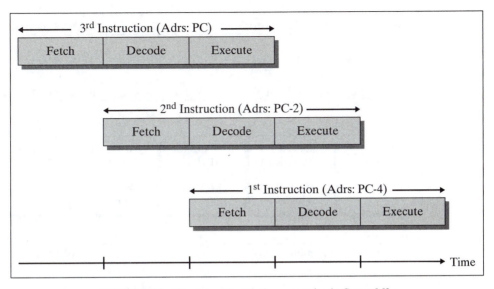

FIGURE 5-14   Overlapped instruction processing in Cortex-M3.

5.4.3 Memory Model

The ARM specification reserves specific regions within the 4-GB memory address space of the Cortex-M3 MCU for code, data, and memory-mapped I/O devices. Specific implementations of the Cortex-M3 specification may implement only portions of each region, but always use the regions in a manner that is consistent with the specification. The memory is byte-addressable, but each memory cycle transfers a full 32-bit word of 4 bytes. Code and data are stored in separate and independent hardware; instructions are fetched over the I-Code bus from a nonvolatile flash memory while the system bus is used to access data in static read/write memory (or peripherals). Since the two memories are physically separate, overall performance is enhanced by a *Harvard*-style architecture with separate data paths that allow simultaneous instruction and data access (Figure 5-15).

5.4.4 Bit-Banding

The 32-bit address bus available in a 32-bit processor provides a 4-GB address space that is much larger than needed for almost any embedded application. The Cortex-M3 design takes advantage of the extra space to implement a hardware feature known as "bit-banding." The technique uses two different regions of the address space to reference the same physical data. Within the primary "bit-band region," each address corresponds to a single byte of data; within the "bit-band alias," each address corresponds to a single bit of that same data.

The advantage of bit-banding is that an individual bit of data can be read or written by a single instruction rather than requiring a sequence of bit-manipulation

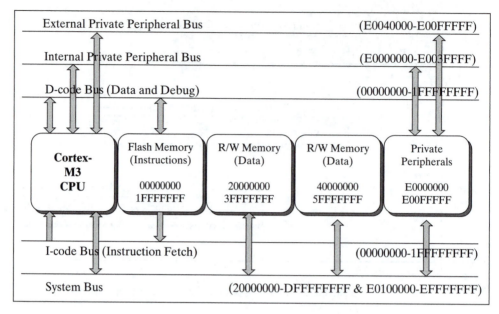

FIGURE 5-15 The Cortex-M3 bus structure.

instructions. For example, an LDR that reads from an address in the bit-band alias region will load a register with either the value 0 or the value 1. In a similar manner, a store register to memory (STR) instruction that writes to an address in the bit-band alias region modifies only a single bit of data in the primary region. Of course the modification requires that the bit-band *hardware* perform a read-modify-write, but only a single instruction (the STR) is fetched and executed.

As shown in Figure 5-16, the first megabyte of the address space for read/write data and the first megabyte of the address space for peripheral devices are designated as bit-band regions. Each of these primary regions has a corresponding 32-MB bit-band alias, and each bit of data in the primary region has a corresponding word address in the alias region. Thus, for every byte in the primary region, there are eight words in the alias region.

The two bit-band alias regions provide an efficient way to access individual status and control bits of I/O devices or to implement a set of 1-bit Boolean flags. Moreover, since the bit-band hardware does not allow its read-modify-write operation to be interrupted by other bus activity, these 1-bit Boolean flags are an efficient way to implement a set of mutex objects (discussed in Chapter 9) used to arbitrate access to shared resources.

Each mod-4 word address in the bit-band alias corresponds to a single bit in the corresponding bit-band region. To access a particular bit in the bit-band region, its corresponding bit-band alias address is calculated as:

```
bit-band alias address = bit-band base + 128 × word offset + 4 × bit number
```

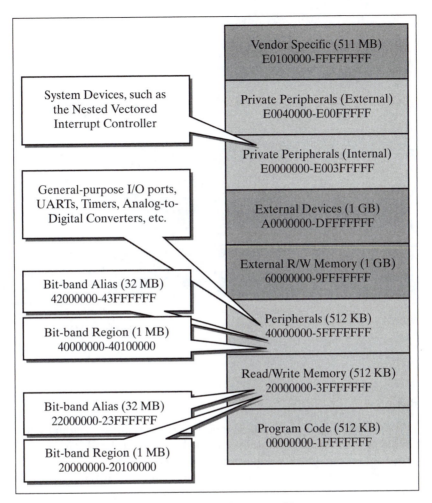

FIGURE 5-16   The Cortex-M3 memory address space.

For example, if bit 3 at address 20001000_{16} is to be modified, the bit-band alias is calculated as:

$$20000000_{16} + 128_{10} \times 1000_{16} + 4 \times 3 = 2208000C_{16}$$

Address 2208000C allows direct access to only bit 3 of the word at address 20001000. A read from that address will provide a word of all zeroes except for the least significant bit, which is a copy of the selected bit from the bit-band region. A write to the same address will ignore all but the least significant bit of the data that is written (Figure 5-17).

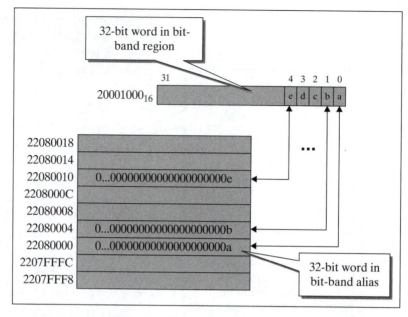

FIGURE 5-17   Bit-banding in the Cortex-M3.

5.5   ARM ASSEMBLY LANGUAGE

Programming in assembly language is a tedious yet occasionally necessary process. What is possible in a single line of code in a high-level language like C inevitably requires several lines of code in assembly. For example, to simply add the content of two integer variables and store their result in a third requires four lines of code in ARM assembly.

The assembly language programmer also has to manage a lot more detail. While a C programmer can let the compiler determine what conversions may be needed when mixing operands of different type, this becomes your responsibility when you program in assembly. Basic operations that we take for granted, such as subscripting an array, parameter passing, and pointer dereferencing, suddenly require the design of sequences of instructions.

Just like learning a foreign language, before learning how to program in assembly, we have to first learn the vocabulary—the instructions that are available, the nuances of their semantics, how they are written, and what options they allow.

5.5.1   Instruction Formats and Operands

The ARM Cortex-M3 processor implements the Thumb and Thumb-2 instruction subsets of the ARM family. In assembly language, ARM instructions are written as an operation code (or simply, "opcode") followed by zero or more operands that may be constants, registers, or memory references. Instructions that transfer data between registers and memory usually specify two operands, as in:

```
LDR  R0,temperature  ;load register R0 from memory location 'temperature'
STR  R1,result       ;store register R0 into memory location 'result'
```

Most ARM instructions perform a calculation between two source operands and specify a third destination operand. For example, the assembly language ADD instruction is written as in:

```
ADD  R2,R3,R4         ;R2 ← R3 + R4
```

Each line of source code in assembly language contains a single machine-language instruction. As shown in Figure 5-18, each line is divided into four fields separated by spaces: the label field, the operation field, the operand(s) field, and the comment field. If a label is used, it must begin in column 1 and is usually terminated with a colon; otherwise, column 1 must be left blank. Comments begin with a semicolon, and the assembler ignores anything to the right of the semicolon.

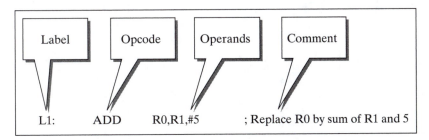

FIGURE 5-18   The four fields in a line of code in assembly language.

The assembler translates each line of source code into the binary representation of a single instruction. The most common error that a new assembly language programmer makes is misunderstand the purpose of the operand field. Executing the following instruction at run time loads the content of a variable called "data" into R0. However, during the assembly process (prior to execution) the value represented by the identifier is its address.

```
LDR  R0,data    ;load register R0 with the content of variable "data"
```

This becomes important when the operand field contains an arithmetic expression. For example, executing the instruction,

```
LDR  R0,data+4 ;load register R0 from an address 4 bytes higher than that of "data"
```

does *not* add the content of data and four and place the sum in register R0. Rather, the addition occurs during assembly; it causes the assembler to add four to the *address* of data and place the sum in the address field of the instruction representation. If, for example, the variable data were stored at address 100 in memory, the instruction shown above would load register R0 from address 104.

In ARM assembly, square brackets are used to enclose more complex address specifications that depend on the content of registers. Thus, whenever you see square brackets, you know that the instruction will access memory.

```
LDR  R0,[R1]   ; register R0 is loaded from memory whose address is given by R1
```

5.5.2 Translating Assembly into Binary

The translation of assembly language source code into binary object code is a two-step process as shown in Figure 5-19. The assembler makes two complete passes over the source code of the program. During the first pass, the assembler builds a symbol table that contains information about programmer-defined identifiers, such as the address of an instruction represented by a label attached to it, or the address of a variable represented by its identifier. During the second pass, the assembler uses this information to assemble the representation of the individual instructions.

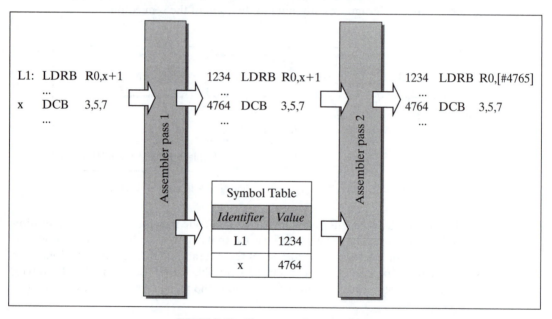

FIGURE 5-19 Two passes of an assembler.

PROBLEMS

1. Which interconnection relationship is incorrect?
   (a) I/O–MEM–CPU
   (b) MEM– CPU–I/O
   (c) CPU– I/O– MEM

2. Which part of the computer puts information on the Address Bus?
   (a) Main memory
   (b) CPU
   (c) ALU

3. How many address lines are required for a memory containing a total of:
   (a) 256 kB
   (b) 2 MB
   (c) 4 GB

4. Fill in the blanks with one of IR, ALU, PC, ACC, MEMORY, FETCH PHASE, or EXECUTE PHASE:
   (a) Data is stored in the _____.
   (b) Programs are stored in the _____.
   (c) To be executed, an instruction is loaded into the _____.
   (d) The address of an instruction to be executed is held in _____.
   (e) Instructions are retrieved during the _____.
   (f) Instructions are interpreted during the _____.
   (g) Arithmetic operations occur in the _____.
   (h) Temporary intermediate results are held in the _____.

5. The fetch phase is preceded by the _____ phase.

6. The fetch phase is followed by the _____ phase.

7. The instruction register (IR) is loaded during the _____ phase.

8. Computation performed by an instruction occurs during the _____ phase.

9. In the ARM architecture, how many bytes are there in:
   (a) A half word?
   (b) A double word?

10. Considering address alignment, what is the worst-case time required to fetch a 4-byte operand from a memory with a 60-nsec cycle time and a data bus that is 16 bits wide?

11. If the data bus connecting the CPU and memory is 4 bytes wide, how many memory cycles are required to read each of the following from memory?
    (a) A 16-bit operand read from decimal address 5
    (b) A 16-bit operand read from decimal address 15
    (c) A 32-bit operand read from decimal address 10
    (d) A 32-bit operand read from decimal address 20

12. Consider the partial view of a 32-bit memory and decimal addresses for an ARM processor shown below:

Address 111	Address 110	Address 109	Address 108
Address 107	Address 106	Address 105	Address 104
Address 103	Address 102	Address 101	Address 100
Address 99	Address 98	Address 97	Address 96

   (a) Shade the word whoose address is 102?
   (b) What is the address of the most significant byte of the word at address 102?
   (c) How many memory cycles are required to read the word at address 102?
   (d) How many memory cycles are required to read the half word at address 102?

13. In a computer that uses little-endian format, which byte of a 16-bit word has the higher address?
   (a) The least significant byte
   (b) The most significant byte

14. In a computer that uses little-endian format, if the 2 bytes of a 16-bit word are at addresses 100 and 101, then what is the address of the entire 16-bit word?

15. Consider a computer that uses little-endian numbering. If a 32-bit operand resides at decimal address N, what is the address of:
   (a) The most significant byte
   (b) The 16-bit operand corresponding to the most significant half

16. If bytes within a word are assigned addresses that increase from the most to least significant byte, the computer is said to use:
   (a) Little-endian numbering
   (b) Big-endian numbering

17. In a computer that uses little-endian numbering, bits within an operand are numbered:
   (a) From least to most significant bit, starting at 0
   (b) From least to most significant bit, starting at 1
   (c) From most to least significant bit, starting at 0
   (d) From most to least significant bit, starting at 1

18. If the first element of a one-dimensional array is located in memory at address 100, what will be the address of the second element if the array contains:
   (a) chars
   (b) short ints
   (c) long ints
   (d) long long ints

19. Which of the following registers of the ARM Cortex-M3 are modified during the fetch phase of the fetch-execute cycle? (Circle all that apply.)
   (a) SP
   (b) PC
   (c) LR
   (d) PSW

20. Which of the following can the Cortex-M3 can access in a memory cycle? (Circle all that apply.)
   (a) A single byte
   (b) A half word
   (c) A word
   (d) A double word

21. In general, the Cortex-M3 processor uses:
   (a) A 1-operand instruction format
   (b) A 2-operand instruction format
   (c) A 3-operand instruction format

22. Which of the following operand types can be used as the left-most operand of an instruction in the ARM Cortex-M3 processor? (Circle all that apply.)
    (a) A memory location
    (b) A constant
    (c) An I/O port
    (d) A register

23. What is the fewest number of Cortex-M3 instructions required to increment a memory location?

24. What is the fewest number of Cortex-M3 instructions required to set a single bit in memory
    (a) Without bit-banding?
    (b) With bit-banding?

25. What address in the bit-band alias of the Cortex-M3 corresponds to bit 7 of the word at address $2004066C_{16}$?

26. What address in the bit-band region of the Cortex-M3 contains the bit that corresponds to word address 22001234_{16} in the bit-band alias?

27. Which of the following are correct? In assembly language, the "value" represented by an identifier used as a label on a memory location that contains data is:
    (a) The contents of the memory location
    (b) The address of the memory location
    (c) Determined at execution time
    (d) Determined during pass 1 of the assembler
    (e) Determined during pass 2 of the assembler

28. When is the opcode portion of the binary representation of an instruction filled in during assembly?
    (a) During pass 1 of the assembler
    (b) During pass 2 of the assembler
    (c) During program execution

C H A P T E R   6

Programming in Assembly
Part 2: Data Manipulation

The ARM processor is an example of a "Load/Store" architecture, which means that all computations (addition, multiplication, and so on) are performed on data held in registers, not in memory. In other words, data must be moved to a register before you can operate on it. The data transfer instructions include those for loading constants into registers, loading and storing memory data, and stack operations.

6.1 LOADING CONSTANTS INTO REGISTERS

The Thumb-2 instruction subset includes instructions for loading a constant into a register. The MOV and MVN instructions embed a constant within the representation of the instruction itself. Such constants are referred to as "immediate" constants since they are immediately available once the instruction has been fetched, without the need to load the constant from a separate memory location.

The MOV instruction copies the constant into a register; the MVN instruction is essentially a "move not," copying the *inverse* of the constant into a register:[1]

```
MOV     R1,#100                  ;R1 ← 100
MVN     R1,#100                  ;R1 ← ~100 (same as R1 ← -101)
```

Constants are always preceded by a pound sign. By default, constants are written in decimal; hexadecimal constants must be preceded by "0x," as in "MOV R1,#0xF3."

Although the MOV instruction of the processor only supports positive constants, if you code a negative constant, the assembler will convert it to an equivalent MVN instruction. For example, the assembler will replace "MOV R1,#–100" by "MVN R1,#99."

Unfortunately, neither the MOV nor the MVN instruction supports the full range of 32-bit values since only a small number of bits of the instruction are used to hold the constant. As a result, the MOV and MVN instructions are limited to constants in the range of 0 to 255 and a "few" other values. When a different value is needed, the only alternative is to store the constant in a separate memory location and load it using a memory reference instruction.

---

[1] The source operand of an MOV or an MVN instruction can be any of a constant, a register, or a shifted register.

The good news is that there is a special "pseudo-operation" that will work for *any* constant up to 32 bits wide. You simply write what appears to be a regular ARM instruction (except that an equal sign is substituted for the pound sign) and let the assembler sort out the most efficient way to achieve your objective:

```
LDR   R1,=10        ;assembler replaces this by MOV R1,#10.
LDR   R1,=-15       ;assembler replaces this by MVN R1,#14.
LDR   R1,=-127435   ;assembler replaces this by a memory reference
                    ;instruction that loads the constant from a
                    ;separate memory location.
```

6.2 LOADING MEMORY DATA INTO REGISTERS

The LDR instruction is used for loading data from memory into a register. The normal LDR instruction loads (copies) a 32-bit value from memory into a register. However, when loading 8- or 16-bit data into a 32-bit register, the operand itself is always right justified within the register and its most significant bits filled according to whether the value is signed or unsigned (Figures 6-1 and 6-2).

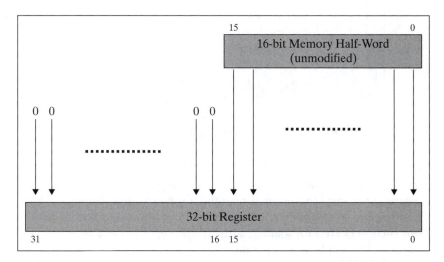

FIGURE 6-1   The LDRH instruction fills bits 16 to 31 with zeroes.

Unsigned operands less than 32 bits wide must fill the extra bit positions with zeroes (called "zero-filling"). This insures that the unsigned interpretation of the register's contents is the same as the unsigned interpretation of the data loaded from memory. For example, the load register with unsigned half word from memory (LDRH) instruction is used with 16-bit *unsigned* integers; it loads a 16-bit half word from memory into the least significant 16 bits of a register and fills the remaining 16 bits with 0's. Similarly, load register with unsigned byte from memory (LDRB) is used with 8-bit unsigned integers; it loads an 8-bit byte from memory into the least significant 8 bits of a register and fills the remaining 24 bits with 0's.

Signed operands less than 32 bits wide must fill the extra bit positions with copies of their sign bit. "Sign-extending" is used because the ARM processor (like most modern processors) uses the 2's-complement representation of signed numbers.[2] For example, the load register with signed half word from memory (LDRSH) instruction is used with 16-bit signed integers; it fills the remaining 16 bits of the register with 16 copies of the sign bit (bit 15) of the memory operand. Similarly, load register with signed byte from memory (LDRSB) is used with 8-bit signed integers and fills the remaining 24 bits of the register with 24 copies of the sign bit (bit 7) of the memory operand.

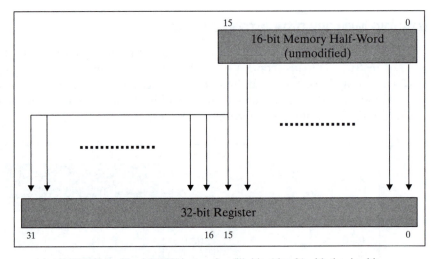

FIGURE 6-2   The LDRSH instruction fills bits 16 to 31 with the sign bit.

Using LDRH and LDRB to zero-fill unsigned values and LDRSH and LDRSB to sign-extend signed values is necessary to produce a numerically equivalent 32-bit representation of the original operand. Of course zero-filling and sign-extending are not needed when loading a 32-bit word or 64-bit double word, so there is only one instruction (LDR) for loading a 32-bit word operand and only one (LDRD) for loading a 64-bit double-word operand.

LDRD loads a pair of registers with the two halves of a 64-bit double-word value. The 64-bit value is stored in little-endian format with the least significant half (bits 0 to 31) stored in byte addresses N through N + 3, and the most significant half (bits 32 to 63) stored in byte addresses N + 4 through N + 7. The least significant half is loaded first into the left-most register listed in the instruction, followed by the most significant half then loaded into the second register (Table 6-1).

---

[2] Other representations of signed integers (such as sign-plus-magnitude) require different techniques for filling the extra bit positions.

TABLE 6-1   ARM Thumb-2 Instructions That Load Registers with Data from Memory

Instruction	Operation	Notes
LDR R_d,<mem>	$R_d \leftarrow mem_{32}[address]$	
LDRB R_d,<mem>	$R_d \leftarrow mem_8[address]$	Most significant bits of register are filled with 0's. (Used for loading 8- and 16-bit unsigned integers.)
LDRH R_d,<mem>	$R_d \leftarrow mem_{16}[address]$	
LDRSB R_d,<mem>	$R_d \leftarrow mem_8[address]$	Most significant bits of register are filled with copies of the sign bit of the memory operand. (Used for loading 8- and 16-bit signed integers.)
LDRSH R_d,<mem>	$R_d \leftarrow mem_{16}[address]$	
LDRD R_t,R_{t2},<mem>	R_{t2},$R_t \leftarrow mem_{64}[address]$	Address must be specified as an immediate constant.

Note: The notation "<mem>" refers to a memory address expression described later in this section.

6.3   STORING DATA FROM REGISTERS TO MEMORY

The LDR instructions had to support not only a variety of different size operands, but also had to operate differently for signed versus unsigned operands. The STR instructions for storing a register to memory, however, only have to worry about size. The normal STR instruction copies 32 bits of data from a register into a 32-bit memory location. The STRB and STRH instructions are used when the destination location in memory is only 8 bits or 16 bits wide, respectively, and only copy the least significant bits of the register to memory. The STRD instruction copies 64 bits from a pair of registers into a 64-bit double word in memory and operates like the reverse of an LDRD (Figure 6-3 and Table 6-2).

When writing a byte or half-word result into memory, all 4 bytes of the register are placed on the 32-bit memory data bus, but only one or two of those bytes are

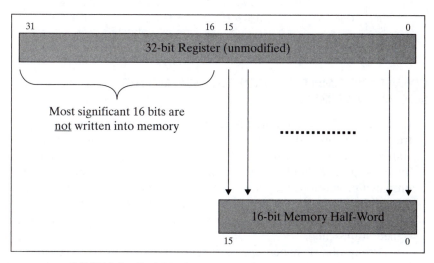

FIGURE 6-3   The STRH instruction writes bits 0 to 15 to memory.

TABLE 6-2   ARM Thumb-2 Instructions That Store Data from Registers to Memory

Instruction	Operation	Notes
STR R_d,<mem>	$R_d \rightarrow \text{mem}_{32}[\text{address}]$	
STRB R_d,<mem>	$R_d \rightarrow \text{mem}_8[\text{address}]$	
STRH R_d,<mem>	$R_d \rightarrow \text{mem}_{16}[\text{address}]$	
STRD R_t,R_{t2},<mem>	$R_{t2}R_t \rightarrow \text{mem}_{64}[\text{address}]$	Address must be specified as an immediate constant.

Note: The notation "<mem>" refers to a memory address expression described later in this section.

enabled to be written during the write cycle. For example, consider what happens when writing a half-word result to address 104: The two memory bytes that should be written are at addresses 104 and 105. However, the 32-bit memory data bus is actually 4 bytes wide, corresponding to addresses 104, 105, 106, and 107. Each byte of the memory data bus has its own write enable; during the memory write cycle, the write-enable signals for addresses 106 and 107 are disabled so that only the bytes at addresses 104 and 105 are modified. The particular type of store instruction determines which bytes of the 32-bit register are written:

Instruction	Operand	Memory Byte Locations Actually Written			
STRB	8 bits				Address N
STRH	16 bits			Address N + 1	Address N
STR	32 bits	Address N + 3	Address N + 2	Address N + 1	Address N
STRD	Lower 32 bits	Address N + 3	Address N + 2	Address N + 1	Address N
	Upper 32 bits	Address N + 7	Address N + 6	Address N + 5	Address N + 4

6.4   CONVERTING SIMPLE C ASSIGNMENT STATEMENTS INTO ARM ASSEMBLY

LDR and STR are the only instructions that can reference memory, and will appear frequently in any code that we write. We start by examining how a simple C assignment statement such as "dst = 5;" or "dst = src;" would be translated into ARM assembly. Table 6-3 gives a number of solutions that cover 8, 16, 32, and 64 operands, signed and unsigned promotions (copying a smaller variable into a larger one), and demotions. A few of the entries in the table must be modified (as indicated by the footnotes) for cases involving the promotion of signed data types; all other entries will work for either signed or unsigned.

Promotion of signed operands requires extending the sign into the most significant bit positions of the destination. When the destination is 16 or 32 bits, the

TABLE 6-3   Translation of Simple C Assignment Statements to ARM Assembly

	8-bit Destination	16-bit Destination	32-bit Destination	64-bit Destination
Source is the constant 5	LDR R0,=5 STRB R0,dst8	LDR R0,=5 STRH R0,dst16	LDR R0,=5 STR R0,dst32	LDR R0,=5 LDR[1] R1,=0 STRD R0,R1,dst64
8-bit source	LDRB R0,src8 STRB R0,dst8	LDRB[2] R0,src8 STRH R0,dst16	LDRB[2] R0,src8 STR R0,dst32	LDRB[2] R0,src8 LDR[4] R1,=0 STRD R0,R1,dst64
16-bit source	LDRB R0,src16 STRB R0,dst8	LDRH R0,src16 STRH R0,dst16	LDRH[3] R0,src18 STR R0,dst32	LDRH[3] R0,src16 LDR[4] R1,=0 STRD R0,R1,dst64
32-bit source	LDRB R0,src32 STRB R0,dst8	LDRH R0,src32 STRH R0,dst16	LDR R0,src32 STR R0,dst32	LDR R0,src32 LDR[4] R1,=0 STRD R0,R1,dst64
64-bit source	LDRB R0,src64 STRB R0,dst8	LDRH R0,src64 STRH R0,dst16	LDR R0,src64 STR R0,dst32	LDRD R0,R1,src64 STRD R0,R1,dst64

[1]Replace with ASR R1,R0,#31 if source operand is a negative constant.
[2]Replace with LDRSB if source operand is signed.
[3]Replace with LDRSH if source operand is signed.
[4]Replace with ASR R1,R0,#31 if source operand is signed.

sign-extension is handled entirely by the LDRSB or LDRSH instruction. However, when the destination is 64 bits wide, creating the upper 32 bits of the sign extension requires that we perform a 31-bit arithmetic right shift of a copy of the lower half; the ASR instruction used to do this will be introduced later in this chapter.

6.5   MEMORY ADDRESS CALCULATIONS

During the execute phase of an instruction such as "LDR R0,data", the instruction must provide the address of the memory operand "data" to memory. Storing the address as a 32-bit constant within the representation of the instruction itself would mean that all LDR and STR instructions were more than 32 bits wide. To conserve memory space and instruction fetch time, these instructions simply specify *how* the address should be calculated from a smaller number of bits. The assembler automatically converts a reference to the variable "data" into a *PC-relative* reference, where the address is calculated as the sum of the program counter (R15) and a small constant stored in the instruction. The constant is known as a *displacement* whose value is the difference between the address of the instruction and the address of the data. The displacement is only 13 bits wide and thus restricted to ±4,095.

PC-relative addressing is a special case of an ARM addressing mode known as "offset addressing." It provides four basic options for calculating an address as summarized in Table 6-4. Examples of how these are used are covered later in this section.

TABLE 6-4   Offset Addressing Options

Syntax	Memory Address	Example
$[R_n]$	R_n	$[R5]$
$[R_n, \text{\#constant}]$	$R_n + \text{constant}$	$[R5, \text{\#}100]$
$[R_n, R_m]$	$R_n + R_m$	$[R4, R5]$
$[R_n, R_m, \text{LSL \#constant}]$	$R_n + (R_m << \text{constant})$	$[R4, R5, \text{LSL \#}3]$

Note: "LDR R0,data" is a special PC-relative case of $[R_n, \text{\#constant}]$

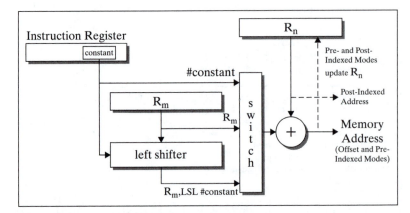

FIGURE 6-4   Conceptual model of ARM address calculation.

When you are writing in assembly, it is important to remember that the operand field of an Instruction that accesses memory is restricted to using either an expression whose value is a constant, such as the address represented by the name of a variable, or one of the four options listed in Table 6-4. For example, the assembler will reject subscripted array names (e.g., LDR R0,data[k]) or the use of a variable name inside an address specification enclosed in square brackets (e.g., LDR R0,[R0+k]).

Figure 6-4 illustrates how offset addressing can use registers, a shifter, and a small constant to generate the address of an instruction operand. Two other addressing modes are simply variations of offset addressing, which are useful in loops that process an array of data. Pre-indexed addressing (specified by following the right square bracket by an exclamation point) simply writes the address back into register R_n at the end of the instruction. Post-indexed addressing (specified by enclosing only R_n in brackets) does the same, but uses the prior content of R_n as the address of the instruction operand.

6.6   MEMORY ADDRESSING EXAMPLES

When an instruction references data in memory, only one of the two possible situations can exist. Either the address of the data is a constant or it is a value that must be calculated at run-time. In C, the only variables whose address is a constant are those that are declared globally (outside of all functions) or inside a function but with the static key-word. Data accessed through a pointer, all function parameters, and any nonstatic vari-ables declared inside a function have an address that must be calculated.

6.6.1 Translating C Pointer Expressions to Assembly

In C, pointers are used to hold the address of some location in memory. They are usu-ally initialized by loading them with the result of applying the "address-of" operator (&) to another variable:

```
int8_t *ptr2byte;  // 32-bit pointer holds address of an 8-bit byte
int8_t data;
ptr2byte = &data;  // store address of data (a constant) in pointer
```

This value of &data is a constant. In ARM assembly, we use a special "ADR" instruction to obtain this constant:

```
ADR     R0,data           ;R0 ← &data
STR     R0,ptr2byte       ;ptr2byte ← R0
```

The source operand field of the ADR instruction can use *any* of same memory reference expressions as the LDR and STR instructions, but it does not actually refer-ence memory—it merely calculates an address without causing a memory read or memory write. In its simplest form (as mentioned earlier), it is similar to an LDR instruction that loads a constant into a register since the address of "data" is a constant. However, this address is actually obtained by adding something to the current value of the program counter.

When you dereference a pointer, you use its content as the address of the data you want to reference. Assuming "ptr2byte" has been initialized with the address of "data," we can store a zero into it by an indirect reference through pointer, as in:

```
*ptr2byte = 0 ;          // store a zero into the byte "data"
```

Note that we are storing the zero at a location whose address is provided by a variable rather than a constant. Thus, in ARM assembly, we must load the content of that variable into a register and then use it inside a pair of square brackets when stor-ing the zero into memory:

```
LDR     R0,=0             ;get the constant zero
LDR     R1,ptr2byte       ;get the address held in "ptr2byte"
STRB    R0,[R1]           ;store the zero into a byte of memory
```

The code above uses an STRB instruction because the pointer was declared to point to data which is 8 bits wide. However, the pointer itself is loaded using a regular LDR instruction since an address is always 32 bits.

It is also important to understand how pointer arithmetic works. Consider the following:

```
int32_t array[100] ; // an array of 32-bit words of 4 bytes each
int32_t *ptr2word ;  // a pointer to a 32-bit word
ptr2word = array ;   // initialize ptr2word with the address of array[0]
```

Since ptr2word contains the *address* of array[0], we know that *ptr2word is a reference to the *content* of array[0]. Similarly, the pointer expression ptr2word + 1 is the address of array[1], and the pointer expression ptr2word + k is the address of array[k]. What is important is to realize that each element of the array consists of 4 bytes so that if the address of array[0] is 1000, then the address of array[1] would be 1004. This means that when we write ptr2word + 1, we are actually adding 4 to the address, not 1. For example, the C assignment statement

```
*(ptr2word + 5) = 0 ;     // equivalent to:  array[5] = 0 ;
```

would be translated to the following ARM assembly:

```
LDR    R0,=0          ;get the constant zero
LDR    R1,ptr2word    ;get the address held in "ptr2word"
STR    R0,[R1,#20]    ;store zero at address 4*5 bytes higher in memory
```

If we replace the constant 5 with an integer variable k, as in:

```
*(ptr2word + k) = 0 ;     // equivalent to:  array[k] = 0 ;
```

then the ARM assembly code becomes:

```
LDR    R0,=0              ;get the constant zero
LDR    R1,ptr2word        ;get the address held in "ptr2word"
LDR    R2,k               ;get the integer held in "k"
STR    R0,[R1,R2,LSL#2]   ;store at address 4k bytes beyond pointer
```

Being able to left shift the content of a register used in the address calculation is an easy way to multiply by a power of 2, and particularly useful because we normally work with data that is 1, 2, 4, or 8 bytes in width.

Also remember that the difference of two pointers is not the difference in the addresses that they hold, but rather the difference in objects. For example, consider the following declarations:

```
int32_t  array[100];            // an array of 100 words of 4 bytes each
int32_t *p1 = &array[10];
int32_t *p2 = &array[20];
```

If the array begins at address 1000, then p1 will be initialized to the address 1040 and p2 to 1080. However, the value of expression p2 − p1 is not 40 (the difference in addresses), but 10 (the difference in objects). To calculate this value in assembly requires a subtraction followed by a division by 4:

```
LDR    R0,p1       ;get the address held in p1
LDR    R1,p2       ;get the address held in p2
SUB    R2,R1,R0    ;R2 ← the difference in addresses
ASR    R0,R2,#2    ;R0 ← R2, arithmetic shift right by 2 (divide by 4)
```

6.6.2 Translating C Subscript Expressions to Assembly

A subscripted array reference shares much in common with pointer dereferencing. In either case, the address calculation involves three components:

1. A starting address (provided either by a pointer or by the name of an array)
2. The value of a subscript or integer offset
3. The size of the objects held in the array or pointed to by the pointer

The only real difference is whether the starting address is a constant or a variable. In fact, you can actually subscript a pointer or dereference an array name.[3] Consider the declarations:

```
int32_t  array[100], *ptr2word, k ;
```

Applying a subscript to the pointer (e.g., ptr2word[k] = 0;) produces the same ARM assembly code we saw earlier for *(ptr2word + k) = 0, and dereferencing the array name (e.g., *(array + k) = 0 ;) is equivalent to the subscripted reference array[k] = 0, which produces very similar assembly code:

```
LDR    R0,=0             ;get the constant zero
ADR    R1,array          ;get the starting address of "array"
LDR    R2,k              ;get the integer held in "k"
STR    R0,[R1,R2,LSL#2]  ;store at address 4k bytes into array
```

6.6.3 Translating Structure References to Assembly

The location of a member element within a structure is obtained by adding a constant (10 in the examples below) to the starting address of the structure. When the reference is specified using the name of a global or statically allocated structure, as in

```
s.m = 5 ;          ;store 5 into member 'm' of structure 's'
```
then the address of the member element is the sum of two constants and may be computed when the code is assembled:

```
LDR    R0,=5             ;get the constant 5
STR    R0,s+10           ;store 5 into the member element
```

However, if the reference to the structure is via a pointer, as in

```
p->m = 5;       ;store 5 into member 'm' of the structure pointed to by 'p'
```

then the address must be calculated at run-time using the value of the pointer:

```
LDR    R0,=5        ;get the constant 5
LDR    R1,p         ;get the address of the structure from the pointer
STR    R0,[R1,#10]  ;store 5 into the member element
```

---

[3] C compilers internally convert a[5] into *(a+5). Since addition is commutative, 5[a] will generate equivalent code.

6.7 STACK INSTRUCTIONS

A stack is a "Last-In, First-Out" (LIFO) data structure in which data is retrieved in the opposite order from which it was written. Processors implement stacks by allocating a region of memory for the stack and maintaining a "stack pointer" (SP) register that holds the address of the next stack location to be accessed, called the *top* of the stack. A "push" operation writes data to the top of the stack and a "pop" operation reads data from the top of the stack. Push and pop operations adjust the SP so that the location designated as the top of the stack automatically moves up and down in memory as push and pop instructions are executed (Figure 6-5).

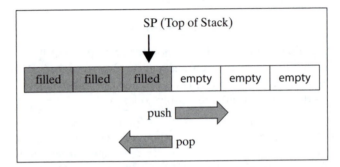

FIGURE 6-5   Implementation of a stack in memory.

In the ARM processor, PUSH and POP instructions transfer one or more 32-bit words between the registers and the stack. The stack grows downward toward lower memory addresses as more and more data are pushed. Each PUSH writes a set of registers to the top of the stack and decrements SP (R13) by four times the number of registers written. Each POP does the reverse—it loads a set of registers from the top of the stack and increments SP by four times the number of registers loaded. When more than one register is written to the stack by a single PUSH instruction, the highest numbered register is written to the highest memory address, and the lowest numbered register to the lowest memory address (Table 6-5).

TABLE 6-5   The ARM Thumb-2 Stack Instructions

Instruction	Operation	Example	Notes
PUSH {reglist}	regs → mem [SP – 4 × #regs]; [SP –= 4 × #regs];	PUSH {R0,R1,R7}	May not include SP or PC.
POP {reglist}	regs ← mem[SP]; SP+ = 4 × #regs	POP {R1,R2,R6,LR}	May not include SP; PC or LR may be included, but not both.

Stacks are a convenient temporary storage because no identifiers are needed for referring to the locations within a stack. C functions make extensive use of the stack for parameters, temporary variables, and to preserve and restore the content of registers that the function must modify. When a function needs to use one or more registers in order to carry out its computation, the function can use a PUSH instruction to preserve their original content and a POP to restore them when finished. When a larger amount of temporary storage is needed, space is allocated on the stack by simply subtracting a constant from SP for the duration of the function.

6.8   DATA-PROCESSING INSTRUCTIONS

The Thumb-2 data-processing instructions of the Cortex-M3 processor perform arithmetic, shifting, and bit manipulation. They share a number of common features, including what they can use as operands and whether or not they affect the flags in the APSR. Almost all of these instructions compute a result from two source operands. The result and one of the operands are held in registers, while the second operand may be a constant (e.g., "ADD R0,R1,#2"), a register (e.g., "ADD R0,R1,R2"), or a register that has been shifted in some way by the barrel shifter (e.g., "ADD R0,R1,R2,ASR #31"). There are five different ways that the second source operand may be shifted (Table 6-6). In the following tables, this operand is simply represented by "<op>".

TABLE 6-6   Second Operand Shift Options

Shift Option	Meaning	Notes
LSL #n	Logical shift left by n bits	Zero fills; $0 \le n \le 31$
LSR #n	Logical shift right by n bits	Zero fills; $1 \le n \le 32$
ASR #n	Arithmetic shift right by n bits	Sign extends; $1 \le n \le 32$
ROR #n	Rotate right by n bits	$1 \le n \le 32$
RRX	Rotate right with carry (n + 1 bits)	Only shifts by 1 bit

6.8.1 Updating the Flags in the APSR

The APSR is used to record the characteristics of a computed value and may be tested later to make branch decisions. Since the LDR, STR, PUSH, and POP instructions simply move data from one place to another, they never modify any of the flags. Many of the other instructions *can* modify the flags, provided that the letter "S" is appended to the end of the instruction mnemonic.

For example, an "ADD R0,R0,#1" instruction will increment the content of register R0 but has no effect on the flags. However, changing the ADD to an ADDS will record information in the flags as to whether or not the result was negative ($N = 1$), zero ($Z = 1$), or resulted a carry out ($C = 1$) or a 2's-complement overflow ($V = 1$).

Although it does not perform any arithmetic computation, the MOVS version of the MOV instruction can be used to capture the characteristics of a value copied into a register. For example, the "MOV R1,R0" instruction will move (copy) the content of R0 into R1, but will not modify any flags. However, changing the MOV to an MOVS will also update the N and Z flags[4] to indicate whether the value was negative ($N = 1$) or zero ($Z = 1$). In the following tables, the column labeled "{S}" indicates whether or not you may append an "S'" and what flags are updated if you do.

---

[4] MOVS will modify the carry flag (C) if the source operand specifies a shift.

6.8.2 Arithmetic Instructions

The Thumb-2 instruction subset provides the four basic arithmetic operations of addition, subtraction, multiplication, and division. In addition, an RSB (reverse subtract) instruction is provided when you need to subtract the value of a register from a constant, and an NEG (negative) instruction when you need to change the sign of a value held in a register (Table 6-7).

TABLE 6-7   Thumb-2 Addition and Subtraction Instructions

Instruction		Operation	{S}	Notes
ADD	$R_d,R_n,$<op>	$R_d \leftarrow R_n + $<op>	NZCV	
ADC	$R_d,R_n,$<op>	$R_d \leftarrow R_n + $<op>$ + C$	NZCV	
SUB	$R_d,R_n,$<op>	$R_d \leftarrow R_n - $<op>	NZCV	
SBC	$R_d,R_n,$<op>	$R_d \leftarrow R_n - $<op>$ + C - 1$	NZCV	
RSB	$R_d,R_n,$<op>	$R_d \leftarrow $<op>$ - R_n$	NZCV	Reverse subtraction
MOV	$R_d,$<op>	$R_d \leftarrow $<op>	NZC	Carry may be affected by <op>
NEG	R_d,R_n	$R_d \leftarrow -R_n$		Always updates: NZCV

The ADC instruction is used to perform multiple precision addition on operands that are more than 32 bits wide. For example, the ADC is used when adding the most significant halves of two 64-bit operands to incorporate the carry resulting from the addition of the least significant halves. The SBC instruction does the same for multiple precision subtraction, using the carry to hold the borrow (Figure 6-6).

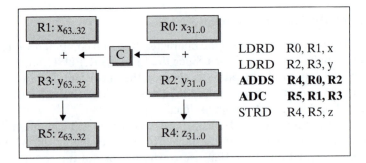

FIGURE 6-6   Double-length 64-bit addition ($z = x + y$;).

There are several instructions for multiplication and a couple for division. The SMULL and SMLAL instructions[5] compute a 64-bit product from 32-bit signed

---

[5] The last "L" in SMULL and SMLAL stands for "Long," which refers to the fact that the product is double-length.

operands; UMULL and UMLAL do the same for unsigned operands. Signed and unsigned multiplication only differs in the most significant half of a double-length product. The MUL, MLA, and MLS instructions only produce single-length products, so these instructions can be used with either signed or unsigned operands. The MLA, MLS, UMLAL, and SMLAL instructions are useful in series approximations, and the MLS instruction can be used to compute the remainder after a division (Table 6-8).

TABLE 6-8   Thumb-2 Multiplication and Division Instructions

Instruction		Operation	{S}	Notes
MUL	R_d,R_n,R_m	$R_d \leftarrow R_n \times R_m$	NZ	32-bit product
MLA	R_d,R_n,R_m,R_a	$R_d \leftarrow (R_n \times R_m) + R_a$		
MLS	R_d,R_n,R_m,R_a	$R_d \leftarrow R_a - (R_n \times R_m)$		32-bit product
UMULL	R_{dlo},R_{dhi},R_n,R_m	$R_{dhi}R_{dlo} \leftarrow R_n \times R_m$		
UMLAL	R_{dlo},R_{dhi},R_n,R_m	$R_{dhi}R_{dlo} \leftarrow R_{dhi}R_{dlo} + R_n \times R_m$		Unsigned 64-bit product
SMULL	R_{dlo},R_{dhi},R_n,R_m	$R_{dhi}R_{dlo} \leftarrow R_n \times R_m$		
SMLAL	R_{dlo},R_{dhi},R_n,R_m	$R_{dhi}R_{dlo} \leftarrow R_{dhi}R_{dlo} + R_n \times R_m$		Signed 64-bit product
UDIV	R_d,R_n,R_m	$R_d \leftarrow R_n / R_m$		Unsigned 32-bit quotient; no remainder
SDIV	R_d,R_n,R_m	$R_d \leftarrow R_n / R_m$		Signed 32-bit quotient; no remainder

To compute the remainder of a division, you must subtract the product of the quotient and divisor from the dividend. For example, consider the following C assignment statement:

```
remainder = dividend % divisor ;
```

Assuming that all variables are 32-bit unsigned integers, the remainder would be calculated in assembly as:

```
LDR     R0,dividend     ;R0 ← dividend
LDR     R1,divisor      ;R1 ← divisor
UDIV    R2,R0,R1        ;R2 ← quotient
MLS     R0,R2,R1,R0     ;R0 ← dividend – divisor × quotient
STR     R0,remainder
```

6.8.3 Bit Manipulation Instructions

Embedded applications frequently process packed information and need an effective set of instructions for manipulating bits. The Thumb-2 instruction subset includes the following basic bitwise NOT, AND, OR, and exclusive-OR operations (Table 6-9):

The familiar bitwise operations in C are easily translated into equivalent ARM assembly. For example, the C statement used to clear bit 5 of "x":

```
x &= ~(1 << 5) ;              // clear bit n of x
```

TABLE 6-9   Thumb-2 bit Manipulation Instructions

Instruction		Operation	{S}	Notes
AND	$R_d,R_n,$<op>	$R_d \leftarrow R_n$ & <op>	NZC	
ORR	$R_d,R_n,$<op>	$R_d \leftarrow R_n \mid$ <op>	NZC	
EOR	$R_d,R_n,$<op>	$R_d \leftarrow R_n \wedge$ <op>	NZC	"Exclusive OR"
BIC	$R_d,R_n,$<op>	$R_d \leftarrow R_n$ & ~<op>	NZC	"Bit Clear"
ORN	$R_d,R_n,$<op>	$R_d \leftarrow R_n \mid$ ~<op>	NZC	"OR Not"
MVN	R_d,R_n	$R_d \leftarrow$ ~R_n	NZC	"Move Not"

would be coded using the BIC instruction, as in:

```
LDR     R0,x            ;get a copy of x
BIC     R0,R0,#20       ;clear bit 5
STR     R0,x            ;store result back into x
```

6.8.4 Shift Instructions

Table 6-10 lists the Thumb-2 shift instructions. Although many other instructions (e.g., ADD, ORR, and so on) can incorporate a shift of one of their operands, the shift amount is restricted to a constant[6] the shift instructions do not have that restriction. They shift a copy of the operand (R_n), a number of bit positions specified by a constant, *or* the contents of another register. In all cases, appending the letter "S" to the instruction mnemonic causes the carry flag (C) to capture the bit shifted out of the operand; in a multi-bit shift, it captures the last bit shifted out.

The shift instructions differ in what they use to fill the vacated bit position on the other end of the operand, as illustrated in Figure 6-7. The logical shift left (LSL) and

TABLE 6-10   Thumb-2 Shift Instructions

Instruction		Operation	{S}	Notes
LSL	$R_d,R_n,$<shift>	$R_d \leftarrow R_n$ << <shift>	NZC	Zero fills
LSR	$R_d,R_n,$<shift>	$R_d \leftarrow R_n$ >> <shift>	NZC	
ASR	$R_d,R_n,$<shift>	$R_d \leftarrow R_n$ >> <shift>	NZC	Sign extends
ROR	$R_d,R_n,$<shift>	$R_d \leftarrow R_n$ >> <shift>	NZC	Right rotate
RRX	R_d,R_n	$R_d \leftarrow R_n$ >> 1	NZC	Right shift, fill w/C

Note: "<shift> " is either a constant or a register and specifies how many bit positions to shift

---

[6] This restriction applies only to the Thumb-2 instruction subset of the Cortex-M3 processor; the more general ARM instruction set allows the shift amount to be determined by the content of a register.

logical shift right (LSR) instructions always insert a 0. The arithmetic shift right (ASR) instruction replicates the most significant bit so that the result has the same sign as the original operand.

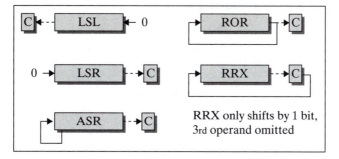

FIGURE 6-7   Shift instructions (Append "S" to modify Carry Flag).

The rotate right instruction (ROR) performs a 32-bit rotation, and thus fills bit 31 with the value that comes out of bit 0. Note that a left rotate of N bits can be achieved by a right of 32-N bits. The rotate right extended (RRX) performs a 33-bit rotation, with the carry flag (C) serving as a 1-bit extension to the operand; all 33 bits are then rotated so that bit 31 is filled with the previous contents of the carry flag.

Shifting a 64-bit double-length operand requires three instructions. For example, to perform a left-shift logical on a double-length operand, begin with a left-shift logical of the upper half. This leaves a 0 in its least significant bit, which must be replaced by the most significant bit of the lower half. A single instruction can both shift a copy of the lower half right by 31 bits and bitwise-OR it into the upper half. Finally, all that is left to do is to left shift the lower half (Figure 6-8).

	R1		R0	
LDRD R0,R1,data64 $\Rightarrow$	b_{63}	b_{32}	b_{31}	b_0
LSL R1,R1,#1 $\Rightarrow$	b_{62}	$b_{32}0$	b_{31}	b_0
ORR R1,R1,R0,LSR #31 $\Rightarrow$	b_{62}	$b_{32}b_{31}$	b_{31}	b_0
LSL R0,R0,#1 $\Rightarrow$	b_{62}	b_{31}	b_{30}	$b_0 0$
STRD R0,R1,data64				

FIGURE 6-8   Double-length 64-bit logical left shift.

An alternative solution is to begin by left shifting the lower half and capturing bit 31 in the carry flag by using an LSLS instruction. Then, shift the upper half left. Finally, use an ADC with a zero as the second operand to get bit 31 that was saved in the carry flag into the upper half. Note, however, that although this approach works for a double-length shift left, it does not work in the other direction. Finding an optimal solution for a double-length rotate is left as an exercise for the reader.

6.8.5 Bit Field Manipulation Instructions

Extraction and insertion of bit fields whose position and width is fixed is easily implemented using Thumb-2 instructions. A single instruction can insert 0's into a bit field of a register, copy the least significant bits of a register into a bit field of another, or extract a bit field from a register and expand it into a 32-bit signed or unsigned value. In each case, the least significant bit (lsb) position and width of the bit field are specified by the last two (constant) operands of the instruction (Table 6-11).

TABLE 6-11   Thumb-2 Bit Field Manipulation Instructions

Instruction		Operation	{S}	Notes
BFC	R_d,#lsb,#width	R_d<bits> ← 0		
BFI	R_d,R_n,#lsb,#width	R_d<bits> ← R_n<lsb's>		
SBFX	R_d,R_n,#lsb,#width	R_d ← R_n<bits>		Sign extends
UBFX	R_d,R_n,#lsb,#width	R_d ← R_n<bits>		Zero extends

For example, Figure 6-9 illustrates how bit field manipulation instructions can be easily used to extract the 6-bit unsigned minutes from the middle of a 16-bit packed representation of time or replace it with a new value taken from another register.

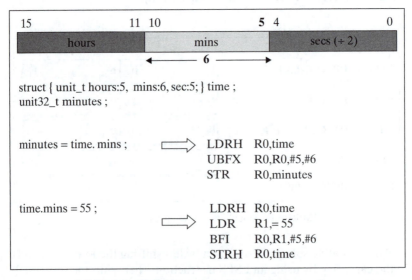

FIGURE 6-9   Bit field insertion and extraction instructions.

6.8.6 Miscellaneous Bit, Byte, and Half-Word Instructions

In addition to the bit, shift, and bit field instructions, the following instructions are occasionally useful in specific situations, such as when converting data between little- and big-endian systems, as is necessary when processing data held in Ethernet packets. These instructions do not modify their operand (R_n) or any of the flags (Table 6-12).

TABLE 6-12   Miscellaneous Thumb-2 Bit, Byte, and Half-Word Instructions

Instruction		Operation	{S}	Notes
CLZ	R_d,R_n	$R_d \leftarrow CountZeroes(R_n)$		# leading zeroes (0–32)
RBIT	R_d,R_n	$R_d \leftarrow RevBits(R_n)$		Reverses bit order
REV	R_d,R_n	$R_d \leftarrow RevByteOrder(R_n)$		Reverses byte order
REV16	R_d,R_n	$R_d \leftarrow RevHalfWords(R_n)$		Reverses bytes in each half word
REVSH	R_d,R_n	$R_d \leftarrow RevLoHalf(R_n)$		Reverses 2 LS bytes, sign extends
SXTB	R_d,R_n	$R_d \leftarrow SignedByte(R_n)$		Sign extends; operand may be R_n or
SXTH	R_d,R_n	$R_d \leftarrow SignedHalf(R_n)$		"R_n,ROR #n", where n = 8, 16, or 24
UXTB	R_d,R_n	$R_d \leftarrow UnsignedByte(R_n)$		Zero extends; operand may be R_n or
UXTH	R_d,R_n	$R_d \leftarrow UnsignedHalf(R_n)$		"R_n,ROR #n", where n = 8, 16, or 24

Dealing with large products

If we do the arithmetic by hand, multiplying two n-bit integers produces a product of 2n bits. However, multiplication in C produces a product of the same data type (and thus the same size) as the operands.[7] Consider the following line of C code:

```
a = (b*c) / d ;
```

If all the variables are 16-bit integers, the generated assembly code will be similar to:

```
LDRSH   R0,b
LDRSH   R1,c
MUL     R0,R0,R1
SXTH    R0,R0      ;Force a 16-bit representation (short × short → short)
LDRSH   R2,d
SDIV    R0,R0,R2
STRH    R0,a
```

Now, consider what happens when b, c, and d each contain a large value like +10,000. Mathematically, the final result should also be +10,000, but the 32-bit product is too large to be represented in 16 bits and thus the division will not yield the correct result.

---

[7] That is why the MUL, MLA, and MLS instructions only keep the least-significant half of a double-length product.

Trying to fix the problem in C by casting the product to a 32-bit value before dividing will not work because it simply extends an incorrect 16-bit product to an equivalent incorrect 32-bit representation. The only solution in C is to cast the operands *before* the multiplication.

It gets even more interesting if the variables are 32-bit integers containing large values like 10^6. Although casting them into 64-bit integers before multiplying will work, there is no 64×64 bit multiply instruction, so the compiler is forced to generate code that calls a library function to do the multiplication. Also note that although you could code in assembly and use the SMULL instruction to produce the 64-bit product from two 32-bit operands, there is no divide instruction that can use a 64-bit dividend.

With that background, now think about trying to write software in C to multiply two 16.16 fixed-point integers x and y to produce a 16.16 fixed-point product, z. Although the operands and product are all 32-bit values, you must calculate a 64-bit product because the 16.16 fixed point product lies in the middle of the 64-bit integer product. Thus, the only way to do this efficiently is in assembly:

```
LDR     R0,x                  ;R0 ← x (a 16.16 fixed-point real)
LDR     R1,y                  ;R1 ← y (a 16.16 fixed-point real)
SMULL   R0,R1,R0,R1           ;R0,R1 ← 64-bit integer product
LSR     R0,R0,#16             ;keep 16 MSBs of least significant half
ORR     R0,R0,R1,LSL#16       ;and 16 LSBs f the most significant half
STR     R0,z
```

PROBLEMS

1. If register SP contains 12348_{10} and then a "PUSH {R1}" instruction is executed, what value will be left in register SP?
   (a) 12347
   (b) 12346
   (c) 12345
   (d) 12344

2. Suppose that you have three 32-bit integers named x, y, and z. Give an appropriate sequence of ARM Cortex-M3 assembly language instructions required to implement the assignment statement $z = x / y$, assuming that the integers are:
   (a) unsigned
   (b) signed

3. Which of the following registers would not be used to hold the subscript of array when accessing the array element? (Circle all that apply.)
   (a) R11
   (b) R12
   (c) R13
   (d) R14
   (e) R15

4. Suppose registers R0 and R1 already hold a single 64-bit quantity with the most significant 32 bits in R1 and the least significant 32 bits in R0. Give a minimum-length sequence of ARM Cortex-M3 instructions that would be required to implement:

   (a) A 64-bit logical right shift by 1-bit position
   (b) A 64-bit arithmetic right shift by 1-bit position
   (c) A 64-bit right rotate (not including the carry flag) by 1-bit position

5. What is the minimum number of instructions needed to implement each of the following four C assignment statements on Cortex-M3 processor?

   ```
   long long int a ;
   long int b ;
   ```

   (a) a = (long long) b ;
   (b) b = (long) a ;
   (c) b += 100 ;
   (d) a += 100 ;

6. For each of the following, give C declarations for each of the variables and C assignment statements which accomplish the same thing. Specify signed or unsigned wherever it can be determined; otherwise leave it off the declaration:

   (a)
   ```
   LDRH R0,red
   ADR R1,blue
   LDR R2,purple
   STRH R0,[R1,R2,LSL #1]
   ```

   (b)
   ```
   LDR R0,green
   ADD R0,R0,#1
   LDR R1,=0
   STRD R0,R1,violet
   ```

   (c)
   ```
   LDRB R0,black
   LDR R1,=5
   UDIV R2,R0,R1
   MLS R0,R1.R2.R0
   STRB R0,white
   ```

   (d)
   ```
   LDRD R0,R1,orange
   LSL R1,R1,#1
   ORR R1,R1,R0,LSR #31
   LSL R0,R0,#1
   STRD R0,R1,yellow
   ```

7. Given the C declaration statements,

   ```
   int8_t  s8 ;        uint8_t  u8, *pu8 ;
   int16_t s16 ;       uint16_t u16 ;
   int32 _t s32 ;      uint32_t u32, *pu32 ;
   int64_t s64 ;       uint64_t u64 ;
   ```

Translate each of the following C assignment statements into Cortex-M3 assembly:

(a) u32 = 100 ;		**(m)** u32 = u8 ;	
(b) u8 = u32 ;		**(n)** pu32 = &u32 ;	
(c) u16 = 100 ;		**(o)** u64 = u32 ;	
(d) s16 = s8 ;		**(p)** pu8 = &u8 ;	
(e) u8 = 100 ;		**(q)** u8 = u16 ;	
(f) s32 = s16 ;		**(r)** ((uint8_t *) &u32)[0] = u8 ;	
(g) u64 = 100 ;		**(s)** u16 = u32 ;	
(h) s32 = s8 ;		**(t)** *pu32++ = 0 ;	
(i) u16 = u8 ;		**(u)** u16 = u8 + 1 ;	
(j) s64 = s32 ;		**(v)** u64 = u64 + 1 ;	
(k) u32 = u16 ;		**(w)** p16 = &u16 + 1 ;	
(l) s64 = −1 ;		**(x)** *p16 = *p16 + 1 ;	

8. Translate each of the following C assignment statements into Cortex-M3 assembly:

(a)
```
signed long long s64 ;
signed long s32 ;
signed char s8 ;
s32 = s64 + s8 ;
```

(b)
```
long k32, *p32, a32[10] ;
k32 = (p32 - a32) + 5 ;
```

(c)
```
long long a64[10] ;
long k32, *p32 ;
p32 = ((long *) &a64[k32]) + 1 ;
```

(d)
```
unsigned long u32 ;
signed long s32 ;
s32 = 10 * u32 ;
```

(e)
```
short int **pp16 ;
*(*pp16 + 1) = 0 ;
```

(f)
```
long k32, a32[10], *p32 ;
k32 = &a32[k32] - p32 ;
```

(g)
```
short a16[10] ;
long k32 ;
++a16[k32 - 1] ;
```

(h)
```
unsigned long u32 ;
unsigned long long u64 ;
u64 = (unsigned long long) u32 ;
```

(i)
```
signed char s8 ;
signed long long s64 ;
s64 = (signed long long) s8 ;
```

(j)
```
signed long long int s64 ;
signed long s32 ;
s64 = (signed long long) s32 ;
```

(k)
```
signed long s32 ;
s32 %= 10 ;
```

(l)
```
unsigned short u16 ;
u16 /= 10 ;
```

CHAPTER 7

Programming in Assembly Part 3: Control Structures

This chapter looks at the implementation of decision structures, loops, and function calls in ARM assembly. Most embedded programs are a mix of C and assembly. The main program and the majority of the procedures are usually implemented in C, with only a handful of low-level support routines written in assembly—typically to optimize performance. Thus, our objective will be to learn how to implement these structures as efficiently as possible.

7.1 INSTRUCTION SEQUENCING

Once the processor is running, it repeats the fetch–execute cycle over and over again. As a result, the default operation of the processor is to execute a straight-line sequence of instructions read from successive memory locations. To accomplish anything useful, however, a program must occasionally depart from this sequence by transferring control (either conditionally or unconditionally) to another part of memory.

In C, transfers of control are created by break, continue, switch, and goto statements, function calls and returns, and implicitly at the end of loops. When the code is compiled, each of these is translated into a branch instruction,[1] as shown in Figure 7-1.

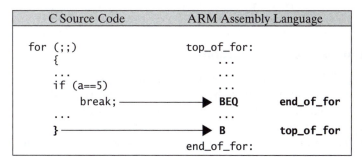

FIGURE 7-1 Branch instructions in code generated by a compiler for a break statement and at the end of a for loop.

---

[1] How switch statements are translated into assembly depends on the number and distribution of case–label constants. Sometimes a multiway jump is formed by indexing into a table of destination addresses; in other cases the switch statement is translated into the equivalent of a cascading sequence of if-then-else statements.

7.2   IMPLEMENTING DECISIONS

Decisions usually begin by evaluating an expression that is either true or false. The expression, called the conditional, may be a simple comparison of two values. Compound conditionals involving more than one comparison are constructed from these basic conditionals by combining them using Boolean operators.

In assembly, each decision is a two-step process: One instruction is used to set the flags, followed by another instruction that uses the flags to make the actual branch decision. Each component of a compound conditional requires this two-part sequence—a compare followed by a conditional branch. In most cases, the first instruction compares two values by computing their difference. The actual value of that difference is not important—only its characteristics. For example, the compare (CMP) computes the difference of two values, discards that difference, but saves its characteristics in the flags.[2] Then by checking the flags (using a conditional branch instruction), we can make a decision regarding the relative magnitude of the two values and alter the flow of execution accordingly.

CMP compares a register to a second operand that may be a constant, a register, or a shifted register. There is also a CMN (compare negative) instruction that adds instead of subtracting the second operand. Both instructions record whether the result is negative, zero, resulted in a carry (or borrow out), or resulted in a 2's-complement overflow.[3] The TST[4] instruction is used to test if one or more bits in a register are non-zero, and the TEQ[5] instruction is used to test if two values are identical without affecting the V or C flags (Table 7-1).

TABLE 7-1   ARM Thumb-2 Compare and Test Instructions

Instruction		Operation	{S}	Notes
CMP	R_n,<op>	R_n − <op>		
CMN	R_n,<op>	R_n + <op>		Always updates: NZCV
TST	R_n,<op>	R_n & <op>		Always updates: NZ; if shifted,
TEQ	R_n,<op>	R_n ^ <op>		<op> may affect C flag

7.2.1 Conditional Branch Instructions

Figure 7-1 includes an example of a conditional branch instruction (BEQ) that makes a decision to branch based on the state of the zero flag (Z). If Z is 1, the equality comparison was true and the instruction breaks out of the loop; otherwise, instruction flow continues sequentially with whatever instruction immediately follows the BEQ. The "EQ" in BEQ is *called a condition code*; there are 15 possible condition codes as summarized in Table 7-2.

---

[2] The CMP is identical to the SUBS instruction, except that the CMP does not store the difference in a register.

[3] Relative magnitude decisions for unsigned operands can be made by simply examining the Z and C flags; making such decisions for signed operands requires examining the Z, V, and N flags.

[4] The TST is identical to the ANDS instruction, except that it does not store the difference in a register.

[5] The TEQ is identical to the EORS instruction, except that it does not store the difference in a register.

TABLE 7-2   ARM Condition Codes

Code	Meaning	Requirements
EQ	**Equal**	**Z = 1**
NE	**Not equal**	**Z = 0**
CS	Carry set	C = 1
CC	Carry clear	C = 0
MI	Minus/negative	N = 1
PL	Plus—positive or zero (nonnegative)	N = 0
VS	Overflow	V = 1
VC	No overflow	V = 0
HI	**Unsigned > ("Higher")**	**C = 1 && Z = 0**
LS	**Unsigned ≤ ("Lower or Same")**	**C = 0 || Z = 1**
GE	**Signed ≥ ("Greater than or Equal")**	**N = V**
LT	**Signed < ("Less Than")**	**N ≠ V**
GT	**Signed > ("Greater Than")**	**Z = 0 && N = V**
LE	**Signed ≤ ("Less than or Equal")**	**Z = 1 || N ≠ V**
AL	Always (unconditional)	*(Rarely used)*

Eight of the condition codes are used much more frequently than others and are indicated in bold in the table. EQ and NE are used for equality and inequality tests. The codes for relative magnitude tests depend on whether the operands are signed or unsigned; condition codes GE, LT, GT, and LE are used with signed operands, while HI and LS are used with unsigned operands.

If you are not sure why two separate sets of condition codes for relative magnitude comparisons are necessary, then ask yourself which is greater: 1101_2 or 0111_2. As 4-bit unsigned values, they represent decimal 13 and 7 so that $1101_2 > 0111_2$; however, as 4-bit signed 2's-complement values, they represent −3 and +7 so that $1101_2 < 0111_2$.

7.2.2 If-Then and If-Then-Else Statements

Consider the following simple C if-then statement shown in Figure 7-2. Since the C code uses an equality comparison (==), you may be tempted to use a BEQ instruction in assembly. If you do, you will have to add an unconditional branch around the two instructions that are the then clause. Instead, a more efficient solution is to use the BNE instruction to eliminate the unconditional branch:

C Source Code	Inefficient Assembly	Efficient Assembly

`int32_t a,b ;`
 	
`if (a == 0) b = 1 ;`
	`        LDR   R0,a`
	`        CMP   R0,#0`
	`        BEQ   Then`
	`        B     EndIf`
	`Then:   LDR   R0,=1`
	`        STR   R0,b`
	`EndIf: ...`
		`        LDR   R0,a`
		`        CMP   R0,#0`
		`        BNE   EndIf`
		`Then:   LDR   R0,=1`
		`        STR   R0,b`
		`EndIf: ...`

FIGURE 7-2   Converting an if-then statement to assembly.

It is important to realize that when a decision is made in assembly, the only possible action is to branch. In other words, to get closer to what is actually done in assembly, we should imagine that the if statement has been rearranged so that the action controlled by the if statement is a goto, which then requires that we reverse the sense of the comparison:

```
if (a != 0) goto L1 ;
b = 1 ;
L1:
```

When coding a relative magnitude comparison, it is important to remember that the opposite of "less than" is NOT "greater than." If a condition includes the equality case, then the opposite condition must not, and vice versa!

You may have noticed that two condition codes for relative magnitude comparison of unsigned values are missing. That is, there is no "higher than or same" (>=) and no "lower than" (<). For example, if the variable "a" in Figure 7-3 were unsigned, we would need a conditional branch instruction with a "higher than or same" condition code (which doesn't exist). There are three possible work-around solutions. The first and second solutions simply reverse the order of the operands in the compare. When the second operand is a constant, however, a third solution is to simply use a constant that differs by 1.

Examples in Figures 7-3 and 7-4 illustrate how an else-less if statement is translated into assembly. When an else is added, an unconditional branch must always be

C Source Code	Incorrect Assembly	Correct Assembly

int32_t a, b;
 	
if (a < 100) b = 1;
	LDR R0,a
	   CMP R0,#100
	   BG L1 ; NO!
	   LDR R0,=1
	   STR R0,b
	L1: ...
		LDR R0,a
		   CMP R0,#100
		   BGE L1
		   LDR R0,=1
		   STR R0,b
		L1: ...

FIGURE 7-3   Correctly choosing the opposite condition code.

included. As shown in Figure 7-5, the unconditional branch must immediately follow the then clause (b = 1;) in order to skip over the else (c = 2;) so that only one of the two will be executed. If omitted, the code simply will not work as intended.

7.2.3 Compound Conditionals

Simple equality tests and relative magnitude comparisons translate from C to assembly in a relatively straightforward manner. However, compound conditionals containing two or more conditionals are a little trickier. First, let us consider comparing a value against the minimum and maximum of a range of values:

```
if (x >= -100 && x <= +100) y = x ;   // Assume that "x" is a signed int.
```

C Source Code	Solution #1	Solution #2	Solution #3

uint32_t a,b;
 	
if (a < 100) b = 1;
	`LDR  R0,a`
	`LDR  R1,=100`
	`CMP  R1,R0`
	`BLS  L1`
	`LDR  R0,=1`
	`STR  R0,b`
	`L1: ...`
		`LDR   R0,a`
		`RSBS` [a] `R0,R0,#100`
		`BLS   L1`
		`LDR   R0,=1`
		`STR   R0,b`
		`L1: ...`
			`LDR  R0,a`
			`CMP  R0,#99`
			`BHI  L1`
			`LDR  R0,=1`
			`STR  R0,b`
			`L1: ...`

FIGURE 7-4 Coding strategies for unsigned compares.

[a]The RSBS may be used here only because we do not need to preserve the content of R0.

C Source Code	Assembly Code

signed int a,b,c;
 	
if (a > 0) b = 1;
else c = 2;
	`      LDR  R0,a   ;Is a > 0 ?`
	`      CMP  R0,#0`
	`      BLE  Else`
	`Then: LDR  R0,=1   ;b ← 1`
	`      STR  R0,b`
	`      B    EndIf   ;skip over the else!!`
	`Else: LDR  R0,=2   ;c ← 2`
	`      STR  R0,c`
	`EndIf: ...         ;end of the if`

FIGURE 7-5 Converting an if-then-else statement to assembly.

Sometimes it is easier to convert this to assembly if the logical AND is replaced by a logical OR. To do so, first replace the conditional by its logical inverse and modify the if statement so that it skips over the assignment (instead of executing it) when the new condition is true:

```
     if (!(x >= -100 && x <= +100)) goto L1 ;
     y = x;
L1:  ...
```

Next, use DeMorgan's law from Boolean algebra to remove the logical NOT. To do so, replace all the logical ANDs (&&) by logical ORs (‖), all logical ORs by logical ANDs (there are none in this example), and all operands (the two conditionals) by their inverse. The result is

```
     if (x < -100 || x > +100) goto L1 ;
     y = x;
L1:  ...
```

Now that the expression is OR'ing the results from the two compares, it is much easier to visualize how to separate the two comparisons into two if statements:

```
     if (x < -100) goto L1;
     if (x > +100) goto L1;
```

```
        y = x;
L1:     ...
```

and thus much easier to visualize how to translate the preceding into assembly language:

```
        LDR   R0,x              ; if (x < -100) goto L1
        CMN   R0,#100
        BLT   L1
        CMP   R0,#100           ; if (x > +100) goto L1
        BGT   L1
        STR   R0,y              ; y = x ;
L1:     ...
```

Now consider a different problem. Suppose that we want to execute the assignment when x was outside (rather than inside) the range. In C, we would simply write the following if statement:

```
if (x < -100 || x > upper_limit) y = x;
```

Separating this into two if statements, each with a single comparison and each controlling a goto, yields

```
        if (x < -100) goto L1 ;
        if (x > +100) goto L1 ;
        goto L2 ;
L1:     y = x ;
L2:     ...
```

We can eliminate one of the goto's (and thus an unconditional branch instruction) by inverting the sense of the last comparison and changing the destination of its goto:

```
        if (x < -100) goto L1 ;
        if (x <= +100) goto L2 ;
L1:     y = x ;
L2:     ...
```

Then, translating into assembly, the final result becomes

```
        LDR   R0,x              ; if (x < -100) goto L1
        CMN   R0,#100
        BL    L1
        CMP   R0,#100           ; if (x <= +100) goto L2
        BLE   L2
L1:     STR   R0,y              ; y = x;
L2:     ...
```

7.2.4 The "If-Then" (IT) Instruction

We learned in Chapter 5 that branch instructions stall the instruction pipeline, causing performance to suffer. When an if statement controls a short sequence of instructions, it often executes faster to always fetch the instructions but simply use the flags to enable or disable their execution phase (Figure 7-6).

The IT instruction makes the execute phase of one to four following instructions conditional. The conditions can be all the same, or some of them can be the logical inverse of the others. The conditional instructions following the IT instruction form the *IT block*.

C Source Code	Assembly Code		
signed int a,b,c;	LDR	R0,a	; is a > 0?
	CMP	R0,#0	
if (a > 0) b = 1;	ITTEE	GT	; controls 4 instructions
else c = 2;	LDRGT	R0,=1	; yes: b ← 1
	STRGT	R0,b	
	LDRLE	R0,=2	; no: c ← 2
	STRLE	R0,c	

FIGURE 7-6   Speeding up an if-then-else statement with an IT block.

The first instruction in the IT block is enabled if the condition code given in the operand field of the IT instruction is true. The remaining instructions in the block are controlled by appending one to three letters to the IT mnemonic. If the letter is a "T" ("then"), the condition code enables the corresponding instruction; if the letter is an "E" ("else"), the opposite of the condition code enables the instruction. All instructions in the IT block must have their enabling condition code appended to their mnemonic.[6]

An instruction within an IT block may modify the flags, but has no effect on whether the remaining instructions in the block are enabled or disabled.

There are three fundamental restrictions regarding IT blocks:

1. An IT block may not contain an IT, CBZ, CBNZ, CPSID, or CPSIE instruction.[7]
2. Instructions that modify the PC may be used only as the last instruction of the block.
3. A branch to an instruction within an IT block is not allowed.

7.3   IMPLEMENTING LOOPS

Loops generally consist of four parts: initialization, test for completion (or continuation), update of the loop control variables, and the body of the loop (the code to be repeated). Sometimes the update is part of the body of the loop. Loops may be distinguished by whether their test for completion is placed before or after the body of the loop. For and while loops test for completion before each iteration and thus repeat zero or more times; do-while loops test after each iteration and always repeat at least once.

Some loops repeat for a fixed number of iterations, specified by either a constant or the value of a variable, such as finding the factorial of a number or computing the average of a set of values. Others repeat until some condition is satisfied that depends on values computed during the loop, such as finding the greatest common divisor (GCD) of two integers or the convergence test in a series approximation.

---

[6] All ARM processors use a single unified assembly language (UAL). Unlike Thumb-2 instructions, appending a condition code to a regular ARM instruction makes its execution conditional without the need for an IT instruction. When assembled for a regular ARM processor, the IT instruction is ignored, and the seemingly redundant requirement for condition codes appended to instructions within the IT block allows the same source code to be used for regular and Thumb-2 code.

[7] CPSID is used to disable interrupts and CPSIE to enable them.

All for loops, while loops, and do-while loops have an implicit branch from the bottom to the top of the loop; this branch instruction becomes explicit when translated into assembly (Figures 7-7 and 7-8).

C Source Code	Assembly Code
```// Computes Greatest` `// Common Divisor` `// of 'a' and 'b'`  `uint32_t a, b, gcd;`  `while (a != b)` ` {` ` if (a > b) a -= b ;` ` else b -= a ;` ` }` `gcd = a ;```	``` LDR R0,a ;initialization` ` LDR R1,b` `top: CMP R0,R1 ;test for continuation (a != b)` ` BEQ done` ` ITE GT ;loop body and update` ` SUBGT R0,R0,R1 ;a -= b` ` SUBLE R1,R1,R0 ;b -= a` ` B top ;implicit branch to the top` `done: STR R0,gcd```

FIGURE 7-7   Translating the components of a while loop into assembly.

C Source Code	Assembly Code
```// Computes n!`  `uint32_t k, fact, n ;`  `fact = 1 ;` `for (k = n; k != 0; k--)` ` {` ` fact *= k ;` ` }```	``` LDR R0,=1 ;initialization (nfact = 1, k = n)` ` LDR R1,n` `top: CMP R1,#0 ;test for continuation (k != 0)` ` BEQ done` ` MUL R0,R0,R1 ;loop body (nfact *= k)` ` SUB R1,R1,#1 ;update (k--)` ` B top ;implicit branch to the top`  `done: STR R0,fact```

FIGURE 7-8   Translating the components of a for loop into assembly.

Counting loops (i.e., loops that repeat for a predetermined number of iterations) are so common that the Thumb-2 instruction set provides two instructions (CBZ and CBNZ) that combine the compare and branch decision of these loops into a single instruction. For example, the CMP and BEQ instructions in the previous example can be replaced by a single "CBZ R1,done" instruction (Table 7-3).

TABLE 7-3   ARM Thumb-2 Compare and Branch Instructions

Instruction	Operation	{S}	Notes
CBZ R_n,label CBNZ R_n,label	Branch to label If $R_n = 0$ Branch to label If $R_n \neq 0$		Cannot be used in an IT block

7.3.1 Speeding Up Array Access

Loops that work with arrays are common and are thus good candidates for optimization. They typically sequence through the elements of an array in order, making it possible to take advantage of the pre- and post-increment addressing capability of the processor. For example, these addressing modes can improve performance when initializing an array to a constant value, scanning an array for a particular value, copying one array to another, or comparing two arrays. All such loops must either load or store an element of the array and then increment or decrement the address; pre- and post-increment combine these two operations into a single instruction.

Pre-increment address mode

The syntax for pre-increment address mode simply adds an exclamation point after the closing square bracket:

```
LDR   R0,[R1,#4]!       ; R1 ← R1 + 4, then R0 ← mem[R1]
LDR   R0,[R1,R2]!       ; R1 ← R1 + R2, then R0 ← mem[R1]
LDR   R0,[R1,R2,LSL #2]!  ; R1 ← R1 + (R2 << 2), then R0 ← mem[R1]
```

Post-increment address mode

The syntax for post-increment address mode simply moves the closing square bracket so that it follows the first register:

```
LDR   R0,[R1],#4        ; R0 ← mem[R1], then R1 ← R1 + 4
LDR   R0,[R1],R2        ; R0 ← mem[R1], then R1 ← R1 + R2
LDR   R0,[R1],R2,LSL #2  ; R0 ← mem[R1], then R1 ← R1 + (R2 << 2)
```

For example, by using post-increment addressing and the CBNZ instruction, copying a NUL-terminated string from one area of memory to another may be implemented as a loop of three instructions:

```
      ADR   R0,source       ; R0 ← starting address of source string
      ADR   R1,destination ; R1 ← starting address of destination string
copy: LDRB  R2,[R0],#1      ; R2 ← char from source string; R0++
      STRB  R2,[R1],#1      ; char in destination string ← R2; R1++
      CBNZ  R2,copy         ; continue until last char copied is a NUL
```

When the data to be copied is known to be a multiple of 4 bytes, copying is even faster using the load multiple and store multiple instructions. Each instruction can transfer 1 or more 32-bit words between registers and memory and update another register that holds the memory address (Table 7-4).

TABLE 7-4 ARM Thumb-2 Load Multiple and Store Multiple Instructions

Instruction	Operation	{S}	Notes
LDMIA[a] R_n{!},<reglist>	$R_{first} \leftarrow mem_{32}[R_n]$, $R_{first+1} \leftarrow mem_{32}[R_n+4]$, $R_{first+2} \leftarrow mem_{32}[R_n+8]$, etc.		R_{first} and R_{last} refer to the order of the registers by register number, not by the order of appearance in the list
LDMDB R_n{!},<reglist>	$R_{last} \leftarrow mem_{32}[R_n]$, $R_{last-1} \leftarrow mem_{32}[R_n-4]$, $R_{last-2} \leftarrow mem_{32}[R_n-8]$, etc.		
STMIA R_n{!},<reglist>	$mem_{32}[R_n] \leftarrow R_{first}$, $mem_{32}[R_n+4] \leftarrow R_{first+1}$, $mem_{32}[R_n+8] \leftarrow R_{first+2}$, etc.		'!' is an optional write-back suffix. If present, the final address that is loaded from or stored to is written back into R_n
STMDB[b] R_n{!},<reglist>	$mem_{32}[R_n] \leftarrow R_{last}$, $mem_{32}[R_n-4] \leftarrow R_{last-1}$, $mem_{32}[R_n-8] \leftarrow R_{last-2}$, etc.		Ex: LDMIA R0!,{R1,R3 to R7}

[a]POP is equivalent to LDMIA SP!,<reglist>
[b]PUSH is equivalent to STMDB SP!,<reglist>

7.4 IMPLEMENTING FUNCTIONS

To write a function in assembly language to be called from a high-level language requires much more than just understanding how control is transferred from the calling program to the function and back. How parameters are passed and how the return value is retrieved are predetermined by the way in which the compiler translates a C function call into a sequence of assembly language instructions. Within the function, we will see that the design of the compiler also establishes certain rules governing the preservation, allocation, and the use of registers for temporary results. We must work within these constraints, but with the fundamental objective of optimizing performance.

7.4.1 Function Call and Return

The two instructions most commonly used to call and return from C functions are shown in Table 7-5. The Branch and Link (BL) instruction saves the return address (the address of the instruction immediately after the BL instruction) in register LR and then branches to the entry point address of the function. LR is then used with the Branch Indirect (BX) instruction to return from the called function by copying the content of LR back into the program counter.

Almost any instruction that copies the return address into PC can be used to cause a return. Although it may seem that "BX LR" is equivalent to "MOV PC,LR," the latter is

TABLE 7-5 ARM Thumb-2 Instructions for Subroutine Call and Return

Instruction	Operation	{S}	Notes
BL label	LR ← return address; PC ← address of label		Subroutine call
BX R_n	PC ← R_n		Subroutine return when R_n = LR

discouraged to maintain compatibility with the original ARM instruction set. As we will see a little later in this chapter, it is often more efficient to POP the return address into PC.

When a function with no parameters and no return value is called from a C program, the compiler generates a single BL instruction. A simple example of such a function that disables the interrupt system is shown in Figure 7-9. The EXPORT directive tells the assembler to make the name of the function known to the linker so that it can resolve references to the function from other source code files.

C function prototype:	`void DisableInterrupts(void);`
Example usage in C:	`DisableInterrupts();`
Function call in assembly:	**BL DisableInterrupts**

Function definition in assembly:	`EXPORT DisableInterrupts`
	`DisableInterrupts:`
	`  CPSID          ;disable interrupts`
	`  BX      LR   ;return from function`

FIGURE 7-9   Function with no parameters and no return value.

Obviously register LR can hold only a single return address, so functions that call other functions must preserve LR at their entry point and restore its original content before returning. The code in Figure 7-10 does this using PUSH and POP instructions. Rather than using a POP to restore LR only to immediately follow it with a BX LR to copy LR into PC, a simple and commonly used optimization is to replace the instruction pair with a single POP directly into PC.

7.4.2 Register Usage

Our objective is to learn how to implement functions in assembly language that can be called by a program written in C. The way we write our code must be compatible with

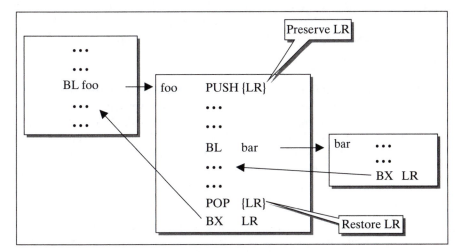

FIGURE 7-10   Preserving register LR during nested function calls.
Note: The last two instructions may be replaced by POP {PC}.

TABLE 7-6   ARM Architecture Procedure Call Standard

Register(s)	AAPCS Name(s)	Primary Use	Use as Scratch?	Preserve?
R0	A1	First function Argument; 8-/16-/32-bit return values	Yes	
R1	A2	Second function Argument; upper half of 64-bit return value	Yes	
R2, R3	A3, A4	Third and Fourth function Arguments	Yes	
R4 to R8	V1 to V5	Register Variables	Yes	Yes
R9 to R11	V6 to V8	Usage depends on compiler	Yes	Yes
R12	IP	Intra-Procedure-call scratch register	Yes	
R13	SP	Stack Pointer (lower end of current stack frame)	*These register have special purposes*	
R14	LR	Link Register		
R15	PC	Program Counter		

the way that the compiler expects functions to operate. Beyond the simple mechanics of transferring control to the subroutine and returning, being compatible also demands that we understand:

1. Where to find parameters that are passed to our function,
2. Where to leave return values so that the caller can find them, and
3. Which registers must be preserved and which may be modified.

Fortunately, these requirements are specified by the ARM Architecture Procedure Call Standard (AAPCS), which is summarized in Table 7-6. It uses registers R0 through R3 to hold the first four words of parameters passed to a function and registers R0 and R1 to hold the return value. R0 is used to return 8-bit, 16-bit, and 32-bit values; 64-bit values are returned in R0 and R1, with R1 holding the upper 32 bits. Registers R0 through R3 may be modified as needed within a function without regard to their original content. Most other registers are available for use as well, but their original contents must be preserved before any modification and restored before the function returns.

7.4.3 Parameter Passing

Registers R0 through R3 are used to pass parameters (Figure 7-11) and are usually sufficient for the kind of small support routines that we write in assembly.[8] The compiler loads each 8-bit, 16-bit, or 32-bit parameter into a single register assigned in left-to-right order; double-word parameters are passed in two consecutive registers (e.g., R0 and R1, R1 and R2, or R2 and R3), with the upper 32 bits in the second register of the pair. The called function may modify the contents of R0 through R3 and so has no obligation to return with the original parameter values still in them.

---

[8] When a function is called with more than four parameters of 32 bits each, the compiler will push the remainder onto the stack prior to the call; it is then the function's responsibility to restore SP to its original value before returning. A popular alternative is to store the parameters in a structure and pass the address of the structure to the function.

C function prototype and call	Generated assembly
| ```
void display(int8_t, int16_t [ ], int64_t);
...
doit(ch, array, bignum) ;
...
``` | ```
...
LDRSB   R0,ch
ADR     R1,array
LDRD    R2,R3,bignum
BL      display
...
``` |

FIGURE 7-11   Parameters are passed in R0 through R3.

7.4.4 Return Values

Functions are expected to return any 8-bit, 16-bit, or 32-bit result in R0, zero-filled or signed filled according to the declared return type (Figure 7-12). Functions that return a 64-bit result must do so with bits 0 to 31 in R0 and bits 32 to 63 in R1 (Figure 7-13). If a function must return multiple results, a common practice is for the caller to pass a pointer to a structure, and let the function use the pointer to store the results into the structure. Although C functions are allowed to return a structure containing more than 64 bits, this is rarely required for a support routine written in assembly.

7.4.5 Temporary Variables

Functions should first try to use registers R0 through R3 for any required temporary variables, since there is no obligation that their content be preserved. Registers R4 through R11 are the second choice, but their original content must be saved at function entry and restored prior to the function return.

When more space for temporaries is required, it may be allocated on the stack. This is accomplished by subtracting a constant from SP at the entry to the function, corresponding

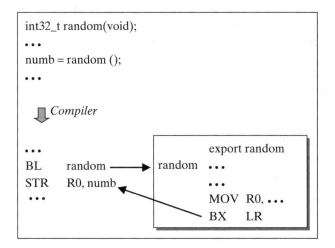

FIGURE 7-12   Returning a 32-bit result in R0.

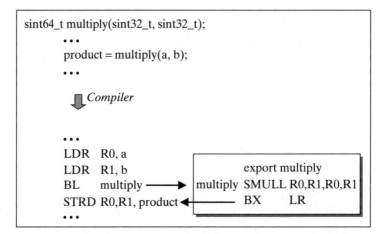

FIGURE 7-13   Returning a 64-bit result in R0 and R1.

to the number of bytes of stack space required,[9] and then referencing the allocated memory locations using positive SP-relative offsets (e.g., [SP,#8]). The original value of SP must be restored by adding the constant back to SP just before the function returns.

There are two good reasons why it is important to use registers or stack space for temporary variables instead of creating fixed locations with labels:

1. *Memory conservation:* The stack space will be automatically released when the function returns so that it can be reused for other needs.

2. *Reentrancy:* Every entry of the function allocates a unique set of memory locations for its temporary variables. Thus, if the function is interrupted, and the interrupting code calls (or reenters) the same function, it is ensured that each invocation will modify only its own set of temporary variables.

Although the memory space just beyond the current top of the stack is not currently in use, it must still be allocated (reserved) before we put our temporary variables there. For example, if our function calls another function, the called function may overwrite an indeterminate amount of this space. Even if no other function is called, a hardware interrupt may occur, invoking an interrupt service routine that overwrites the space. Thus, to protect the temporary variables we place in this "unused" portion of the stack, we must first adjust the stack pointer (and restore it later when the variables are no longer needed).

7.4.6 Preserving Registers

Functions that modify registers must generally preserve and restore their previous contents on the stack. However, since the stack is stored in memory, and since memory cycles are the primary performance bottleneck, it is important to preserve as few registers as possible.

---

[9] To preserve address alignment, the constant should be a multiple of four.

The ideal situation is a function such as function f1 in Figure 7-14, which does not itself contain a function call and which modifies no registers other than R0 through R3. In this case, no registers need to be preserved.

When a function modifies any register other than R0 through R3, it is required to preserve their original content. The best way to do this is to push those registers onto the stack immediately upon entering the function, and to pop them back just before the function returns as is done in function f2 of Figure 7-14.

When a function calls are nested, the second call will overwrite the current return address held in LR. Thus when one function (such function as f3 in Figure 7-14) contains a call (BL) to a second function (f4), the first must push the content of LR at its entry and pop it back just before it returns. Note that since LR is already on the stack, the BX LR instruction normally used to return to the caller may be eliminated by replacing LR by PC in the POP instruction.

Registers R0 through R3 are not a good place for functions that call other functions to keep information. For example, in Figure 7-14, the call to function f4 may require parameters to be placed in R0 through R3, and/or may modify their content before return. Therefore, a common practice is for f3 to move its parameters and temporaries into R4 through R11, preserving their original content on entry to f3 and restoring them just before it returns.

```
;Function f1          ;Function f2 does          ;Function f3 contains a call to a second
;modifies             ;not call any functions,   ;function (f4). The BL used to call f4
;only R0-R3           ;but modifies one or       ;modifies LR, which contains f3's return
;and does             ;more registers other      ;address, so we must preserve LR on the
;not call any         ;than R0-R3; their         ;stack. That value is then POP'd into PC
;functions.           ;original content must     ;to cause a return. Also, since f4 may
                      ;be preserved.             ;modify R0-R3,
f1 ...                                           ;
   ...                f2 PUSH {R4,..}            ; (1) f3's parameters should be moved to
   ...                   ...                     ;     R4-R7 for use,
   BX  LR                ...                     ; (2) any temporary variables should be
                         ...                     ;     allocated from R4-R11, and
                      POP   {R4,..}              ; (3) any of R4-R11, that are used should
                      BX    LR                   ;     be preserved on entry to f3 and
                                                 ;     restored just prior to return.
                                                 
                                                 f3 PUSH {R4,..,LR}  ; preserve
                                                    MOV  R4,R0       ; move parameter to R4
                                                    ...
                                                    BL   f4          ; may modify R0-R3
                                                    ...
                                                    POP  {R4,...,PC} ; restore and return
```

FIGURE 7-14   Summary of when a function needs to preserve registers.

PROBLEMS

1. Write a sequence of Cortex-M3 instructions that will form the sum of the numbers 1 through 100.

2. Write a sequence of Cortex-M3 instructions that corresponds to the following statements, where x, y, and z are labels on 32-bit memory locations whose contents are *unsigned* integers:

(a) `if (x < y) z = 6 ; else z = x ;`
(b) `x = (13 * y) / 3 ;`
(c) `x = 0; for (y = 0; y < 1000; y = y << 1) x += y ;`
(d) `if (x > 10) if (x < 20) y = 1 ; else z = 0 ;`

3. Convert the following into a sequence of ARM Thumb-2 Instructions without using an IT block:

(a) `unsigned short int a, b ;`
`    if (a > 0 && a < 100) b = b << 2 ;`

(b) `signed long int a, b ;`
`    if (a > 100 || a < 50) a = a & b ;`

(c) `unsigned long int a, b, c ; //Careful!`
`    if (a > 200)`
`        if (b > 0) c = 5 ;`
`    else c = -5 ;`

4. Use an IT block to convert the following into a sequence of ARM Thumb-2 Instructions:

(a) `signed short int a, b, c ;`
`    if (a > b) c = b + 2 ;`

(b) `unsigned short int a, b, c ;`
`    if (a == b) c = 0 ; else c = a - b ;`

(c) `signed long int a, b, c ;`
`    a = (b < c) ? b : c ;`

(d) `unsigned long int a, b, c ; //Careful!`
`    if (a > 200)`
`    if (b > 0) c = 5 ;`
`    else c = -5 ;`

5. Write a sequence of Cortex-M3 instructions that corresponds to the following statements, where *ch* is the label on an 8-bit memory location whose content is an ASCII character, and x, y, and z are labels on 32-bit memory locations whose contents are *signed* integers:

(a) `if (x < y && y < z) z = 6; else z = x;`
(b) `if (-10 < x && x < +10) goto L1 ;`
(c) `if (x < 10 || x > 20) y = 0 ; else y = 1 ;`
(d) `if ('a' <= ch && ch <= 'z') ch = ch - 'a' + 'A' ;`
(e) `x = y / 5 ;`

6. Convert the following into a sequence of Cortex-M3 instructions:

(a) `int f1(long, long) ;        // function prototype`
`    x = f1(a, 125) ;        // function call`

(b) `void f2(char) ;        // function prototype`
`    f2(c) ;        // function call`

(c) void f3(char *) ;   // function prototype
       f3(&c) ;   // function call

(d) uint64_t Add(uint64_t a, uint64_t b)
       {
       return a + b ;
       }

(e) uint64_t foo(uint32_t, uint32_t *) ;
       uint64_t n64 ;
       uint32_t n32 ;
       ...
       n64 = foo(100, &n32) ;

(f) uint32_t green(uint32_t) ;
       uint32_t blue(uint32_t a)
       {
       return a + green(5) ;
       }

(g) int32_t GetAndClear(int32_t *p)
       {
       int32_t temp = *p ;
       *p = 0 ;
       return temp ;
       }

(h) unsigned long u32 ;
       signed long s32 ;
       if (u32 > 10) s32 = s32 - 1 ;
       else s32 = s32 + 1 ;

(i) signed long s32 ;
       if (-10 < s32 && s32 < +10) s32 = 0 ;

(j) unsigned long u32, min, max ;
       if (u32 < min || u32 > max) u32 = 0 ;

(k) long s32, extra(long) ;
       s32 = s32 + extra(s32) ;

(l) void swap(long *p1, *p2)
       {
       long temp = *p1 ;
       *p1 = *p2 ;
       *p2 = temp ;
       }

(m) long Red(long a, long b)
       {
       return Blue(a) + Blue(b) ;
       }

7. Write a sequence of Cortex-M3 instructions to implement this function so that it counts and returns the number of bits that are 1 in its argument.

```
unsigned CountOnes(uint32_t) ;
```

C H A P T E R 8

Programming in Assembly
Part 4: I/O Programming

Many of the external input/output (I/O) devices, such as keypads, solenoids, and relays, attached to embedded systems are typically mechanical. Their response time is characterized by the time required for physical movement, which is orders of magnitude slower than the speed of a computer's CPU or main memory. Another common I/O device is an analog-to-digital (A-to-D) converter that takes a voltage as input and provides a digital representation of its value for use in computation. Conversion involves executing an algorithm implemented in the hardware of the A-to-D converter, but which still runs much slower than the speed of the computer.

The bottleneck that usually limits the speed of I/O data transfer is the speed of the external device, and the computer must not transfer data faster than the device can process it. A few I/O devices, however, can transfer data at very high rates that require a thorough understanding of the capabilities and limitations of the various options for how a processor performs I/O.

All I/O devices operate asynchronously with respect to the CPU. In other words, the events that determine when an input device has data available or when an output device is ready to accept more data are independent of the CPU. Most I/O programming, therefore, requires quite a bit of "handshaking" between the CPU and the I/O device to coordinate the transfer so that data is transferred reliably.

The time behavior of I/O data transfer varies considerably from one device to another as shown in Figure 8-1. For example, a keypad provides data at a very low rate and with data bytes arriving at somewhat random times. Data received by a modem arrives at a relatively low rate, but with a reasonably constant time between bytes (periodic). High data rate devices sometimes transmit an entire "block" of several bytes at once. The size of the block may be fixed or variable and, as with slower devices, blocks may arrive randomly or periodically.

Data Rate	Occurrence	Increasing Time →			
Low	Random	⊥ ⊥ ⊥		⊥ ⊥⊥	⊥
	Periodic	⊥ ⊥ ⊥ ⊥ ⊥ ⊥ ⊥ ⊥ ⊥ ⊥ ⊥ ⊥ ⊥ ⊥			
High	Random	⊥⊥⊥⊥⊥⊥		⊥⊥⊥ ⊥⊥⊥⊥⊥⊥⊥⊥⊥⊥⊥⊥	
	Periodic	⊥⊥⊥⊥⊥⊥ ⊥⊥⊥⊥⊥⊥	⊥⊥⊥⊥⊥⊥	⊥⊥⊥⊥⊥⊥	

FIGURE 8-1   Different types of time behavior in I/O data transfers.

8.1 THE CORTEX-M3 I/O HARDWARE

Desktop computers typically have separate instructions for accessing memory and peripherals. Their memory-reference instructions cannot access I/O devices, and their I/O instructions cannot reference memory. As a result, the only way to access an I/O device in C is to write a support routine in assembly using I/O instructions and then call the function from C anytime we want to transfer data to or from the device.

The Cortex-M3, however, uses a memory-mapped architecture as described at the beginning of Chapter 5. This establishes a unified address space for both memory and I/O that allows either to be referenced by regular LDR or STR instructions. Writing software in C to access an I/O device with memory-mapped I/O is really no different than accessing a location in regular memory using a pointer. It is merely a matter of initializing the pointer with the address of the I/O device and then using the deference operator to access the device indirectly via the pointer.

8.1.1 Interrupts and Exceptions

Consider the following situation: You are working at your desk at home on your income taxes. The phone rings (an interrupt). You stop work on your taxes and answer the phone (you accept the interrupt). It is your friend, who wants to know the name and phone number of your auto mechanic so she can call to arrange a service for her car. You give her the name and number (you process the interrupt request immediately). You then hang up and go back to work on your taxes. The additional time it will take you to complete your taxes is minuscule, yet the amount of time for your friend to complete her task may be significantly reduced. This simple example clearly illustrates how interrupts can drastically improve response time in a real-time system. Using interrupts requires that we first understand how the CPU processes an interrupt so that we can select the most appropriate software solution for each I/O device.

Interrupts are a special case of *exceptions*. Besides interrupts, exceptions can also be triggered by certain internal errors, such as division by zero, an undefined instruction, or an illegal unaligned memory access. When an exception occurs, the processor executes a special sequence of instructions known as an *exception handler*. The term *interrupt service routine* (ISR) is often used to refer to exception handlers for interrupts.

Writing handlers often requires writing code in assembly, even when the processor uses memory-mapped I/O. Although they share much in common, handlers and regular C functions are inherently different. An exception can occur at any time — between any two instructions or even in the middle of executing a single instruction. Unlike a regular C function, handlers must preserve and restore the content of *all* registers, including the program status register so that the handler may return to the interrupted code as if nothing has happened other than the passage of time.

For this reason, handlers have traditionally been written entirely in assembly, as a mix of C and inline assembly, or as a regular C function defined with a special *interrupt* keyword that causes the compiler to generate code that saves and restores all registers. The Cortex-M3, however, has been designed in such a way that the hardware takes care of the differences so that handlers may be written as a regular void function with no parameters.

8.1.2 Thread and Handler Modes

The Cortex-M3 processor operates in one of two modes. During the execution of the main program or a thread, the processor is in *thread mode*; during the execution of a handler the processor is in *handler mode*. When executing code, this "Dr. Jeckyl and Mr. Hyde" behavior allows the processor to behave one way for a regular C function and a somewhat different way for a handler. Thread mode and handler mode are distinguished by bits 0 to 8 of the processor status word (PSR). In thread mode, these bits are all zeroes; in handler mode, they hold a nonzero number that identifies the exception type.

8.1.3 Entering the Exception Handler

When an exception is recognized by the processor, it automatically responds with a specific sequence of actions:

1. *Stacking*: The contents of R0 to R3, R12, the return address, and the contents of the PSW and link register (LR) are pushed onto the stack. (Note that the PSW and registers R0 to R3 and R12 are exactly those registers that the AAPCS[1] does not require functions to preserve.)

2. In parallel with the stacking operation, the processor identifies the exception, records its identity as an exception number in the PSW, and uses that number to locate and copy the starting address of the corresponding handler from the *vector table*[2] into the program counter (PC).

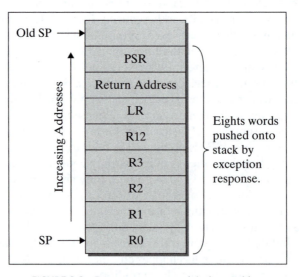

FIGURE 8-2   Processor state saved during stacking.

---

[1] The ARM Architecture Procedure Call Standard (AAPCS) is defined in Chapter 7.

[2] By default, the vector table is stored starting at address 0 but may be relocated by changing the contents of the vector table offset register.

3. Register LR is loaded with all 1's except for the least significant 4 bits; these bits record the mode of the processor (thread or handler) prior to the exception. (*Note:* LR does not contain the return address! The value stored in LR (known as EXC_RETURN) is a special value recognized and used by the processor to restore the previous mode when the handler returns.)
4. Handler mode is enabled.
5. Execution of the handler begins.

8.1.4 Returning from the Exception Handler[3]

The processor initiates the return sequence when the handler executes an instruction (such as "BX LR") that loads the PC with the EXC_RETURN value. That value signals the processor to start the return sequence and determines whether the processor returns to thread or handler mode. The return sequence then pops eights words from the stack, using them to restore registers R0 to R3, R12, LR, and the PSW, and to load the PC with the return address.

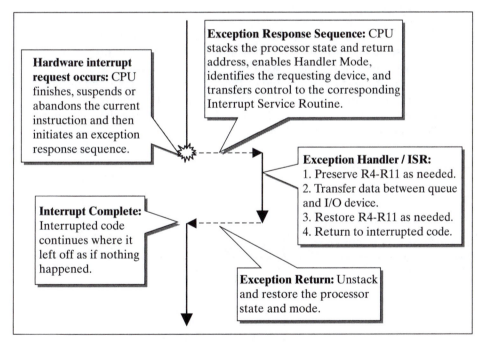

FIGURE 8-3   Hardware interrupt processing.

8.1.5 Latency Reduction

The Cortex-M3 uses three techniques to reduce interrupt latency—the time from the interrupt request until the corresponding handler begins to execute.

---

[3] Some exceptions are so serious as to be fatal, so that there is no reason for the handler to return.

Suspending or abandoning instruction execution

When an interrupt request arrives, the processor is likely to be in the middle of executing an instruction. That instruction is allowed to complete if it can do so in a single clock cycle. Instructions such as LDM, STM, PUSH, and POP that transfer multiple words to or from memory can be suspended and continued after the interrupt. All other instructions are abandoned and restarted after the interrupt so that in all cases the exception request is processed within a single processor clock cycle.

Late arrival processing

Suppose the processor has begun an interrupt response sequence only to have another interrupt of higher priority suddenly arrive during the stacking operation. Rather than completing the response and entering the handler for the first interrupt only to have it preempted by the late arriving interrupt of higher priority, the processor will redirect the remainder of the interrupt response so that it handles the late arrival first.

Tail chaining

The data rate capability of interrupt-driven I/O suffers somewhat from the overhead cost associated with saving and restoring the eight word of processor state information. In most processors, when two ISRs execute back-to-back, the state information is popped off the stack at the end of the first interrupt only to be pushed back onto it at the beginning of the next. The Cortex-M3 completely eliminates this useless pop–push sequence with a technique called *tail-chaining*, reducing the ISR transition time from 24 clock cycles down to only 6.

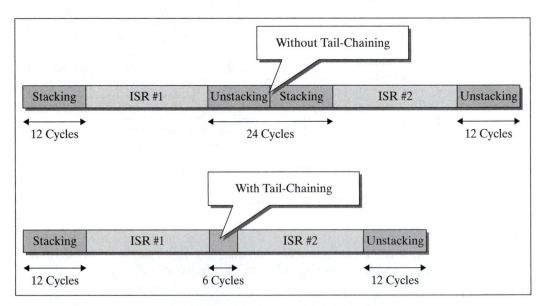

FIGURE 8-4   Cortex-M3 tail chaining.

8.1.6 Priorities and Nested Exceptions

Some interrupts are more important than others. For example, when you slam on the brakes in your car, you cannot afford to wait for the processor to finish what it may be working on—even if it is executing an ISR for some other device. It is critical that the antilock braking system start working without delay. Real-time applications like antilock braking have hard deadlines, and to insure that these deadlines are met requires that we assign priorities to interrupts and allow higher-priority interrupts to preempt those of lower priority.

The Cortex-M3 processor incorporates a device called the nested vector interrupt controller (NVIC) that implements a priority system among the various exceptions and interrupts. As shown in Table 8-1, lower numbers are assigned to higher priorities, with interrupts from external devices having lower priority than other kinds of exceptions.

There is a special hardware interrupt called the nonmaskable interrupt (NMI) whose purpose is to handle catastrophic events such as an impending power failure or a memory parity failure. It has a priority greater than any other interrupt and cannot be disabled.

Most priority numbers are software configurable from 0 (highest) to 255 (lowest), except those for reset, NMI, and hard faults. Until modified by software, the default priority of any exception whose priority is configurable is 0. If two interrupts are assigned the same priority, the one with the lower interrupt number is treated as having a higher priority.

TABLE 8-1   Exception Priorities and Vector Table Positions

Exception Type	Exception #[a]	IRQ #	Priority	Comment
				Initial SP value (loaded on reset)
Reset	1		−3 (fixed)	Power up and warm reset
NMI	2		−2 (fixed)	NMI
Hard fault	3		−1 (fixed)	
Memory mgmt.	4			
Bus fault	5			Address/memory-related faults
Usage fault	6	n/a		Undefined instruction
Reserved	7–10		Configured through system handler priority registers	
SVCall	11			Software interrupt (SVC instruction)
Debug monitor	12			
Reserved	13			
PendSV	14			
SysTick	15			System timer tick
Ext. interrupts	16–255	0–239	Configurable	

[a] Vector table entries are ordered by exception number, with the first entry reserved for the initial SP value. IRQ # is the interrupt request number (same as the exception number minus 16).

Priority numbers for the twelve system exceptions (4–15) are stored one per byte in the NVIC, starting at address $E000ED18_{16}$, and can be modified by code equivalent to:

```
((uint8_t *) 0xE000ED18)[exception_number - 4] = priority ;
```

Priority numbers for up to 240 external interrupts are also stored one per byte in the NVIC, starting at address $E000E400_{16}$, and can be modified by code equivalent to:

```
((uint8_t *) 0xE000E400)[IRQ_number] = priority ;
```

Once configured, the priority numbers determine which exceptions can preempt the handlers for other exceptions. For example, if the processor is executing the handler for an external interrupt, that handler can be preempted by a hard fault exception because it has a higher priority.

Enabling and disabling external interrupts

Interrupts can be either entirely or selectively enabled or disabled. To enable or disable all external interrupts, use one of the following two instructions:

```
CPSIE    i     ; Enable external interrupts
CPSID    i     ; Disable external interrupts
```

Individual external interrupts are controlled by two sets of eight registers within the NVIC, called the set enable registers (starting at address $E000E100_{16}$) and clear enable registers (starting at address $E000E180_{16}$). Each register is 32 bits wide, with 1 bit per interrupt. Setting a bit to 1 in a set enable register will enable the corresponding interrupt, while setting the corresponding bit to 1 in a clear enable register will disable it. For example, an individual interrupt can be enabled in the NVIC by code equivalent to:

```
((uint32_t *) 0xE000E100)[IRQ_number / 32] |= 1 << (IRQ_number % 32) ;
```

8.2 SYNCHRONIZATION, TRANSFER RATE, AND LATENCY

The CPU and I/O devices are physically independent. Events occurring within an I/O device that determine when data is available for input or when the device is ready to receive output data are not under the control of the computer. To transfer data to or from an I/O device requires *synchronizing* the CPU to the I/O device by somehow checking the status of the device and waiting until it is ready to transfer.

Transfer rate is simply a measure of the number of bytes per second transferred between the CPU and an external device. The fastest transfer rates are provided by direct memory access (DMA), but at the expense of some additional hardware complexity. Polled waiting loops are the easiest to implement and provide good transfer rates but are rarely used in real-time applications. Interrupt-driven I/O is the slowest due to the overhead of saving and restoring the machine state (especially if only 1 byte of data is transferred per interrupt) but is the most commonly used technique of the three.

Latency is a measure of the delay from the instant that the device is ready until the time the first data byte is transferred. Latency is thus equivalent to "response time." Latency can be very high or even unpredictable with polled waiting loops, is manageable with interrupt-driven I/O, and is very low with DMA.

Even if the CPU is capable of transferring data at a very high rate, it may be useless if it takes too long to begin. For example, if a sequence of several data bytes arrives as a contiguous block of data on a serial line, the CPU must recognize the availability of the first data byte and remove it from the input before the second byte arrives. If the computer is busy performing some other task when the block begins to arrive, many of the first data bytes within the block may be lost.

Polled waiting loops have long and usually unpredictable latency, since the computer may not even be checking the device for arrival of new data at the moment that it arrives. Latency is dramatically reduced with interrupt-driven I/O but still imposes a software overhead with more latency than DMA.

8.3   BUFFERS AND QUEUES

Interrupt-driven I/O inherently separates the ISR that handles the actual I/O transfers from the background code that processes the data, but the two communicate with each other by passing the data through a region of memory referred to as a buffer. For example, an ISR that handles keyboard interrupts stores coded representations of keystrokes into a buffer; a background routine then retrieves these keystrokes from the buffer and interprets them as numbers, lines of text, or editing commands.

A common special case is a "first-in, first-out" (FIFO) buffer, known as a queue. As shown in Figure 8-5, the amount of data in a queue at any moment varies depending on how frequently data arrives for insertion and how fast that data is removed for processing. This "elastic" property of a queue helps decouple the timing relationship between the code that fills the queue and the code that empties it, allowing each to operate more asynchronously.

Data is inserted (enqueued) at the "rear" of the queue and removed (dequeued) in the same order from the "front" of the queue. The queue is implemented as an array (q.bfr), with two subscripts to identify the current front (q.dq) and rear (q.nq) positions as shown in Figure 8-6. Two more integers are required to keep track of the size of the queue (q.size) and how much data it presently contains (q.count). When data is entered at the rear or removed from the front, the corresponding subscript is advanced. If a subscript advances beyond the end of the array, it gets reset to 0 so that the queue behaves in a circular manner. The code that uses this data structure is shown in Figure 8-7.

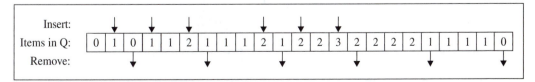

FIGURE 8-5   Using a queue to decouple time of data arrival from time of data processing.

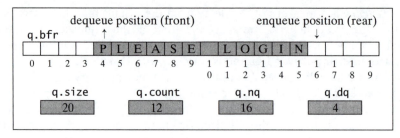

FIGURE 8-6 Using an array to implement a queue.

```c
typedef struct
    {
    uint32_t  nq ;  // insertion index
    uint32_t  dq ;  // removal index
    uint32_t  count ; // #items in queue
    uint32_t  size ; // buffer capacity
    uint8_t bfr[1] ;  // buffer array
    } QUEUE ;
```

```c
QUEUE *CreateQueue(uint32_t  bfrsize)
    {
    uint32_t bytes;
    QUEUE *q ;

    bytes = (sizeof(QUEUE) - 1) + bfrsize ;
    q = (QUEUE *) malloc(bytes) ;
    if (q != NULL)
        {
            q->nq = q->dq = q->count = 0 ;
            q->size = bfrsize ;
        }

    return q ;
    }
```

```c
BOOL Enqueue(QUEUE *q, uint8_t data)
    {
    BOOL full ;

    disable() ;
    full = q->count == q->size ;
    if (!full)
        {
        q->bfr[q->nq] = data ;
        if (++q->nq == q->size)
            {
            q->nq = 0 ;
            }
        q->count++ ;
        }
    enable() ;

    return !full ;
    }
```

```c
BOOL Dequeue(QUEUE *q, uint8_t *ptr2data)
    {
    BOOL empty ;

    disable() ;
    empty = q->count == 0 ;
    if (!empty)
        {
        *ptr2data = q->bfr[q->dq] ;
        if (++q->dq == q->size)
            {
            q->dq = 0 ;
            }
        q->count-- ;
        }
    enable() ;

    return !empty ;
    }
```

FIGURE 8-7 C functions to implement a FIFO queue.

Since both Enqueue and Dequeue modify the same queue data structure, interrupts must be disabled within both[4] functions, or else the data could become corrupted. Interrupts are disabled on entry to Enqueue and Dequeue by calling the C library function disable, and re-enabled on exit by calling enable.

8.3.1 Double Buffering

Cycle stealing DMA is usually used to fill a buffer with a large block of data (such as the 512 bytes of data stored in one sector of a hard disk) with processing of the data delayed until the buffer is full. Although the DMA proceeds concurrently with other computation, the rate at which blocks of data can be processed is slowed by the time required to fill the buffer, as shown in Figure 8-8.

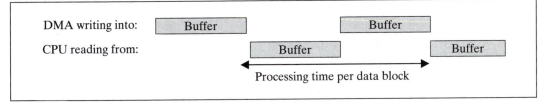

FIGURE 8-8   Single-buffered DMA.

We learned how a queue could be used to decouple two asynchronous threads of code that communicate through a shared buffer. Although we could use a queue in which each entry is a block of data, the amount of memory required may be unjustified. A common compromise is a special case of a queue containing exactly two blocks, called *double buffering*. While DMA is filling one of the buffers, the CPU is retrieving data from the other. Once both the DMA and the CPU are finished using their buffers, the buffers are swapped and the process is repeated. As shown in Figure 8-9, the time required to transfer data via DMA in one buffer is overlapped with that required for the CPU to process the data in the other, thus effectively doubling the overall processing rate.

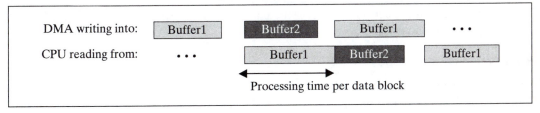

FIGURE 8-9   Double-buffered timing

---

[4] For the current example of an input ISR, Dequeue is the only one that must be protected against interrupts that cause Enqueue to be called. However, if these queue functions were used for an output ISR, the opposite would be true. Thus, it is better to disable interrupts in both so that the routines can be general purpose.

8.4 ESTIMATING I/O PERFORMANCE CAPABILITY

I/O software design must consider the requirements and limitations of the I/O device. In general, there are three strategies: polled waiting loops, interrupt-driven I/O, and DMA. The strategy we choose must be *capable* of data rates fast enough to keep up with the demands of the device, and usually at the lowest possible cost and complexity.

Estimating I/O performance requires knowing how fast our code will execute. Table 8-2 summarizes the execution time of Cortex-M3 instructions in terms of processor clock cycles. There are exceptions, such as executing any instruction that effectively branches by loading a new value into the program counter. However, the table should apply to vast majority of instructions.

TABLE 8-2   Cortex-M3 Instruction Clock Cycles[a]

Instructions		Clock Cycles
PUSH, POP, LDM, STM		1 + #regs
SDIV, UDIV		2–12
SMLAL, UMLAL		4–7
SMULL, UMULL		3–5
Unconditional branch (B, BL, BX)		2–4
Conditional branch	Successful	2–4
	Failed	1
LDRD, STRD		3
ADR, MLA, MLS, & all LDR's and STR's		2
All other instructions		1

[a]Assumes memory and processor run at the same speed.

The execution time of some instructions is given as a range. For example, the time required to execute a multiply or divide depends on the values of the operands. In most cases we want to use the worst-case value so that our estimate of execution time is conservative. When a conditional branch instruction is used in a loop, however, it is usually more accurate to consider whether the majority will branch or fall through and use the corresponding cycle count.

8.4.1 Polled Waiting Loops

Polled waiting loops use software to test the status of a device before transferring each data byte, as shown in Figure 8-10. Note the use of the keyword *volatile* on the third parameter of the function. That parameter is a pointer to the memory-mapped address space of the UART. The UART status ports are read-only but change to reflect changing UART hardware status. The keyword volatile is required to prevent certain compiler optimizations that would cause the code to fail. Without it, optimized code would read the status port into a register once prior to entering the while loop, and the loop condition converted to a test of the register contents rather than reloading the UART status from memory on each iteration of the loop.

The fastest possible transfer rate occurs when the code is designed to transfer a block of data in a tight loop as shown in Figures 8-10 and 8-11 . However, for either input or output, the software must repeatedly test that the device is ready before each byte of data is transferred. The time required to execute one iteration of the for loop determines the minimum time per transfer and thus the maximum data rate. Latency, however, is unpredictable because there is no guarantee that the program will have entered the function and be waiting on the device when it becomes ready to transfer the first byte of data.

```c
//  TXFE (bit 7 of status port) =1 if transmitter holding register empty
#define TXFE (1 << 7)

// RS232 Data Port    = rs232 base address + 0
// RS232 Status Port  = rs232 base address + 24

void rs232Output(uint8_t *ptr2data, int bytes, volatile uint32_t *rs232base)
        {
        for (int byte = 0; byte < bytes; byte++)
                {
                while ((*(rs232base + 6) & TXFE) == 0)
                        {
                        // do nothing (wait for data to arrive)
                        }
                *rs232base = (uint32_t) *ptr2data++ ;
                }
        }
```

FIGURE 8-10   Synchronizing data transfers on a serial line using polled waiting loops.

```
            EXPORT rs232Output
    rs232Output:

            ; R0 contains the parameter 'ptr2data'
            ; R1 contains the parameter 'bytes'
            ; R2 contains base address of RS232 device

    Repeat:  CBZ   R1,Return      ; more data to send?
    OutWait: LDR   R3,[R2,#0x18]  ; get status word
             TST   R3,#0x80       ; TXFE = 1?
             BZ    OutWait        ; loop until ready
             LDRB  R3,[R0],#1     ; get next byte & update pointer
             STR   R3,[R2]        ; send data to device
             SUB   R1,R1,#1       ; decrement byte count
             B     Repeat         ; do it all again
    Return:  BX    LR             ; return
```

FIGURE 8-11   Polled waiting loop optimized in assembly.

The polled waiting loop function can be reprogrammed in assembly as shown in Figure 8-12 to reduce the execution time and thus increase the maximum data rate. The fastest execution of function rs232Output in Figure 8-12 occurs when the device is always ready, meaning that the conditional branch (BZ) of the waiting loop will fail to branch and instead will fall straight through. Under this condition, each iteration of the loop executes a total of eight instructions (none of which reference named memory locations), two conditional branch instructions that both fall straight through, and one unconditional branch. As detailed in Figure 8-12, one pass through the code is estimated to take 14 clock cycles. Typical Cortex-M3 devices place the program memory on the same chip as the processor, with the memory cycle times the same as the processor clock cycle. With a 50-MHz chip, there are 20 nsec/clock cycle, so that the total execution time of one iteration of the for loop (the time to transfer 1 byte of data) will be about 280 nsec (280×10^{-9} sec). The maximum data rate is simply the inverse of this time, or about 3.6 MB/sec.[5] To put this in context, the fastest RS232 serial device operates at 115,200 bits/sec (~10 KB/sec), or 360 times slower than the maximum data rate capability of polled waiting loop I/O.

```
        EXPORT  rs232Output     ;   Clock
rs232Output:                    ;   Cycles

Repeat:   CBZ   R1,Return       ;   1 (Fail)
OutWait:  LDR   R3,[R2,#0x18]   ;   2
          TST   R3,#0x80        ;   1
          BZ    OutWait         ;   1 (Fail)
          LDRB  R3,[R0],#1      ;   2
          STR   R3,[R2]         ;   2
          SUB   R1,R1,#1        ;   1
          B     Repeat          ;   4

        Clock cycles:  14
     Execution time:  14 × 20 nsec = 280 nsec
 Maximum Data Rate:  10^9÷280 = 3.6 MB/sec
```

FIGURE 8-12   Estimating data rate performance.

8.4.2 Interrupt-Driven I/O

A typical (although perhaps simplified) version of an ISR for an RS232 serial input device is given in Figure 8-13. Immediately upon entry, the ISR reads the data byte from the device and then proceeds to store it into a queue for later processing. In

---

[5] Although an RS232 serial output device (like most I/O devices) accepts only 1 byte per transfer, it is conceivable that a different kind of device might accept a full 32-bit word per transfer; in this case, our maximum data rate would have been 40 MB/sec.

```
                                                                      Clock
    Rs232InputHandler:                                                Cycles

        ADR   R0,rs232InpDataPort   ; R0 ← rs232 device address        2
        LDR   R0,[R0]               ; R0 ← rs232 input data byte       2

        LDR   R2,rs232InputNQIndex  ; update enqueue index             2
        ADD   R2,R2,#1                                                 1
        AND   R2,R2,#0x3F           ; increment & wrap (0 to 63)       1
        STR   R2,rs232InputNQIndex                                     2

        LDR   R3,rs232InputQueue    ; R3 ← address of buffer           2
        STRB  R0,[R3,R2]            ; store data into buffer           2

        LDR   R2,rs232InputCount    ; update #items in queue           2
        ADD   R2,R2,#1                                                 1
        STR   R2.rs232InputCount                                       2

        BX    LR                    ; return                           4

    Tail-chaining time between successive ISRs:                        6

       Clock cycles: 29
    Execution time: 29 × 20 nsec = 580 nsec
Maximum Data Rate: 10⁹÷580 = 1.7 MB/sec
```

FIGURE 8-13   Performance analysis of a RS232 serial interrupt handler.

practice, the code for inserting the data into the queue would most likely be a call to a routine in a real-time kernel that also changes the state of a pending thread and may possibly result in a context switch. This additional complexity is omitted here for simplicity but means that our resulting estimate of maximum data rate performance will be somewhat optimistic.

The maximum data rate corresponds to back-to-back interrupts from the same device and presumes that no other higher-priority interrupts or exceptions preempt this code. The total time from one transfer to the next will then be the sum of the execution time of the ISR and the tail-chaining between any two ISRs. Using the same assumptions about clock rate and memory speed as before, the total time will be approximately 580 nsec, yielding a maximum data rate of 1.7 MB/sec.

One way to improve the data-transfer rate of interrupt-driven I/O is to transfer an entire block of data inside the ISR, using code similar to that used with the polled waiting loop method. This approach avoids the substantial overhead associated with processing an interrupt for *every* data byte to be transferred by processing several data bytes during each interrupt.

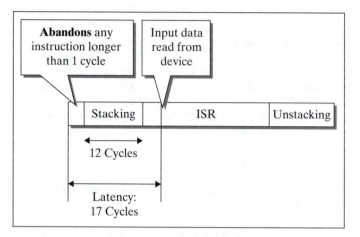

FIGURE 8-14   Interrupt latency.

Estimating the worst-case latency from time of interrupt request to the moment that data is read from the device is relatively straightforward. We simply add one cycle to complete or abandon the current instruction, the time required for stacking and the rest of the exception response, and the execution time of the first two instructions in the ISR required to actually read the data from the device. As shown in Figure 8-14, this adds to a total of 17 clock cycles, or 340 nsec.

8.4.3 Direct Memory Access

DMA is a high-performance, low-latency I/O data-transfer method. A special hardware DMA controller attached to the processor handles the actual transfers. The extra cost of the controller causes it to be omitted unless it is required by the demands of the attached I/O devices.

DMA controllers must be initialized through software to specify the source and destination of each transfer and the number of bytes to be transferred. The transfers may be from an input device to memory or from memory to an output device. Once initialized, the DMA controller takes over and performs the transfer without further assistance from the processor. Once all the bytes have been transferred, the DMA controller issues a hardware interrupt to the CPU to signal completion.

DMA controllers operate in basically one of two modes: either block transfer or cycle stealing. In block transfers, the DMA controller takes control of the memory bus from the CPU, transfers all of its data, and then returns the bus to the CPU. In cycle stealing mode, the DMA controller transfers a single byte whenever it can steal the bus from the CPU, then returns the bus to the CPU and waits for the next opportunity.

Although we have previously assumed a memory with a cycle time of one 20 nsec processor clock cycle, that was only feasible between a processor and a memory that were both on the same chip. DMA is more often used in situations where the memory and I/O device are physically separate, with cycle times corresponding to two or three processor clock cycles. Thus, a reasonable estimate of maximum DMA data rate probably requires using 60 nsec/cycle. If each cycle transfers a full 32-bit word of 4 bytes, the data rate would be $4 / (60 \times 10^{-9})$ bytes/sec, or about 66 MB/sec.

DMA transfers can occur between any two memory cycles so that the maximum latency for DMA is no more than the time required for one DMA memory cycle.

8.4.4 Comparison of Methods

Our execution-time performance estimates of latency and transfer rate for the various types of I/O as well as a relative comparison of hardware cost and software complexity are summarized in Table 8-3. These results assume all bus access to memory and I/O are completed in a single processor clock cycle.

TABLE 8-3   Performance Estimates and Relative Cost of Three I/O Strategies

	Polled Waiting Loop	Interrupt-Driven I/O	Direct Memory Access
Maximum transfer rate	~ 3.6 MB/sec	~ 1.7 MB/sec	~ 66 MB/sec
Best-case latency	Unpredictable	340 nsec	~ 60 nsec
Hardware cost	Least	Low	Moderate
Software complexity	Low	Moderate	Moderate

Programmed I/O is rarely used in real-time embedded systems, due to the unpredictable latency for input devices and the inability to do any other useful work while waiting for a device to be ready for a data transfer. DMA is rarely used in small-scale embedded systems, due to the extra cost of the DMA controller and because the interrupt-driven data rates are usually sufficient for most applications.

The example code we have used for estimating performance capability was written in assembly. However, we have seen that the Cortex-M3 has a number of features that make it possible (and desirable) to write an ISR in C with little or no loss of performance. ISRs transfer data between an I/O device and memory but have no input parameters or return value. In C, an ISR for the Cortex-M3 is written as a regular void function that contains hard-coded references to a specific memory-mapped I/O device and a buffer or queue located in memory. The one and only detail that requires some unusual C code is to locate the vector table at physical address zero.[6] Almost every C compiler provides some sort of extended syntax that allows this to be specified in the declaration, but it usually varies from one compiler to another. If not, one can always resort to creating the vector table in assembly.

---

[6] The vector table may be relocated once the processor is up and running but must initially reside at address zero.

PROBLEMS

1. Which of the following I/O methods has the highest possible data rate?
   (a) Polled waiting loop
   (b) Interrupt-driven I/O
   (c) DMA

2. Which of the following I/O methods has the least latency?
   (a) Polled waiting loop
   (b) Interrupt-driven I/O
   (c) DMA

3. Which of the following I/O methods requires the most additional hardware?
   (a) Polled waiting loop
   (b) Interrupt-driven I/O
   (c) DMA

4. The fundamental limit on how fast instructions can be executed is the:
   (a) Number of instruction pipeline stages
   (b) Number of instructions to be executed
   (c) Maximum memory bandwidth
   (d) Average number of operands per instruction

5. Assuming a single-cycle (zero wait state) memory, what is the worst-case number of clock cycles required to execute each of the following Cortex-M3 instructions?
   (a) LDRB   R0,[R1]
   (b) ADR   R0,data
   (c) ADDS   R0,R1,#100
   (d) PUSH   {R1–R4}
   (e) BEQ   Finish

6. In addition to the bytes required to represent the instruction, how many additional bytes are transferred to or from memory during the execution of the following instructions?
   (a) LDRB   R0,[R1]
   (b) ADR   R0,data
   (c) ADDS   R0,R1,#100
   (d) PUSH   {R1–R4}
   (e) BEQ   Finish

7. Which of the following must be true in order for the Cortex-M3 to respond to an interrupt request? (Circle all that apply.)
   (a) The device must request an interrupt.
   (b) The device must not have its interrupt request masked by the NVIC.
   (c) Must not be executing the handler of a higher-priority exception.
   (d) Interrupts must have been enabled by a CPSIE instruction.
   (e) Execution of the current instruction must be completed.

8. Which of the following are true statements for the Cortex-M3? (Circle all that apply.)
   (a) Interrupts may occur between any two adjacent memory cycles.
   (b) Interrupts may occur between any two adjacent instructions.
   (c) Interrupts may occur between any two adjacent C statements.

9. Which of the following are true statements? (Circle all that apply.)
   (a) DMA may occur between any two memory cycles.
   (b) DMA may occur between any two assembly language instructions.
   (c) DMA may occur between any two C statements.

10. Which of the following registers are pushed on the stack when the Cortex-M3 responds to an interrupt? (Circle all that apply.)
    (a) R0
    (b) R4
    (c) R12
    (d) LR
    (e) PSW

11. Which of the following provide the index used to retrieve the handler address from the vector table for an external interrupt?
    (a) A hard-coded constant built into the CPU
    (b) The next instruction in the pipeline
    (c) The NVIC

12. Which of the following provide the index used to retrieve the handler address from the vector table for exceptions that are not external interrupts?
    (a) A hard-coded constant built into the CPU
    (b) The next instruction in the pipeline
    (c) The NVIC

13. True/False: Register LR contains the return address during the execution of an event handler.

14. Which of the following reduce the time between two back-to-back exceptions?
    (a) Abandoning
    (b) Tail-chaining
    (c) Late arrival processing

15. Which of the following redirect the exception response sequence?
    (a) Abandoning
    (b) Tail-chaining
    (c) Late arrival processing

16. Which of the following are true? (Circle all that apply.)
    (a) The starting address of the vector table is always zero.
    (b) The starting address of the vector table is stored in the vector table offset register.
    (c) The starting address of the vector table is different for internal versus external interrupts.

17. Assume that an ISR is currently executing and interrupts are enabled. For each of the following, circle the appropriate adjective to indicate when the CPU will respond to a second interrupt:
    (a) If the second interrupt is of (lower/higher) priority, then only after the ISR returns.
    (b) Immediately if the second interrupt is of (lower/higher) priority.

18. The hardware of our ARM processor was designed so that exception handlers (including ISRs) could be written in C like any other function. Which registers did this require to be saved on the stack during the hardware response to the interrupt request?

19. Both interrupt-driven I/O and polled waiting loop I/O are implemented in software, yet the maximum data rate of interrupt-driven I/O is almost an order of magnitude slower. What causes this?

20. For input devices, latency is defined as the time from the moment that data is available at the device until the time that the data is read from the device. What determines latency when:
    (a) Interrupt-driven I/O is used, interrupts are enabled, and no other ISRs are currently executing?
    (b) Interrupt-driven I/O is used and interrupts are enabled, but other ISRs are currently executing?
    (c) DMA is used?
    (d) Polled waiting loop is used?

21. Write an instruction loop that transfers 1,000 bytes of data from one area of memory to another as fast as possible, and estimate how long it will take to execute on a Cortex-M3 with a zero wait-state memory.

CHAPTER 9

Concurrent Software

9.1 FOREGROUND/BACKGROUND SYSTEMS

In many systems where response time is critical, it is common to organize the program as a foreground/background system, as shown in Figure 9-1. Most of the actual work is performed in the "foreground," implemented as one or more interrupt service routines with each ISR processing a particular hardware event. As we learned in Section 8.4, this arrangement allows the system to respond to external events with a predictable amount of latency. To the extent that the external events are independent, there may be no or little communication between the various interrupt service routines (ISRs).

The main program performs the necessary initialization and then enters the "background" portion of the program, which is often nothing more than a simple loop that waits for interrupts to occur.

9.1.1 Thread State and Serialization

Sometimes previous events that have occurred will determine how an input event should be processed. As a simple example, consider an external device that is sent a

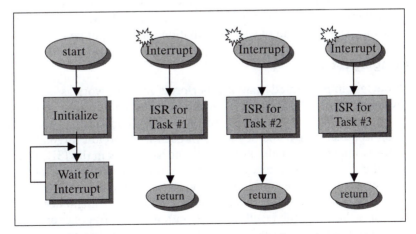

FIGURE 9-1   Organization of a foreground/background system.

Note: No program termination path is indicated, since once started, most embedded applications run indefinitely.

```
unsigned int byte_counter  ;

void Send_Request_For_Data(void)
    {
    byte_counter = 0 ;
    outportb(CMD_PORT, RQST_DATA_CMD) ;
    }

void Process_One_Data_Byte(void)
   {
   BYTE8 data = inportb(DATA_PORT) ;

   switch (++byte_counter)
     {
     case 1: Process_Temperature(data); break ;
     case 2: Process_Altitude(data);    break ;
     case 3: Process_Humidity(data);    break ;
     ...
     }
   }
```

> This counter holds *state* information. It allows us to distinguish data bytes according to the order in which they are received.

FIGURE 9-2   Example of state information within an ISR.

request for data and then returns an entire set of data values in response. Each data byte in the set might be associated with a particular measurement, with bytes distinguished only by the relative order in which they arrive. If each byte causes a new interrupt request, then processing the data properly requires that the corresponding ISR provide a counter that is reset to zero when the original command is issued and then incremented on each input interrupt. The counter shown in the example of Figure 9-2 provides a simple form of state information for the input task.

9.1.2 Managing Latency

If the task implemented by an ISR performs all of the work associated with an external event, it may have quite a bit of work to do. It then becomes important to implement an interrupt priority system in hardware and to re-enable higher-priority interrupts as soon as possible near the beginning of each ISR. Do not forget, however, that lower-priority interrupts remain disabled as long as we stay in the ISR! If the ISR contains a lot of code, then the latency times imposed on lower-priority interrupts may still be intolerable if they are not re-enabled until the end of the ISR.

For example, an ISR that handles an input device might need to process the input data and then send the results to some output device. But of course you cannot write to the output device until it is ready. If the ready status of the output device is polled inside the ISR, as shown in Figure 9-3, any pending lower-priority interrupts will have to wait an unspecified amount of time. This is obviously unacceptable.

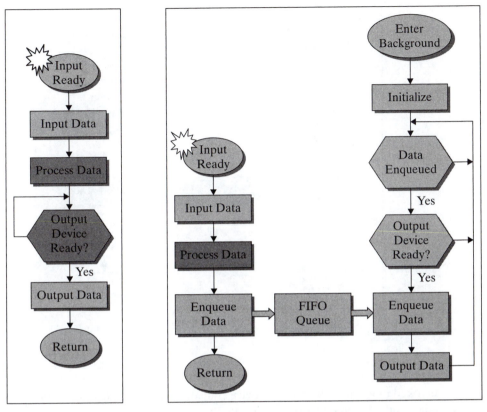

FIGURE 9-3   Waiting loop to be removed from ISR.

FIGURE 9-4   Writing into a queue from inside an ISR and subsequently emptying it in the background loop.

One solution is to have the ISR write the output data into a queue. The data can be removed from the queue by a background task, as shown in Figure 9-4. The ISR then becomes straight-line code that imposes a more predictable latency on lower-priority interrupts.

Using interrupt-driven input and polled waiting loop output is an intuitive solution, since the data flow from input to output is initiated by the input device. Unfortunately, the overall response time (from input to output) of such systems is far from optimal, since the background loop can be suspended by even the lowest priority interrupt. Rather than waiting for the background to output the result, a faster response time can be achieved by using interrupt-driven input/output (I/O) for both input and output.

The general structure of a fully interrupt-driven architecture is shown in Figure 9-5. There is one minor detail that must be resolved when using a queue in this manner. Output devices request an interrupt when they finish processing the current output byte to indicate that they are now ready for the next byte. In other words, the output ISR is

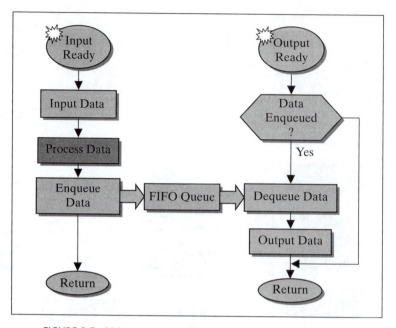

FIGURE 9-5   Using an output-ready ISR to empty the output queue.

invoked only when the output device transitions from a "busy" condition to a "ready" condition. This creates two problems:

1. When the input ISR puts the first data into the first-in, first-out (FIFO) queue, the output device is idle and already in the "ready" state, so no interrupt request from the output device is about to occur. The output ISR will not be invoked and the data will not be removed from the queue.

2. If somehow started, the "interrupt–dequeue–output" cycle will repeat as long as there is data in the queue. However, if the output device ever becomes ready when the queue is empty, no subsequent interrupt will occur to remove the next data placed in the queue.

Assume for the moment that it is possible to determine whether the output device is busy processing a data byte. This information might be obtained from a device status port, or by a software busy flag that is set when data is sent to the device and cleared when the device-ready interrupt is returned. Except for re-enabling interrupts and clearing the flag, replace the rest of the output ISR by a CALL to a procedure (e.g., SendData) that actually outputs the data.

The input ISR checks the output busy flag every time it writes data into the queue. If the device is busy, then a device-ready interrupt is expected and nothing needs to be done; otherwise, the input ISR calls SendData to "kick start" the output process. The flowchart given in Figure 9-6 illustrates the process.

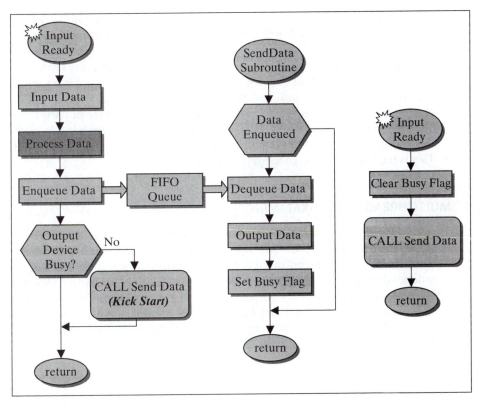

FIGURE 9-6   Kick starting an interrupt-driven output routine.

9.1.3 Interrupt Overrun

Now consider the box labeled "Process Data" in the input-ready ISR of Figure 9-6. If all the substantial work is done in the ISRs, this box may correspond to a lengthy computation, causing interrupts with the same or lower priority to remain disabled for a very long time. If this situation (called interrupt overrun) occurs, one needs to consider whether the processor and algorithms are really fast enough for the data-rate demands of the external devices. Occasionally, however, missing one or more interrupts may not be that disastrous. For example, a missed interrupt of periodic samples taken from a slowly changing analog signal can often be replaced by averaging the previous sample with the next.

9.1.4 Moving Work into the Background

A somewhat obvious way to reduce latency is to move any non-time-critical work (such as updating a display) into the background thread. Data to be processed is written into a queue by the foreground ISR, and then read from the queue for background processing. This sometimes provides a much-needed alternative when the system cannot tolerate ignoring one or more interrupts as the result of interrupt overrun.

Getting the best possible performance out of a foreground/background system requires moving as much work as possible into the background thread. The latter becomes a collection of queues and associated routines to process the data. While this may optimize the latency of the individual ISRs, the greater workload that has been moved to the background begs for a managed allocation of processor time. Just like the external interrupts that initiated them, each background task has a different level of importance, and thus should be assigned a different percentage of CPU time. While the queues can be checked with differing frequency to implement a crude priority system, this is usually the point at which one should consider a more sophisticated approach. This is the subject of the remaining chapters.

9.2 MULTITHREADED PROGRAMMING

As the software for embedded real-time applications becomes more complex, a better strategy for managing processor time is needed. Consider the organization of a multithreaded program, shown in Figure 9-7. The program is structured as a collection of independent threads that process data in the background, with ISRs merely filling input queues and emptying output queues. Moving the data processing from ISRs to the background reduces latency by minimizing the time spent executing ISRs. In addition, it allows the ISRs to be designed as simple "straight-line" code, without the need for any waiting loops.

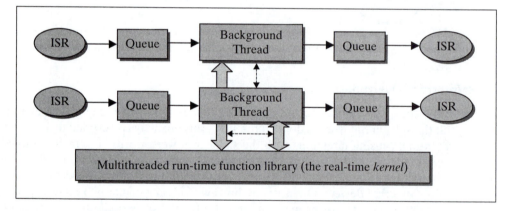

FIGURE 9-7   Organization of multithreaded real-time embedded software.

In an embedded system, each thread is usually implemented as a function that performs some initialization and then enters an infinite processing loop. At the top of the loop, the thread typically waits for data to become available, an external event to occur, or a condition to become true.

Threads make calls to a library of run-time routines (known as the real-time *kernel*) that is designed to manage resources in a multithreaded program. The kernel provides mechanisms to switch from one thread to another, as well as for establishing coordination, synchronization, communications, and priority among the threads. Often the library will also include routines to manage queues, and it may even interface with the ISRs to further improve response time.

9.2.1 Concurrent Execution of Independent Threads

Each thread in a multithreaded program runs *as if* it had its own processor separate from those of the other threads. For the most part, threads are designed, are programmed, and behave as if they are the only thread running. The ability to partition the background into a set of independent threads in this manner greatly simplifies the design of any one thread, and thus the total complexity of the program as well.

An important but sometimes difficult design goal is to partition the background software into threads in a manner that minimizes interthread linkages and thus maximizes thread independence. Occasionally, however, threads will need to share information or coordinate their execution. Kernels provide services for these needs in a disciplined manner that facilitates good program architecture and reduces complexity.

Only one thread runs at a time, while the others are *suspended*. However, the processor switches from one thread to another so quickly that (to the external environment) it appears that all threads are running simultaneously. In reality, the threads are said to be running *concurrently*. The programmer assigns a priority to each thread according to its importance and a kernel routine called the *scheduler* uses this information to determine which thread to run next.

9.2.2 Context Switching

Each thread has its own stack and a special region of memory referred to as its *context*. As shown in Figure 9-8, the context includes memory for the thread's stack and copies of the contents of all the CPU registers when the thread was last suspended.

As shown in Figure 9-9, a *context switch* from thread A to thread B first saves all CPU registers in context A and then reloads all CPU registers from context B. Since the CPU register set includes the stack pointer (SP) and program counter (PC), reloading context B in effect causes a reactivation of thread B's stack and a return to where it left off when it was last suspended.

9.2.3 Non-preemptive (Cooperative) Multithreading

In non-preemptive multithreading, threads must explicitly call a kernel routine to perform the context switch. By calling this routine, the thread relinquishes control of the processor, thus allowing another thread to run. The context switch call is often referred to as a *yield,* and this form of multithreading is often called *cooperative* multithreading.

When an external event occurs, the processor may very well be executing a thread other than the one designed to process the event, and the first opportunity to execute the needed thread will not occur until the current thread reaches the next yield. When the yield actually does occur, it is possible that several other threads may be scheduled to run first. In most cases, this makes it impossible or extremely difficult to predict the worst-case response time of non-preemptive multithreaded systems.

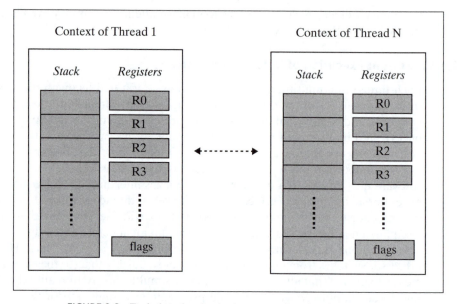

FIGURE 9-8 Each thread maintains its own stack and register contents.

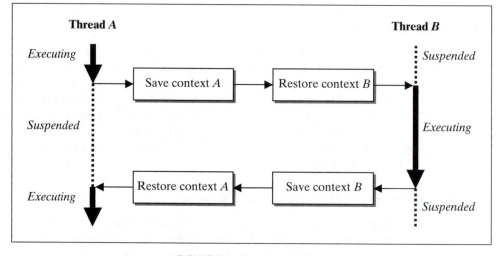

FIGURE 9-9 Context switching.

Obviously, the programmer must call the yield routine frequently, or else system response time may suffer. At a minimum, yields must be inserted in any loop where a thread is waiting for some external condition, as in Figure 9-10. A yield may also be needed inside other loops that take a long time to complete (such as reading or writing a file), or distributed periodically throughout a lengthy computation.

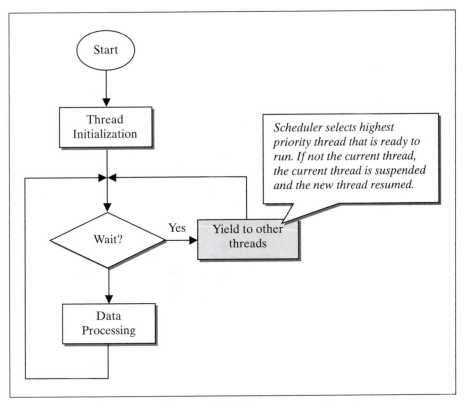

FIGURE 9-10   Context switching in a non-preemptive system.

9.2.4 Preemptive Multithreading

In *preemptive* multithreading, hardware interrupts are used to trigger the context switch, as shown in Figure 9-11. When an external event occurs, an associated hardware ISR is invoked. The ISR includes a call to a kernel routine that lets the thread that is waiting for the data know that it is now available. The kernel then makes a decision about which thread needs the processor the most (which is usually the one to process the data), and performs a context switch so that the ISR returns to it instead of the interrupted thread. System response time is significantly improved because the sequencing of threads is appropriately driven by the order of external events.

Preemptive multithreading eliminates the programmer's obligation to include explicit calls to the kernel to yield the processor within the various background threads. The programmer no longer needs to worry about how frequently the yield routine is called; it is called only when needed—that is, in response to external events.

9.3   SHARED RESOURCES AND CRITICAL SECTIONS

Consider what would happen if two or more threads simultaneously sent data to the same (shared) disk, printer, network card, or serial port. If access were not coordinated

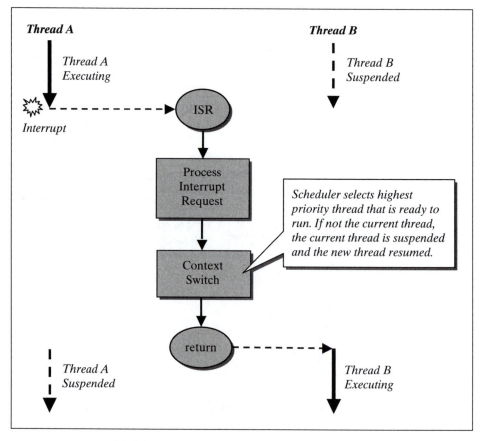

FIGURE 9-11 Context switching in a preemptive system.

so that only one thread used the resource at a time, the data streams might get mixed together, as shown in Figure 9-12, producing nonsense at the destination.

A sequence of instructions that manipulates a shared resource forms what is known as a *critical section* and must be protected against preemption by other (asynchronous) code that manipulates the same resource. Otherwise, associated data and proper operation of the program can become corrupted. Once protected, a critical

FIGURE 9-12 Unarbitrated access to a shared printer.

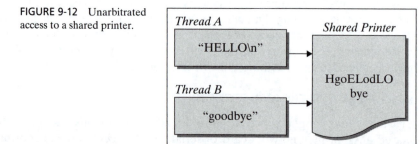

section becomes an *atomic* operation that is guaranteed to execute to completion without interference or data corruption.

In multithreaded applications, two or more threads often communicate with each other by passing information through a common data structure. The data structure is a special case of a shared resource called *shared memory*. Asynchronous access to such shared memory can occur in three fundamental ways:[1]

1. Memory may be shared between a thread and an ISR. Data corruption can occur if the thread's critical section is interrupted to execute the ISR.

2. Memory may be shared between two ISRs. Data corruption can occur if the critical section of one ISR can be interrupted to execute the other ISR.

3. Memory may be shared between two threads. Data corruption can occur unless execution of their critical sections is coordinated.

Non-preemptive systems inherently afford greater protection than preemptive systems against such errors because the programmer has explicit control over where and when a context switch may occur. The programmer merely has to ensure that no kernel functions that could cause a context switch are called (either directly or indirectly) in the middle of a sequence that manipulates the resource.

In preemptive systems, however, the programmer has no control over when and where a context switch may occur, since they can be triggered by an interrupt. In addition to avoiding kernel calls, the programmer must arbitrate access to the resource using techniques such as those discussed below.

9.3.1 Disabling Interrupts

When an ISR accesses a shared resource, the *only* way to protect against corruption is to disable interrupts during any *other* access. However, disabling interrupts can also be an appropriate choice when *no* ISR is involved, provided that interrupts are disabled only for a very few lines of code. Note that the longest duration of disabled interrupts will add to the worst-case response time of every task. However, the overhead of disabling and enabling interrupts is extremely small compared to any other technique.

9.3.2 Disabling Task Switching

Disabling interrupts during the execution of a long critical section can significantly degrade system response time. Doing so blocks the execution of all other threads and ISRs, even if they do not need access to the shared resource. A slightly different approach that still blocks all other threads but leaves interrupts enabled is to disable task switching during the critical section. Most kernels provide a couple of very fast functions for this purpose. Disabling task switching can protect critical sections in competing threads, but since it does not disable interrupts, it cannot protect a shared resource manipulated by an ISR.

---

[1] Note that these examples simply consider memory shared by exactly two asynchronous code sequences. More complex variations involving more than two asynchronous code sequences are certainly possible.

9.3.3 Spin Locks

Another choice is to leave both interrupts and task switching enabled and to *arbitrate* execution of the competing critical sections so that they do not interfere with each other. In other words, while one thread is in a critical section, other threads should be blocked if they arrive at the entry point of a critical section that manipulates the same resource.

One simple strategy is to associate a single Boolean flag with each shared resource. As shown in Figure 9-13, the flag is set before entering a critical section and cleared on exit; while the flag is set, all other access to the same resource is blocked. Blocking is provided by a tight loop that "spins" while the flag is set. The wait loop's testing of the flag and its subsequent setting must together form a single atomic operation called a "test-and-set"; otherwise, if the flag is clear and a context switch to a competing thread occurs between the test and the setting of the flag, then neither thread may be blocked.

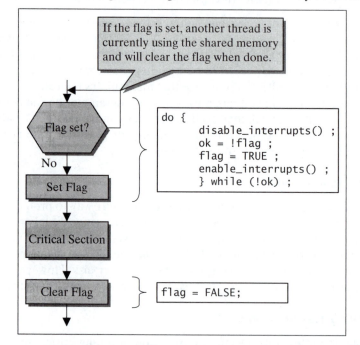

FIGURE 9-13   Using a "spin lock" to protect a critical section.

Although not shown in Figure 9-13, all spin lock loops should include a kernel call. For preemptive kernels this is usually a call to put the thread to "sleep" for a few milliseconds before testing the flag again and improves performance by reducing the overhead of frequent context switching. The call is absolutely necessary for non-preemptive systems to give other threads a chance to run; without this call, the lock would never be released (by the thread that locked it) and the program would effectively stop.

9.3.4 Mutex Objects

Although spin locks allow unrelated code to continue, the kernel must occasionally perform a context switch back to the spin lock to retest the flag and then return via another context switch if it is still locked. The overhead of context switching is much greater than that of disabling and enabling interrupts, and it does not lead to productive work as long as the flag remains locked. Mutex[2] objects eliminate this overhead by moving the test-and-set operation into the kernel so that it does not switch back to the blocked thread until the lock is released.

Coordinating entry into critical sections using a mutex requires calling a kernel function on either side of the critical section. Just before entering the critical section, the first kernel call (called a "pend" or "take") causes the thread to block until the specified mutex can be acquired. When available, the mutex is taken and the thread continues. When the thread reaches the end of its critical section, a second kernel call (called a "post" or "give") releases the mutex so that other threads waiting for the same mutex may proceed. Only a single thread may own a mutex at any one time; when a thread acquires a mutex, it is the only one that can release it.

9.3.5 Semaphores

A semaphore is similar to a mutex in that it can cause a thread to block (or suspend) until a condition is satisfied but is different in that a semaphore is *typically* used to manage events rather than to arbitrate access to a shared resource. Semaphores provide a mechanism for one thread to signal another thread. The first thread is thought of as the "producer" and the second as the "consumer" (although no actual data is produced or consumed). In many cases the producer is an ISR and the consumer is a thread that is waiting for the interrupt to occur.

Semaphores contain a count that is incremented by the producer and decremented by the consumer. The count cannot go below 0 or above some value "N" that is established when the semaphore is created. When the count is zero, consumers are blocked until a producer performs a post that increments the count. When the count is N, producers are blocked until a consumer performs a pend to decrement the count.

One common use of semaphores is to count events. Initially the count is set to zero. An event handler records each event by executing a post (or give) that increments the count, while another thread that processes the event executes a pend (or take) that decrements the count. Semaphores can also be used to manage a set of N identical resources. Initially the count is set to N, corresponding to the number of available resources. When a thread needs a resource, it executes a pend that decrements the count. When the resource is released, it executes a post that increments the count. Note that the semaphore has no knowledge of *which* resource is allocated, only how many.

A "binary semaphore" is a special case in which the count can only be 0 or 1 and is more commonly used than the more general "counting semaphores." Although a binary semaphore may be used in place of a mutex to arbitrate access to a shared resource, there is a subtle but important difference: A corresponding pair of mutex pend and post operations must be called from within the same thread, which allows the kernel to know *which* thread (if any) owns the mutex at any instant. Semaphores have no such notion of ownership.[3]

---

[2] The phrase "mutex object" (or simply "mutex") is short for "mutual exclusion object." A mutex is sometimes referred to as a "critical section object."

[3] There is disagreement among practitioners about the difference between a mutex and a semaphore, with some describing a mutex as equivalent to a binary semaphore.

PROBLEMS

1. Which of the following is appropriate for protecting only *short* critical sections?
   (a) Disabling interrupts
   (b) Disabling task switching
   (c) Spin locks
   (d) Mutex objects
   (e) Semaphores

2. Which of the following causes unnecessary context switching?
   (a) Disabling interrupts
   (b) Disabling task switching
   (c) Spin locks
   (d) Mutex objects
   (e) Semaphores

3. Which of the following methods protect data that is shared between a thread and an ISR? (Circle all that apply.)
   (a) Disabling interrupts
   (b) Disabling task switching
   (c) Spin locks
   (d) Mutex objects
   (e) Semaphores

4. Some processors have two sets of registers: one for integer operations and one for floating-point operations. The integer registers are always saved and restored during every context switch in a preemptive kernel. Under what conditions must the context switch also save and restore the floating-point registers? (Circle all that apply.)
   (a) The floating-point registers must always be saved and restored.
   (b) If floating-point operations are used only in a single thread.
   (c) If floating-point operations are used in more than one thread.

5. True/False: Each thread in a multithreaded application must have its own stack.

6. When a *non-preemptive* kernel is used, the context switch occurs
   (a) Only by an explicit call to a kernel function
   (b) Only because of a hardware interrupt
   (c) Either of the above

7. When a *preemptive* kernel is used, the context switch occurs
   (a) Only by an explicit call to a kernel function
   (b) Only because of a hardware interrupt
   (c) Either of the above

8. Which of the following provides better system response time?
   (a) Non-preemptive kernel
   (b) Preemptive kernel

9. Which of the following situations would never cause data corruption in a multithreaded application?
   (a) Two threads, both reading a shared data structure stored in memory
   (b) Two threads, one reading and the other writing a shared data structure stored in memory
   (c) Two threads, both writing and reading a shared data structure in memory

10. Circle as many of the following that could be appropriate choices of how to arbitrate access to a shared resource in a multithreaded application:
    (a) Disabling/enabling the interrupt system
    (b) Disabling/enabling the context switching (via kernel function calls)
    (c) Using a semaphore or mutex (via kernel function calls)
    (d) Spin locks

11. Which kind of real-time kernel gives better overall response time to external events?
    (a) Preemptive
    (b) Non-preemptive (cooperative)

12. In which of the following two types of real-time kernels are you able to predict exactly where a context switch will occur in the code?
    (a) Preemptive
    (b) Non-preemptive (cooperative)

13. Which of the following two types of real-time kernels requires that you insert calls to the kernel to "yield"?
    (a) Preemptive
    (b) Non-preemptive (cooperative)

14. The minimum number of threads required to have a critical section is _____.

15. The minimum number of shared resources to have a critical section is _____.

16. The following function transmits a packet of information over a serial communications line but may transmit corrupted packets when called by more than one thread in a multi-threaded application. Describe what changes (if any) are required and why (a) when a *preemptive* kernel is used and (b) when a non-preemptive kernel is used. [*Hint: Do not forget that the function Send1Byte might yield while waiting for the device to be ready!*]

```
void SendPacket(int type, char *packet, int length)
{
Send1Byte(0xFF) ;
Send1Byte(type) ;
Send1Byte(length) ;
while (length--) Send1Byte(*packet++) ;
}
```

C H A P T E R   1 0

Scheduling

Multithreaded programming is a common strategy for embedded software. Partitioning an application into separate threads of execution with careful management of communications among the threads tends to simplify the design of each thread. Once partitioned, it is appropriate to consider how these threads compete for their share of processor time.

10.1 THREAD STATES

We begin by recognizing that only one thread can be running, and that the rest must be waiting for their turn, as shown in Figure 10-1. The job of a *scheduler* is to manage turn-taking in a manner that meets performance requirements.

To compete for processor time, each thread must be made known to the scheduler by making a call to the kernel. Before that call is made, the thread is unknown to the scheduler and is said to be *inactive*. As shown in Figure 10-2, threads are thus in one of three states (*inactive*, *running*, or *ready*), with the kernel managing transitions of threads from one state to another.

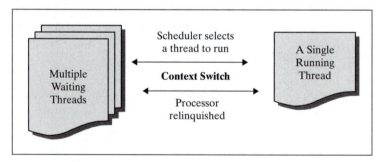

FIGURE 10-1   Scheduler selects thread to run while others wait.

A simplistic scheduling algorithm called *time-slicing* runs each thread for the same fixed amount of time. When a thread reaches the end of its allocated time slice, the kernel simply gives control to the next thread in the sequence, repeating the sequence over and over again. While time slicing may be an appropriate strategy for some types of applications, real-time systems require a kernel that is much more responsive to external events.

FIGURE 10-2   Initial thread state
diagram.

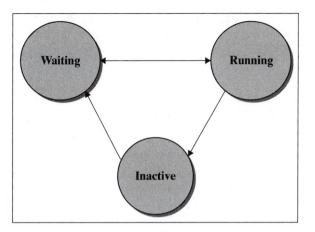

10.2   PENDING THREADS

To optimize processor utilization, scheduling must recognize that threads often have to wait for some event to occur or some shared resource to become available. When this happens, the scheduler should run a different thread while the first one waits. Simply moving the delayed task back into the ready state is not appropriate, however, because the thread may be selected to run again later, only to discover that it must continue to wait, thus adding unnecessary task switching overhead.

The solution is to introduce a fourth state called *pending,* shown in Figure 10-3. When a running thread reaches a point where it cannot proceed until some specific condition is satisfied (such as the occurrence of an external event or the release of a shared resource), another kernel call is used to change the thread to the pending state; the scheduler then selects and runs one of the other threads from the ready list. When the pending condition is ultimately satisfied, another kernel call to the scheduler moves the pending thread to the ready state.

FIGURE 10-3   Revised thread
state diagram.

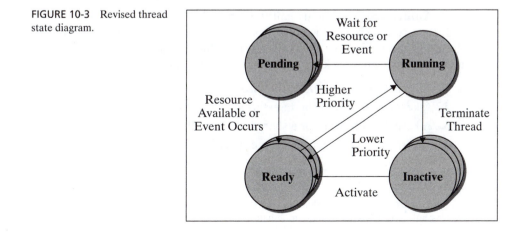

Most threads cycle through these three states (ready, running, and pending) as long as the embedded application is running. Some threads, however, are normally inactive; they are occasionally made ready when needed, are run to completion, and are then returned to the inactive state.

10.3   CONTEXT SWITCHING

A *non-preemptive* context switch is shown in Figure 10-4. Initially, thread A is running and thread B is waiting in the pending state for a specific event to occur. When the event occurs, it triggers an interrupt service routine (ISR), which records the event by executing a semaphore "post" call to the kernel. The kernel knows that thread B has been pending (waiting for the event to occur) and changes its state from pending to ready. The ISR then returns and continues execution of thread A. Sometime later, thread A makes a kernel call to yield the processor, providing an opportunity for the scheduler to context switch to thread B.

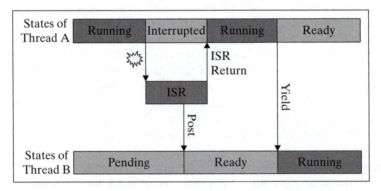

FIGURE 10-4   Non-preemptive context switch.

A thread may explicitly call the scheduler at any time to give other threads a chance to run; such a call is known as a *yield*. The yield call simply moves the current thread to the ready state and calls the scheduler, as shown in Figure 10-5. However, there are other kinds of kernel calls that may implicitly call the scheduler:

1. A kernel call to terminate the thread.[1]
2. A kernel call to wait for an external event to occur.
3. A kernel call to wait for a shared resource that is currently in use.
4. A kernel call to "sleep" for some specified amount of time.

---

[1] Control implicitly transfers back to the scheduler when the function that implements a thread returns; no kernel call is necessary to terminate the thread.

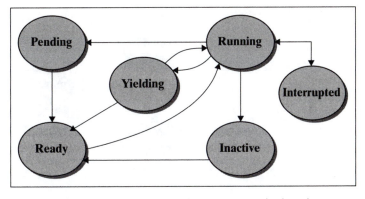

FIGURE 10-5   Thread states in a non-preemptive kernel.

Non-preemptive systems have to make frequent kernel calls in order to achieve good response time. Threads running under a *preemptive* kernel, however, are not *required* to make kernel calls in order to yield. Context switching within the interrupt routine allows preemptive kernels to immediately activate the thread that processes the event. This provides a drastically improved and predictable response time that is critically important for real-time systems that depend on completion of their tasks within certain deadline constraints.

For example, Figure 10-6 illustrates how a preemptive system context switches from one thread to another when an interrupt occurs. Thread B is waiting in the pending state for some external event. As in the non-preemptive example of Figure 10-4, the event triggers an ISR that makes a semaphore post kernel call, changing the state of thread B from pending to ready. Just before returning, however, the ISR makes a second kernel call to the scheduler to check whether a context switch should occur, and changes the ISR's return address if necessary. As shown in Figures 10-5 and 10-7, both preemptive and non-preemptive kernels allow running threads to move temporarily to an "interrupted" state. Unlike non-preemptive kernels, however, a preemptive kernel allows the interrupted thread to move back to the ready state so that a different thread can resume when the interrupt is completed.

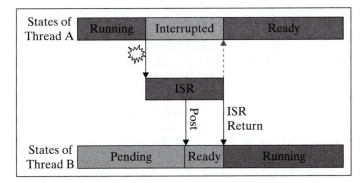

FIGURE 10-6   Interrupt-triggered context switch in a preemptive kernel.

FIGURE 10-7 Thread states in a
preemptive kernel.

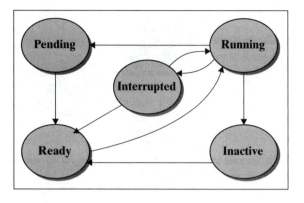

10.4 ROUND-ROBIN SCHEDULING

Scheduling refers to the process by which the kernel selects one of the ready threads to run. The simplest scheduling algorithm is called round-robin scheduling. The kernel maintains a queue containing a list of threads that are ready to run. When the scheduler needs to select a thread to run, it merely removes the next thread from the front of the queue; threads are entered at the rear of the queue as they change to the ready state.

Round-robin scheduling simply treats all threads as having equal importance. In most real-time applications, however, certain threads are more important than others. For example, a task that updates a display can certainly be delayed relative to a task that applies brake pressure in an antilock braking system.

10.5 PRIORITY-BASED SCHEDULING

Scheduling algorithms for real-time systems select which thread to run based on priority numbers that the programmer assigns to each of the threads. *Static* priorities never change during the execution of the application; we will see, however, that *dynamic* priorities are necessary in order to make system response time fast and predictable.

10.5.1 Resource Starvation

A poorly designed multithreaded system can sometimes suffer from a situation called starvation. Starvation occurs when a thread is never scheduled to run because it cannot acquire one (or more) of the resources it needs—usually the CPU. For example, a high-priority thread that never yields or blocks will always be given the CPU in preference to any lower-priority thread. The lower-priority thread is then said to be CPU starved.

Note that it is not necessary for threads to explicitly yield or block to prevent starvation. If two threads have the same priority, neither will starve the other if the scheduler is designed to cycle through equal priority threads in round-robin style to insure that each has a chance to run. However, assigning the same priority to multiple threads would be inappropriate if they have different response time requirements. In this case, we must be careful to design the system so that no resource is perpetually dominated by a single thread.

10.5.2 Priority Inversion

High-priority threads are intended to have precedence over low-priority threads. However, a situation called *priority inversion* can temporarily defeat this intention and is said to exist whenever the completion of one task is delayed by a second task of lower priority.

Priority inversion involves two threads that use the same (shared) resource. For example, let us assume that the low-priority thread in Figure 10-8 had previously acquired and still holds exclusive access to such a resource. Even though the high-priority thread is now running, when it attempts to acquire that same resource, the high-priority thread is placed in the pending state and must wait until the low-priority thread completes its critical section and relinquishes the resource. This simple form of priority inversion exists no longer than the duration of the lower-priority thread's critical section (where it owns the resource). It is referred to as *bounded* priority inversion because the execution time of the low-priority thread's critical section should be designed to be predictable, short, and of fixed duration.

Unbounded priority inversion occurs when a third (medium-priority) thread pre-empts the low-priority thread during the inversion, thus delaying the high-priority thread even more. (This is exactly what happened during the Mars Pathfinder[2] mission.) It is called "unbounded" because it will persist as long as the medium-priority thread has all the resources it needs to continue running, which is unrelated to the resource shared by the other two threads and can be unpredictable. There are two well-known solutions to this particular problem: the priority inheritance protocol (PIP) and the priority ceiling protocol (PCP). Both are based on the ability to modify thread priorities at run-time.

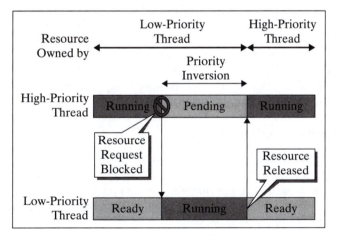

FIGURE 10-8   Example of a priority inversion.

---

[2] The Mars Pathfinder software included three threads (among others): a high-priority bus management thread that ran quickly and frequently, a medium-priority communications thread that ran for a much longer time, and a low-priority meteorological thread that ran infrequently. To publish its data the meteorological thread had to acquire the (shared) bus. Then the communications thread woke up and preempted the meteorological thread. Finally, the bus management thread woke up and was blocked because it could not acquire the bus; when it could not meet its deadline, an alarm went off that reinitialized the computer via a hardware reset.

Consider a system in which a low-priority thread has acquired a shared resource. As long as this thread maintains ownership, higher-priority threads that attempt to acquire the same resource will be blocked. The objective of both PIP and PCP is to limit how long blocking persists by preventing medium-priority threads from preempting (and thus delaying) the low-priority threads until they relinquish ownership of the resource.

Arbitration for a shared resource is implemented by an associated mutex that is unlocked when the resource is available, and locked when it is in use. Threads request exclusive access by making a kernel call to attempt to lock the mutex. If the mutex is already locked, the attempt fails and the thread is placed in the pending state until the mutex is unlocked. Otherwise, the kernel locks the mutex and allows the thread to continue. The thread is then said to *own* the mutex until it makes a subsequent kernel call to unlock it.

10.5.3 The Priority Ceiling Protocol

PCP specifies that the priority of a thread be raised immediately when it acquires a shared resource and restored to its original value when it releases the resource. The temporary priority is a value predetermined by the programmer as the highest among all the threads that access the same resource and is referred to as the priority *ceiling*.

An interesting aspect of PCP is that it can be easily implemented in the source code of the thread. All that is required is a call to a kernel library function to raise priority before acquiring the resource and another to lower the priority after the resource is released. If PCP is implemented in the kernel instead, the ceiling is simply provided as a calling parameter when the mutex is created and kept within an associated data structure maintained by the kernel. This approach is preferred because PCP then becomes transparent to the application except for the initial mutex creation.

The disadvantage of PCP is that it *always* raises the priority, whether a higher-priority thread is blocked or not, and may thus delay the execution of other threads unnecessarily. Moreover, when there are more than two threads that access the resource, raising the priority all the way to the ceiling value may be more restrictive than required.

10.5.4 The Priority Inheritance Protocol

PIP is implemented in the kernel code that locks and unlocks the mutex. If and when a thread fails to lock a mutex, the kernel looks up which thread owns the mutex.[3] If the owner has a priority lower than the thread now blocked, the kernel temporarily raises the priority of the owner to match that of the blocked thread until the resource is released.

PIP is transparent to the source code of the thread since it is implemented entirely in the kernel. Overall system response time performance is better with PIP than PCP. PIP raises the priority of the low-priority thread only when it begins to block a higher-priority thread, and thus delays the execution of other threads only when necessary.

---

[3] Note that this is not possible if a binary semaphore is used to arbitrate access instead of a mutex.

Moreover, when the priority must be raised, PIP only raises it to that of the blocked thread, which may be lower than the ceiling.

10.6 ASSIGNING PRIORITIES

The primary challenge in scheduling is to assign priority numbers in a manner that guarantees that the system meets real-time performance criteria. In real-time systems, faster response times are generally more desirable than slower response times. However, this does not always mean that we must compute every output response as fast as possible. Computing all output responses within their corresponding deadline constraints is a somewhat different objective.

In conventional multiuser systems, we usually try to keep users satisfied with system performance by running the shortest computations (tasks) first with the objective of minimizing the average overall response time. For example, consider the case of two people who submit requests at the same moment—one that needs 1 sec of CPU time and another that needs 6 sec. As shown in Figure 10-9, if the longer task runs first,[4] the response times will be 6 and 7 sec and one user will be significantly delayed; however, if the shorter task runs first, the response times are 1 and 7 sec and both users are satisfied.

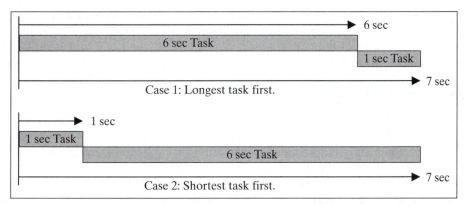

FIGURE 10-9   Scheduling to minimize average response times.

10.6.1 Deadline-Driven Scheduling

The shortest-first policy may not be appropriate for real-time systems with response time deadlines. Associated with every task are two times: (1) the minimum time required to compute the response as determined by CPU speed and the complexity of the computation and (2) the maximum time allowed by external constraints (the deadline).

---

[4] In practice, tasks do not run serially as in Figure 10-9; rather the CPU continuously switches back and forth, devoting a percentage of its time to each task. The example shown represents the extreme case of allocating 100% to one task and 0% to the other. Actual allocations would fall somewhere in between the two cases indicated.

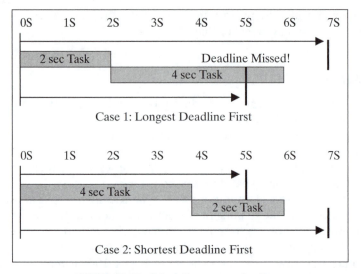

FIGURE 10-10 Scheduling to meet deadlines.

For example, consider two tasks, both initiated at the same instant. One is a 2-sec task with a deadline of 7 sec, and the other is a 4-sec task with a deadline of 5 sec. As Figure 10-10 shows, both deadlines can be met only if the *longer* (4-sec) task runs first. This form of scheduling is known as deadline driven because it schedules the thread with the earliest deadline first.

10.6.2 Rate-Monotonic Scheduling

If we restrict ourselves to tasks that are periodic with fixed-length execution times, a popular technique called rate monotonic analysis (RMA)[5] can be used to analytically determine whether a given system will meet its deadlines. A complete treatment of RMA is beyond the scope of this text.

The primary result of using RMA is that tasks with the shortest execution *periods* are assigned the highest priorities, without regard to how critical each task might be. Such an assignment helps to insure that the faster-executing tasks meet their deadlines by deterring preemption by slower tasks.

For example, a task that processes the arrival of serial data packets will have a period that is related to the serial data rate. As the rate increases, complete packets are assembled and become ready for processing more frequently—meaning that the period between successive packets decreases and that (according to RMA) the priority of the task should thus be higher.

RMA also provides the ability to estimate processor utilization. This is a measure of how much of the processor's capability is being used and indicates whether a faster

[5] Klein et al., "A Practitioners Handbook for Real-Time Analysis: Guide to Rate Monotonic Analysis for Real-Time Systems." Kluwer Academic Publishers, Boston, MA, 1993.

processor is needed or whether a slower (and less expensive) one would suffice. As you might expect, as processor utilization increases, so does the probability that the tasks will not be able to meet their deadlines. A general rule of thumb is to try to keep utilization below 80%.

10.7 DEADLOCK

Deadlock is a situation in which two or more threads are blocked because they are waiting on each other's resources. It can occur only when each of these threads requires exclusive access to two or more shared resources simultaneously (Figure 10-11).

Consider two threads T1 and T2 that share two resources R1 and R2. Since the resources are shared, the threads use mutex objects M1 (for resource R1) and M2 (for resource R2) to protect their critical sections. Suppose that thread T1 has locked mutex M1 because it is using resource R1, and that thread T2 has locked mutex M2 because it is using R2. This corresponds to the beginning of Figure 10-12, where both threads are still active and neither is blocked.

The problem begins when each thread attempts to lock the other mutex without first unlocking the one it already owns. For example, when T2 attempts to lock M1, the kernel puts T2 into the pending state since M1 is already locked by T1. T1 continues to run but then attempts to lock M2; since M2 is already locked by T2, the kernel puts T1 into the pending state too. With both threads now blocked and pending, neither can complete its critical section in order to release its lock.

Our example was based on only two threads for simplicity. After a little thought, you will soon realize that an N-way deadlock with *more* than two threads is also possible (as in Figure 10-11). As N increases, our ability to recognize a potential deadlock

FIGURE 10-11   Deadlock.

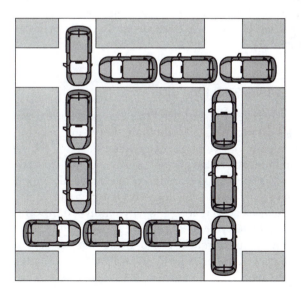

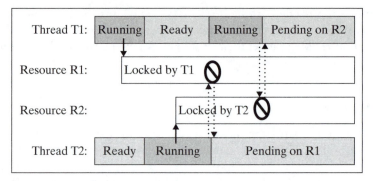

FIGURE 10-12 A sequence of events creating deadlock.

situation diminishes rapidly. Fortunately, development tools do exist that can analyze software and detect such situations automatically, but it is still the programmer who has to find a solution to the problem.

It is important to realize that deadlock simply is not possible when critical sections are protected by turning off task switching or by disabling interrupts. Unfortunately, these techniques are only appropriate for short critical sections. A mutex is the *only* reasonable way to protect long critical sections without affecting the response time of other tasks.

There are several different strategies for dealing with deadlocks. A common approach is to require all threads to acquire resources in the same order. However, even though the specific order chosen is arbitrary, it often causes resources to be locked for longer than necessary. Occasionally there is no order that can be found that is convenient for all threads. When this happens, an alternative strategy is to require a thread to release *all* of its acquired resources and start over if any one resource cannot be acquired. There are even algorithms for detecting when a deadlock has occurred, but breaking a deadlock once it has been detected is not practical in most real-time systems.

10.8 WATCHDOG TIMERS

Priority inversion and deadlock can cause a real-time system to fail. Although strategies exist to avoid such problems, they sometimes are not implemented due to expense, complexity, or oversight. Even when they are, the system may still fail because of programming errors, hardware failure, or unanticipated situations.

If continuous operation of the embedded application is critical, and if the failure is only temporary, then a watchdog timer can be used to provide a primitive recovery mechanism. A watchdog timer is simply a hardware counter that counts down toward zero at a fixed rate. The software is expected to periodically restart the counter so that it never actually reaches zero. If the counter *does* reach zero, a failure is assumed to have occurred. The watchdog hardware then sends a reset signal to the CPU, causing the system to reinitialize. In safety-critical applications, the watchdog hardware must also be responsible for putting everything into a safe state, since the CPU itself may have failed.

In a real-time multithreaded application, it is important that the watchdog timer verify more than just the fact that the CPU is executing instructions. It is tempting to restart the watchdog using a few lines of code added to the system timer tick's ISR. However, this interrupt and its ISR could easily continue to work properly in the presence of a deadlock or a priority inversion, and thus would *not* verify that tasks are meeting their deadlines.

When triggered by an event, the time a task requires to compute the corresponding output response must be less than the specified deadline. It does not matter whether the task is executed periodically, sporadically, or infrequently. Thus, the software that restarts the watchdog counter must do so only after verifying that all such deadlines have been met.

One effective software strategy is illustrated in Figures 10-13 and 10-14. It associates an integer representation of time ("deadline") and two Boolean flags ("busy" and "failed") with every task. All such flags are cleared to false during system initialization. Whenever an event occurs that triggers the execution of the task, the event computes the future deadline for the task, records it in the integer, sets busy to true, and then makes the kernel call that releases the pending task. Once the task has finished computing the output response, it sets its failed flag to true if it missed its deadline, and it unconditionally clears its busy flag to false.

The watchdog software periodically checks each task, as shown in Figure 10-14. A task has missed a deadline if either its failed flag is true or its busy flag is true and the current time is greater than its posted deadline. If none of the tasks has failed, the watchdog software restarts the hardware counter. These checks are relatively simple and fast to compute and can usually be run as a relatively infrequent but high-priority task without much impact on the rest of the system.

Task trigger (e.g., ISR or different thread)	Task to compute output response
| ```
...
deadline[TASK] = current_time() + LIMIT ;
busy[TASK] = true ;
SemaphorePost(...) ;
...
``` | ```
while (true)
{
SemaphorePend(...) ;

... // Compute output response
if (current_time() > deadline[TASK])
{
failed[TASK] = true ;
}
busy[TASK] = false ;
}
``` |

FIGURE 10-13   Monitoring the deadline of a task.

```
while (true)
    {
    int now, task ;

    sleep(...) ;  // for less than counter period ...

    now = current_time() ;
    for (task = 0; task < tasks; task++)
        {
        if (failed[task]) break ;
        if (busy[task] && now > deadline[task]) break ;
        }

    if (task == tasks) restart_counter() ;
    }
```

FIGURE 10-14   Watchdog task to restart hardware counter.

PROBLEMS

1. Which thread *owns* the shared resource during a bounded priority inversion?
   (a) The high-priority thread
   (b) The low-priority thread

2. A bounded priority inversion *begins* when:
   (a) The low-priority thread acquires the shared resource.
   (b) The high-priority thread starts to wait ("pends") for the shared resource.

3. A bounded priority inversion *ends* when:
   (a) The low-priority thread releases the shared resource.
   (b) The high-priority thread releases the shared resource.

4. An *unbounded* priority inversion among three threads, one each of low, medium, and high priority, requires a resource shared by:
   (a) The low- and medium-priority threads
   (b) The low- and high-priority threads
   (c) The medium- and high-priority threads
   (d) All three threads

5. Which of the following solutions to unbounded priority inversion minimizes the length of time that the priority of the lower-priority thread is raised?
   (a) The priority inheritance protocol
   (b) The priority ceiling protocol

6. Consider a multithreaded application consisting of three threads. Initially, a low-priority thread is running and owns a shared resource. A high-priority thread is pending (waiting)

on the same resource. Sometime before the low-priority thread releases the resource, a medium-priority thread becomes ready. Give each of your answers below as an algebraic expression that is the sum of one or more of the following terms, as appropriate:

N = no wait.
L = minimum time for the low-priority thread to complete its critical section.
M = minimum time for the medium-priority thread to complete its task.
H = minimum time for the high-priority thread to complete its critical section.

What is the *maximum* time that the *high*-priority thread must wait if using:
(a) Fixed-priority protocol?
(b) Priority ceiling protocol?
(c) Priority inheritance protocol?

7. What determines the *maximum* time that the *medium*-priority thread must wait if using:
(a) Fixed-priority protocol?
(b) Priority ceiling protocol?
(c) Priority inheritance protocol?

8. What determines the *maximum* time that the *low*-priority thread needs to complete its critical section if using:
(a) Fixed-priority protocol?
(b) Priority ceiling protocol?
(c) Priority inheritance protocol?

9. What determines the *maximum* time that the *medium*-priority thread needs to complete its task if using:
(a) Fixed-priority protocol?
(b) Priority ceiling protocol?
(c) Priority inheritance protocol?

10. Show how threads can become deadlocked by completing the following sequence of thread states. List states as "Ready," "Pending," or "Running." If the state is "Pending," state which resource the thread is waiting to acquire.

	State of thread A	State of thread B	Resource 1 owned by	Resource 2 owned by
Start:	Running	Ready	Thread	No
Event 1:				
Event 2:				
Event 3:				

11. Indicate the minimum number of threads and the minimum number of shared resources for each of the following to occur?
(a) Bounded priority inversion
(b) Unbounded priority inversion
(c) Deadlock

12. Assume that unbounded priority inversion is occurring in a multithreaded application. Which solution has the least negative impact on system response time?
    (a) Priority ceiling protocol
    (b) Priority inheritance protocol

13. Assume that unbounded priority inversion is occurring in a multithreaded application. Which changes a thread's priority at the beginning of a critical section?
    (a) Priority ceiling protocol
    (b) Priority inheritance protocol

14. Assume that unbounded priority inversion is occurring in a multithreaded application. Which requires support built into the run-time kernel?
    (a) Priority ceiling protocol
    (b) Priority inheritance protocol

15. Assume that deadlock is occurring in a multithreaded application. Which solution requires that threads test to see if a resource is locked?
    (a) Changing the order of mutex acquisition
    (b) Releasing mutexes and retrying later

16. Which of the following priority assignment strategies makes it possible to calculate whether response time deadlines will be met?
    Assign the highest priorities to those threads that …
    (a) Have the shortest deadlines.
    (b) Contain the shortest critical section.
    (c) Require the shortest total time to execute.
    (d) Are triggered by events that occur most frequently.
    (e) Require the fewest number of shared resources.

17. Consider a multithreaded application with only two threads that compete for a single shared resource. Assume that the critical section of the low-priority thread has an execution time of "L" seconds, and that the critical section of the high-priority thread has an execution time of "H" seconds. What will be the maximum possible duration of priority inversion?

18. Repeat problem 17, but suppose a third, medium-priority thread is added that does not use any shared resources. Assume that neither PCP nor PIP is used, and that the medium-priority thread never runs for more than "M" seconds without yielding the processor.

19. Repeat problem 17, but assume that:
    (a) Priority ceiling protocol is used.
    (b) Priority inheritance protocol is used.

CHAPTER 11

Memory Management

Although memory-resource management is of concern in any programming project, it is even more crucial for embedded systems. We have seen how multithreaded code is essential to meet the response time demands of real-time systems, and how it can often simplify the design of complex applications by partitioning the software into a set of smaller and simpler (but related) tasks.

In multithreaded code, each thread operates on its own *private* data but often communicates with other threads by accessing a small amount of *shared* data. Any data that is manipulated by more than one thread or Interrupt Service Routine (ISR) creates a situation known as "shared memory" and demands careful coordination of access, or else data corruption can and will occur. Unfortunately, the really frustrating difficulty about programming a multithreaded application is that it is relatively easy to accidentally create unintentional instances of shared memory without even realizing it.

This chapter reviews those features of C that manage data and its creation, initialization, deletion, and accessibility. Establishing a clear understanding of these features (including their relative advantages, disadvantages, and alternatives) will prepare us to build robust multitasking software that protects the integrity of its data. The goal of this chapter is not only to master the familiar use of scope to limit accessibility of private data, but also to develop a foundation for a thorough treatment of shared-memory issues in the next chapter so that we can recognize and avoid those programming practices that create unintentional shared memory.

11.1 OBJECTS IN C

In the original C programming language, an *object* was defined as a region of memory that can be examined and modified. This predates the development of object-oriented programming that expanded the notion of object. For the purposes of this text, however, you may simply think of objects as variables—either scalar (e.g., char, int, or pointer) or aggregate data types (e.g., struct or union).

Every object possesses a number of different attributes, as summarized in Table 11-1. The most familiar of these include their data type, name, value, and address. The less familiar notions of *scope* and *lifetime* are important object attributes even in regular desktop-application programming, but they are even more important for us because they provide the fundamental mechanisms for shared data and restricted access.

Scope and lifetime are the "where and when" of objects. Programmers speak of the scope of an object using words such as *local* and *global* to refer to *where* within the

TABLE 11-1   Attributes of Objects Stored in Memory

Attribute	Description
Type	char, int, unsigned int, etc. (*also implies size, range, and resolution*)
Name	The identifier used to access the object
Value	The data held within the object
Address	The location in memory where the object resides
Scope	That part of the source code where the object's name is recognized
Lifetime	A notion of when the object is created and destroyed, and thus when it is available for use

source code the object may be referenced. The manner in which memory is allocated for the object determines its lifetime and places a second restriction on *when* such references may occur during program execution.

11.2   SCOPE

Most programmers really do not take full advantage of the capability to limit accessibility provided by scope. Declarations are usually placed only in one of two locations: (1) outside of all functions to create global variables or (2) immediately following a function header to create temporary variables local to the function.

A more enlightened knowledge of scope, however, allows us to further restrict accessibility, providing better defense against accidental misuse of an object (Figure 11-1).

```
int a ;        /* global object (accessible by any function) */

void f( )
    {
    int b ; /* temporary local (accessible only inside f) */
    ...
    b = ...
    ...
    }
```

FIGURE 11-1   Typical use of global and local scope.

11.2.1 Refining Local Scope

Simply stated, local scope refers to objects declared within a containing *block*. Blocks (which may be nested) begin with an opening curly brace and end with a matching closing curly brace. The scope of an object *begins at its point of declaration* and ends at the closing curly brace of its containing block. Objects declared within a block may not be referenced outside of that block. Thus:

1. The same identifier may be used for more than one object, as long as the objects are declared in different blocks; the correspondence between

identifiers and the objects to which they refer is resolved by the block in which they appear.

2. Maximum restriction of access to an object is achieved when its declaration appears in the innermost block possible. (Rather than placing all local declarations at the beginning of a function, consider moving them into the body of a loop or into the *then* or *else* block of an if statement.)

3. When blocks are nested, an object declared within an inner block takes precedence over ("hides") an object declared with the same identifier in an outer block.

These principles are illustrated in Example 11-1.

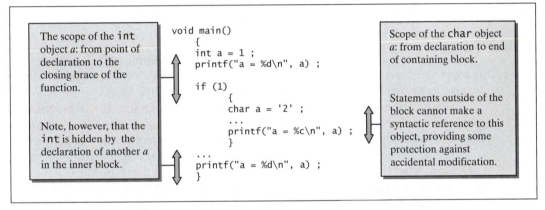

EXAMPLE 11-1   Two objects with the same identifier but nested scope.

11.2.2 Refining Global Scope

In C, objects declared outside of all functions are said to have global scope. These declarations are usually placed at the top of the source file (or in a header file included at the top of the source file).

But global really means that the identifier is accessible only from the point of declaration to the end of the file. Thus, one simple way to reduce the scope of a global variable (within the context of the file) is to position its declaration as near to the end of the source file as possible (i.e., just before the first function that uses it). The syntax rules of the language will then protect against any accidental misuse of the identifier occurring in the statements prior to the declaration.

When a program consists of multiple source files as in Figure 11-2, global objects defined in one file can be referenced by code in any other file, provided that two conditions are satisfied:

1. The file containing the *reference* to a global object must declare it using the extern keyword (or else a separate instance may be created).

2. The file containing the *definition* of the global must not use the keyword static in its declaration.

```
/*                                      /*
        defining file; do                      referencing file; no
        initializations here ...               initializations here ...
*/                                      */

int a = 123 ; /* externally visible */  void f2( )
static int b = 0 ; /* local to file */          {
                                                extern int a ;
void f1( )
        {                                       a = ... /* actual reference */
        ...                                     }
        }
```

FIGURE 11-2   Accessing data across multiple source-code files.

Within the referencing file, the identifier's scope is determined by the position of the extern declaration. If the declaration is global, then the identifier is global to the file; placing the declaration within a block makes it local to that block.

Although the keyword extern is *required* to establish an interfile reference to a global object, it leaves control in the hands of the reference rather than the definition. It offers no protection against interfile references that the programmer had not intended.

Adding the keyword static to the declaration of a global object restricts its scope to the file in which it is declared.[1] This nonintuitive feature of the static keyword causes the object's identifier to be hidden from the link process, and it eliminates any possibility of a syntactic reference from within other files.

Since this feature of the static keyword is not particularly intuitive, many programmers create a macro to make their intention clear, as in the following code:

```
#define LOCAL2FILE static
...
LOCAL2FILE int b = 0; /* This 'b' is not accessible from other files! */
```

Functions are inherently global. Although a function-prototype declaration is usually necessary in the referencing file to specify the number and type of parameters, the prototype does not need to include the keyword extern to establish an interfile reference. The linker automatically resolves interfile function references unless the function definition begins with the keyword static.

11.3   LIFETIME

Objects are created, initialized, used, and destroyed. The notion of lifetime refers to the *duration* of an object's existence (i.e., *when* it is accessible), determines *how* objects are

---

[1] Global objects always use static allocation, regardless of whether the static keyword appears in their declaration.

TABLE 11-2   Types of Memory Allocation Available in C

Method	Object Is Created ...	Object Is Initialized ...	Object Is Destroyed ...
Automatic	Each time the program enters the *function* in which it is declared	If specified in the declaration, initialization occurs *each* time the program enters the *block*	*Each* time the function *returns*
Static	*Once*: When the program is first loaded into memory	*Once*: Just before the program starts to run	*Once*: When the program stops
Dynamic	By calling the library function malloc	By writing executable statements that modify its content	By calling the library function free

created and destroyed, and thus determines whether the management of their memory is automatic or the programmer's responsibility.

A region of memory is allocated to an object when it is created. C offers three basic types of memory allocation as summarized in Table 11-2: *static*, *automatic*, and *dynamic*. Each was designed for a different purpose; understanding their behavior is crucial in order to take advantage of their capability.

11.4   AUTOMATIC ALLOCATION

Automatic memory allocation is the *default* allocation method inside functions. Although not required, the keyword auto may be added as a declaration prefix to make the allocation method explicit.

Automatic objects are created when memory is allocated for them from the stack; this occurs on *every* entry to their containing *function*. If initialization is specified, it occurs on every entry to the containing *block*. For example, the automatic object called "y" in Figure 11-3 is created on entry to function "foo," and is initialized on every iteration of the for loop. The memory location of an automatic object remains fixed during the execution of the function, but the object is destroyed and its memory released on return from the function; this allows the same region of memory to be reused when needed for other automatic objects. Functions may return the *value*[2] of an automatic variable, but should not return its *address,* since the variable no longer exists once the function has returned.

The obvious *disadvantage* of automatic allocation is the lack of persistence. That is, an automatic object declared within the body of a function will not retain its value from one invocation of the function to another. The *advantage* of automatic allocation is conservation of memory through reuse. More importantly, the program manages the reuse of this memory resource automatically in a manner that is transparent to the programmer.

---

[2]Actually, a copy of the value is returned, since the memory containing the original is released.

C	Assembly
```void foo(void) { int32_t x[10]; ... for (;;) { int32_t y[10] = {10}; ... } }```	```foo PUSH {LR} ;preserve return address SUB SP,SP,#80 ;allocate both x and y on stack ... L1: ;top of the for loop ... MOV R0,SP ;R0 ← address of y LDR R1,=40 ;R1 ← number of bytes to zero BL memclr ;library routine to clear memory ;body of for loop ... B L1 L2: ADD SP,SP,#80 ;release allocated memory POP {LR} ;restore return address RET ;return from function```

FIGURE 11-3   Creation, initialization, and destruction of automatic objects.

11.4.1 Storage Class "Register"

The keyword *register* is an explicit alternative to the explicit or implicit use of keyword auto. The only difference is that the compiler *attempts* to allocate one of the registers of the CPU rather than a region of memory and thus provides faster access to the object. In effect, the keyword allows a programmer to tell the compiler something about how to optimize the code. Register allocation may sound tempting to a real-time programmer who needs maximum performance, but compiler technology has improved tremendously since C was first introduced, and the need for programmer-assisted optimization is no longer as important.

Knowing when to register-allocate an object is deceptively nonobvious. Register allocation is local within each function. When one function calls another, there is no way to know what the second function may do to the registers, and so all register variables must be preserved in (and later restored from) memory during the call. The resulting overhead often offsets any performance gain. Worse yet, it is not always obvious when such function calls occur. Some deceptively simply C operators are actually implemented by library routines that are called to evaluate expressions in which no function call appears.

Use of the keyword register does not guarantee that a register will be allocated. The C language allows compilers to simply ignore the keyword and use automatic memory allocation instead. Of course requests to register-allocate (large) aggregate objects will fail because their size is normally larger than the number of bits in a register. More significant is the fact that most CPUs have a very limited number of registers available for allocation (perhaps two or three); once they have been allocated, additional requests must be converted to automatic allocation.

11.5   STATIC ALLOCATION

Static objects are allocated (and possibly initialized) *once* when the program is first loaded into memory. Their location in memory never changes during the entire execution of the program, and thus static objects are not destroyed until the program terminates.

The *advantage* of static allocation is persistence of values. Unlike objects that use automatic allocation, a value stored in a static object will remain from one execution of a function to another.

The *disadvantage* of static allocation is the inability to reclaim the memory for other purposes once the object is no longer needed. Extensive use of static objects can thus result in programs that require lots of memory. An inexperienced programmer's attempt to avoid dealing with scope restrictions by declaring all objects global will ultimately produce very "fat" programs.

Every global object inherently uses static allocation. Inexperienced programmers will also sometimes make an object global just to retain its value from one invocation of a function to the next. However, a better way to accomplish the same thing without global scope *may* be to simply add the keyword static to the declaration of a local object, as shown in Figure 11-4.

Bad	Good
``/*   These two objects are */
/*   global to this file!   */

unsigned total = 0 ;
unsigned count = 0 ;

void Enter_Score(unsigned score)
    {
    total += score ;
    count++ ;
    printf("average score = %u\n",
            total / count) ;
    }``` | ```void Enter_Score(unsigned score)
    {
    /* These two objects are   */
    /* local to this function!   */

    static unsigned total = 0 ;
    static unsigned count = 0 ;

    total += score ;
    count++ ;
    printf("average score = %u\n",
            total / count) ;
    }``` |

FIGURE 11-4   Good and bad ways to retain a value.

Problems can occur, however, when static objects are modified by more than one thread. It is natural to be concerned about this possibility when the object is global. However, moving them into the local scope of a function does not prevent it. If you are not used to using static locals, you may be tempted to keep your static objects global rather than learning *why* restricting their scope does not help. But the real problem has nothing to do with their scope; rather, it is the fact that they are static. Thus, the first priority should be to try to change their allocation method to automatic or dynamic if possible.

11.6   THREE PROGRAMS TO DISTINGUISH STATIC FROM AUTOMATIC

Sometimes it is easier to understand something that you have seen in action. The output from the three programs shown in Example 11-2 provides a bit of insight into how static and automatic allocation differ with respect to creation, initialization, and destruction of objects.

```
#include <stdio.h>

void f1()
    {
       auto int a ;
    static int s ;

    printf(" &auto = %08X\n", &a) ;
    printf("&static = %08X\n", &s) ;
    }

void f2() { auto int x; f1() ; }

int main() { f1() ; f2() ; f1() ; return 0 ;}
```

Program Output:

```
  &auto = 0008E8BC
&static = 0000BA28

  &auto = 0008E89C
&static = 0000BA28

  &auto = 0008E8BC
&static = 0000BA28
```

EXAMPLE 11-2   Creation of automatic versus static objects.

11.6.1 Object Creation

Example 11-2 is intended to provide some insight into how object *creation* differs between objects with automatic allocation and those with static allocation. The program consists of functions main, f1, and f2. Function f1 declares two integer objects: one called "a" with automatic allocation and another called "s" with static allocation. Function f1 is called three times: first by the main program, then by f2 (which is called by main), and then from main again.

In all three cases, the address of the static object "s" remains unchanged, which indicates that there is a single instance of "s" whose location in memory remains fixed throughout the entire execution of the program.

The address of the automatic object "a," however, changes when f1 is called indirectly by f2 as opposed to when it is called directly by the main program. Therefore, its location clearly does *not* remain fixed, which indicates that it is created (and destroyed) several times during the execution of the program.

11.6.2 Object Initialization

Example 11-3 is intended to provide some insight into how object *initialization* differs between objects with automatic allocation and those with static allocation. The program consists of functions main, f1, f2, f3, and f4.

In functions f1 and f2, the allocation method used for the integer object has no effect on the function behavior. In both functions, the integer is reset to zero each time the function is invoked by an executable statement in the body of the function.

```
#include <stdio.h>                              Program Output:

int f1() {  auto int a ; a = 0; return ++a ; }  f1(): 1 1 1
int f2() {static int s ; s = 0; return ++s ; }  f2(): 1 1 1
                                                f3(): 1 1 1
int f3() {  auto int a = 0 ; return ++a ; }     f4(): 3 2 1
int f4() {static int s = 0 ; return ++s ; }

int main()
    {
        printf("f1(): %d %d %d\n", f1(), f1(), f1()) ;
        printf("f2(): %d %d %d\n", f2(), f2(), f2()) ;
        printf("f3(): %d %d %d\n", f3(), f3(), f3()) ;
        printf("f4(): %d %d %d\n", f4(), f4(), f4()) ;
        return 0 ;
    }
```

EXAMPLE 11-3   Initialization of automatic versus static objects.[3]

Functions f3 and f4 are similar except that the initial value of the integer is speci-fied in its declaration. This kind of initialization is performed at the time of object cre-ation; whether object creation happens when the function is invoked or when the program is first loaded into memory (i.e., before execution) depends on the memory-allocation method used by the object.

Automatic objects are created each time execution enters their containing block and are destroyed on its exit from the block. This means that the integer "a" in function f3 is created and *reinitialized* each time f3 is called, as evidenced by its constant return value of 1.

Static objects, however, are created (and initialized) only once, when the program is first loaded into memory. Thus, the first invocation of f4 returns 1, the second returns 2, and so on.

11.6.3 Object Destruction

Example 11-4 is intended to provide some insight into how object *destruction* differs between objects with automatic allocation and those with static allocation. Unfortunately, the term "object destruction" is a bit misleading. What actually happens when an object is "destroyed" is that its memory is made *available* for other uses; the object's data may continue to reside in that memory for some time until the memory is allocated for some other purpose and then written into.

---

[3] The C programming language allows the order in which function parameters are evaluated to vary from one compiler to another. Although the sequence of values shown in the fourth line of output in Example 11-3 indicates that the parameters were processed right to left, other compilers may process them left to right, causing the values to appear in the opposite order.

```
#include <stdio.h>

int *f1()
      {
      static int s = 12345 ;
      return &s ;
      }

int *f2()
      {
      auto int a = 12345 ;
      return &a ;
      }

void Demo(int *(*f)())
      {
      int *p = (*f)() ;
      printf("Address=%08X, Contents=%d\n", p, *p) ;
      printf("Address=%08X, Contents=%d\n", p, *p) ;
      printf("\n") ;
      }

int main() { Demo(f1) ; Demo(f2) ; return 0 ;}
```

Program Output:

```
Address=0008E88C, Contents=12345
Address=0008E88C, Contents=12345

Address=0000AECC, Contents=12345
Address=0000AECC, Contents=583820
```

EXAMPLE 11-4   Destruction of automatic versus static objects.

The program shown in Example 11-4 consists of functions main, f1, f2, and Demo. Functions f1 and f2 each create an integer object, initialize it to the value 12345, and return the object's address; the only difference is that the object created by f1 uses static allocation, while the one created by f2 uses automatic allocation.

Function Demo stores the object's address returned by either f1 or f2 in pointer "p" and accesses the contents of that location by dereferencing the pointer. Then the address and contents are displayed using a call to library function printf. Note that there are two identical calls to printf within Demo. When Demo uses f1, the two printf calls display identical values for the address (p) and its contents (*p). However, when Demo uses f2, the first and second printf calls display different values for the content.

The automatic object in f2 is released (destroyed) and its memory made available for other purposes when f2 returns. The memory has not yet been reallocated or its value overwritten when it is retrieved (*p) as a parameter to be passed to the first printf call.[4] However, during the execution of printf, that memory is reused, as evidenced by the modified value displayed by the second printf. The static object, however, does not get released until the program terminates, and thus its value remains unaffected.

---

[4] Although unlikely, it *is* possible that the memory released on return from f2 might be reallocated and overwritten by a hardware-interrupt service routine that happens to be triggered just before calling printf.

11.7   DYNAMIC ALLOCATION

Dynamic objects are allocated from a region of memory known as the *heap* using the library function malloc. The *sizeof* operator is normally used to determine the amount of memory required to hold an object of the desired type, and this result is provided as a parameter to malloc. An unused portion of the heap large enough to accommodate the request is allocated, and a pointer to the beginning of the allocated memory is returned.[5] This pointer is usually recast and saved in a pointer to data of the desired type.

When the object is no longer needed, it is the programmer's responsibility to release the memory by calling the library function free, giving it the same pointer value that was originally provided by malloc. Until released, the location of the object in memory never changes.[6]

The use of malloc and free is illustrated in Figure 11-5. Although the figure suggests that an object's lifetime is a range of lines of code, it is a dynamic property—not a property of program syntax. Lifetime is more correctly understood in terms of elapsed time and as a consequence of program *behavior*. In fact, the pointer may be passed from function to function, with malloc and free invoked within different functions or even in different threads.

```
#include <stdlib.h>                    /* required to use malloc and free. */
#define NULL        ((void*) 0)        /* may not be defined in stdlib.h   */
...
typedef ... ANYTYPE ;
...
ANYTYPE *p ;

p = (ANYTYPE *) malloc( sizeof(ANYTYPE) ) ; /* object created */
if (p == NULL) Error("Insufficient heap space") ;
      ...
      ...   } The object is initialized and used here via the pointer p.      Object
      ...                                                                     Lifetime.
free(p) ;            /* object destroyed */
```

FIGURE 11-5   Dynamic memory allocation.

The *advantage* of dynamic allocation is that it offers both the persistence of static allocation and memory conservation through reuse. The *disadvantage* is the burden it places on the programmer to balance each call to malloc with a corresponding call to free. Failure to do so can result in a slow "memory leak" that can be very difficult to debug.

11.7.1 Fragmentation

After a large number of calls to malloc and free, the allocated blocks in the heap may become separated by free blocks that are too small to be useful. This *fragmentation* can

---

[5] When insufficient heap space is available, malloc returns a null pointer as an indication of failure.

[6] The realloc function is used when the programmer wishes to change the size of the allocated block. If more memory space is required, realloc may relocate the block to a larger area of the heap.

ultimately cause an allocation request to fail even though the total amount of free memory available is sufficient. Unfortunately, malloc cannot simply rearrange the heap to combine the free blocks, because the allocated blocks must remain stationary.

Worst-case fragmentation occurs when the allocated blocks are small and have large free blocks in between. Given enough blocks, the largest single free block may be only a small fraction of the total amount of free memory. Whether this actually happens depends on the variety of block sizes and the sequence in which they are allocated and released during program execution.

The probability of allocation failure due to fragmentation increases with the number and range of different block sizes. It has been suggested[7] that embedded applications use far fewer block sizes than desktop applications, since file and string handling are much less common in embedded systems.

In most cases, the pragmatic solution is simply to use a heap that is "somewhat" larger than required, and extensive testing to verify that the size is large enough. However, embedded applications that must guarantee failure-free operation over a long period of operation may need to consider other techniques to manage memory.

11.7.2 Memory Allocation Pools

One common strategy for eliminating heap fragmentation is to use allocation pools. A memory allocation pool is a collection of equal-size memory blocks. Multiple pools are usually employed, with each pool using a different block size. Memory is allocated from the pool with the smallest block size that satisfies the request. An entire block is always allocated, even if it means allocating more than the size requested.

Implementation of pool-based allocation schemes is usually best left to the application programmer. The programmer's knowledge of the application places him or her in a unique position to determine the optimum block sizes, number of pools, and blocks per pool. Once determined, the entire memory required for each pool is then preallocated from the heap at the beginning of program execution. Pool memory is never returned to the heap unless its block size is no longer required. Allocation and release of blocks are managed by functions layered on top of the normal heap-management routines.

11.8 AUTOMATIC ALLOCATION WITH VARIABLE SIZE (alloca)

The less we use the heap, the less we have to worry about fragmentation. The most common reason to allocate dynamic memory from the heap is for objects whose sizes are not known until execution time. If this object is needed only as a temporary during the execution of a function, then we can avoid the heap by allocating automatic memory from the stack using the library function alloca,[8] as shown in Figure 11-6.

---

[7] Niall Murphy, "Memory Management," Embedded Systems, Chicago, IL., Feb. 28 to Mar. 2, 2000.

[8] Not all C compiler run-time libraries provide alloca.

```
FILE *OpenFile(char *name, char *ext, char *mode)
        {
        int size = strlen(name) + strlen(ext) + 2 ;
        char *filespec = (char *) alloca(size) ;
        sprintf(filespec, "%s.%s", name, ext) ;
        return fopen(filespec, mode) ;
        }
```

FIGURE 11-6   Allocating automatic memory with all alloca.

There are other *advantages* to using alloca. First, it is extremely fast. Unlike the heap, there is no list of blocks to be searched for an unallocated block of sufficient size. In most cases, compilers simply translate the alloca call into a single machine instruction that merely adjusts the value held in the stack-pointer register. Second, there is no need to explicitly release memory that has been allocated with alloca. Since a function return always restores the stack pointer, any automatic memory allocated within a function is inherently released, completely eliminating any chance of a memory leak. This is especially convenient when there are multiple return statements within the function.

Of course, using alloca does have some *disadvantages*: Memory allocated with alloca does not persist across functions (i.e., you cannot allocate it in one function and release it in another), and thus it is not a replacement for dynamic memory allocated with malloc. But perhaps the most significant disadvantage of alloca is that there is no indication of failure when sufficient stack space is not available to satisfy a request. Instead, the contents of the stack are simply overwritten, and the application will most likely crash.

Since alloca modifies the stack pointer, you must be careful not to call it inside the argument list of another call, as in f(a, alloca(n), b). Doing so causes unpredictable results because it modifies the stack pointer in the middle of pushing the function arguments onto the stack.

11.8.1 Variable-Size Arrays

Another way to achieve what alloca accomplishes that is supported by some C compilers is to use variable-size arrays (VSA), as shown in Figure 11-7. Rather than declaring an array with fixed dimensions, some compilers allow those dimensions to be computed at run-time. In most cases, a VSA can be used as a direct replacement to calling alloca and provides the additional advantage of a cleaner syntax.

```
FILE *OpenFile(char *name, char *ext, char *mode)
        {
        char filespec[strlen(name) + strlen(ext) + 2] ;
        sprintf(filespec, "%s.%s", name, ext) ;
        return fopen(filespec, mode) ;
        }
```

FIGURE 11-7   Allocating automatic memory by using VSAs.

Besides the difference in syntax, however, there is also a subtle difference in lifetime. Function alloca allocates memory on every call, but it does not release *any* memory that it has allocated until the function that called alloca returns. VSAs, on the other hand, allocate memory on entry to their block and release it on exit from the block. Thus, the alloca call on the left in Figure 11-8 accumulates a total of 10 allocated blocks of n bytes each, whereas the VSA on the right never has more than a single block of n bytes allocated at any one time. That is, an alloca call appearing within a loop has no VSA equivalent.

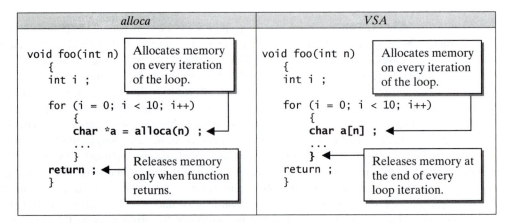

FIGURE 11-8   The subtle difference between memory allocated with alloca versus VSAs.

11.9   RECURSIVE FUNCTIONS AND MEMORY ALLOCATION

A recursive function is one that calls itself, either directly or indirectly. For example, the function shown in Figure 11-9 outputs a number as a sequence of hex characters; the digits are calculated as the remainders of division by 16, and recursion is used so that these digits are produced in the proper left-to-right order.

Function parameters, like other temporary objects, use automatic memory allocation. Since parameters are allocated on entry to the function block, they exist until the function returns. Each time the function calls itself, another set of parameter values is calculated, and another set of locations in memory is allocated to hold them. Thus, at the deepest nested level of a sequence of recursive calls, a number of different parameter sets will have been created and will coexist. The memory allocated for each set is released as the function backs out of these levels by returning from the calls in reverse order (Figure 11-9).

In contrast, however, note that static allocation is used for the character array of hex digits in Figure 11-10. This array converts a small number in the range 0 to 15 into its corresponding hex character by using the number as an index into the array. Making the array *static* guarantees that only a *single* copy exists, since static objects are allocated only once, when the program is loaded into memory.

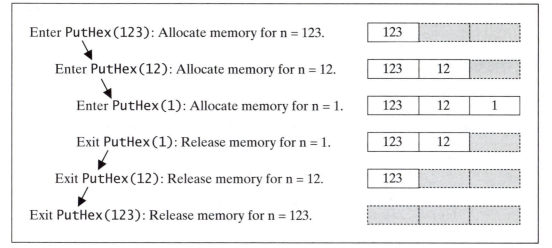

Enter `PutHex(123)`: Allocate memory for n = 123.

Enter `PutHex(12)`: Allocate memory for n = 12.

Enter `PutHex(1)`: Allocate memory for n = 1.

Exit `PutHex(1)`: Release memory for n = 1.

Exit `PutHex(12)`: Release memory for n = 12.

Exit `PutHex(123)`: Release memory for n = 123.

FIGURE 11-9   Recursive calls and memory allocation for parameters.

```
void PutHex(unsigned n)
        {
        static const char digits[] = "0123456789ABCDEF" ;

        if (n >= 16) PutHex(n / 16) ; /* display most significant digits first */
        putchar(digits[n % 16]) ; /* then display least significant digit. */
        }
```

FIGURE 11-10   Recursive function to display a number in hex format.

PROBLEMS

1. Fill each cell of the following table with the correct choice:

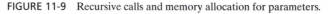

	auto	static	VSA	dynamic	alloca
Created (allocated) when? *(Program load, Entry to function, Entry to block, or Determined by programmer)*					
How many object instances are created by multiple invocations of a function that uses an object of this kind? *(Single or Multiple)*					
Destroyed (released) when? *(Program termination, Return from function, Exit from block, or Determined by programmer)*					
Initialized when? *(Program load, Entry to function, Entry to block, or Only by assignment statement)*					
Allocated where? *(Stack, Heap, or Data segment)*					

2. The code that follows compiles without fatal errors, but does not execute as intended. Provide a corrected version.

```
int *AddressOfCopy(int value)
    {
    int copy = value;
    return &copy;
    }
```

3. For each of the following, your answer should be one or more of the following kinds of memory allocation: automatic, register, static, dynamic, alloca, VSAs, or none of these. Which of the following memory-allocation methods
   (a) Support conservation of memory through reuse?
   (b) Are possible outside of all functions?
   (c) Perform initialization after program load but before execution?
   (d) May cause the same object to be initialized more than once during execution?
   (e) Require calling a function to allocate memory?
   (f) Destroy objects transparently during program execution?
   (g) May be used to maintain a value in an object from one invocation to the next of the same function?
   (h) Can lead to a "memory leak" if used improperly?
   (i) Prevent application of the "address of" operator to an object?
   (j) Is the default inside a pair of curly braces?
   (k) May be silently converted to automatic allocation by the compiler?
   (l) Require that the allocated object be referenced indirectly through a pointer?
   (m) Are not available inside a function?
   (n) Are used for function parameters?

4. Which of the following three programs requires the most memory?
   (a) `void f1(void) {auto char a[100000]; }`
       `void f2(void) {auto char a[100000]; }`
       `int main(void) { f1(); f2(); return  0; }`

   (b) `void f1(void) {static char  a[100000]; }`
       `void f2(void) {static char  a[100000]; }`
       `int main(void) { f1(); f2(); return  0; }`

   (c) `int main(void)`
       ```
           {
           char *p;
           p = (char *) malloc(100000);  free(p);
           p = (char *) malloc(100000);  free(p);
           p = (char *) malloc(100000);  free(p);
           }
       ```

5. Which of the following three programs requires the most memory?
   (a) `void f1(void) {auto char  a[100000]; }`
       `void f2(void) {auto char  a[100000]; }`
       `int main(void) { f1(); f2();  return 0; }`

   (b) `void f1(void) {auto char  a[100000]; }`
       `void f2(void) {auto char  a[100000]; f1(); }`
       `int main(void) { f2(); return 0; }`

(c)
```
void f1(void) {auto char a[100000]; }
void f2(void) {auto char b[100000]; }
void f3(void) {auto char  c[100000]; }
int main(void) { f1(); f2(); f3(); return 0; }
```

6. Consider the C program shown below. The amount of memory allocated from the stack grows and shrinks as statements cause memory to be allocated or released. How much stack space is allocated as the program reaches each of the numbered points shown below? *Note*: Your answers should be given as multiples of 1,000 bytes.

```
int main(void)                      void f1(int bytes)
    {                                   {
    ❶                                   static int k ;
    f1(1000) ;                          for (k = 1; k <= 2; k++)
    ❺                                       {
    if (...)                                char array[k*bytes] ;
        {                                   ❷
        char array[1000] ;                  }
        ❻                               ❸
        f2(1000) ;                      for (k = 1; k <= 2; k++)
        }                                   {
    ❿                                       char *p = alloca(k*bytes) ;
    return 0 ;`                             ❹
    }                                       }
                                        }
```

```
void f2(int bytes)
    {
    static int k ;
    for (k = 1; k <= 2; k++)
        {
        char *p = alloca(k * bytes) ;
        ❼
        }
    ❽
    for (k = 1; k <= 2; k++)
        {
        char array[k * bytes] ;
        ❾
        }
    }
```

7. What does each of the four printf statements print?

```
int foo(void)         int bar(void)          int main(void)
    {                     {                       {
    auto int x = 0;       static int x = 0;       printf("%d", foo());
    x = x + 1;            x = x + 1;              printf("%d", foo());
    return x;             return x;               printf("%d", bar());
    }                     }                       printf("%d", bar());
                                                  return 0;
                                                  }
```

8. Compile and run the following program, then answer the questions that follow, based on the output of the program:

```
#include <stdio.h>
int main(void)
    {
    go(3);
    return 0;
    }


void go(int n)
    {
    static int s = 0;
    auto int a = ++s;
    show("Enter", &n, &a, &s) ;
    if (n != 0) go(n - 1);
    show("Leave", &n, &a, &s) ;
    }


void show(char *label, int *pn, int *pa, int *ps)
    {
    printf("%s: Object Address     Contents\n", label) ;
    printf(" n %08X %d\n", pn, *pn) ;
    printf(" a %08X %d\n", pa, *pa) ;
    printf(" s %08X %d\n", ps,  *ps) ;
    printf("\n") ;
    }
```

(a) What is the maximum number of instances of the function parameter "n" that coexist at any one time during the execution of the program?

(b) What is the maximum number of instances of static integer "s" that coexist at any one time during the execution of the program?

(c) What is the maximum number of instances of automatic integer "a" that coexist at any one time during the execution of the program?

(d) Which two of the three objects ("n," "s," and "a") are allocated from the same region of memory?

9. What does each of the six printf statements print?

```
int x;
void one(void) { int x; x = 1; }
void two(int x) { x = 2; }
void three(void) { x = 2; }
void four (int *p) {*p = 3; }
int main(void)
    {
    printf("%d", x);
    x = 4; one();
    printf("%d", x);
    x = 5; two(x);
    printf("%d", x);
    x = 6;
        {
        int x = 7; three();
        printf("%d", x);
        }
    printf("%d", x);
    x = 8; four(&x);
    printf("%d", x);
    return 0;
    }
```

10. Rearrange the following code so that the scope of all variables is restricted as much as possible:

```
#include <stdio.h>
int old_value = 0;
int average;
void f(int value)
    {
    if (value != old_value)
        {
        average = (value + old_value) / 2;
        printf("average = %d\n", average);
        }
    old_value = value;
    }
```

11. Consider the C program shown below. The amount of memory allocated from the stack grows and shrinks as statements cause memory to be allocated or released. How much stack space is allocated as the program reaches each of the numbered points shown below?

```c
int main(void)
    {
    static int k = 500 ;
    static char *p ;
    ❶
    if (1)
        {
        char b[4*k] ;
        ❷
        }
    ❸
    if (1)
        {
        char a[1000] ;
        ❹
        p = alloca(8*k) ;
        ❺
        }
    ❻
    return 0 ;
    }
```

12. Which lines of the following C function cause the compiler to produce an error message (not just a warning message)?

```c
int *f(int p)
    {
    register int r1 = 0;
    register int r2 = r1 + 1;
    auto int a1 = 0;
    auto int a2 = a1 + 1;
    static int s1 = 0;
    static int s2 = s1 + 1;
    if (r1 == 0) return &r1;
    if (a1 == 0) return &a1;
    if (s1 == 0) return &s1;
    return &p;
    }
```

C H A P T E R   1 2

Shared Memory

When two or more asynchronous instruction sequences access the same data, that data is called *shared memory*. Access to shared memory must be carefully coordinated or else data corruption can occur. Minimizing the use of shared memory, identifying what data *must* be shared, and then protecting it are some of the greatest challenges of the multithreaded programming style that is the cornerstone of real-time embedded systems.

The term *asynchronous* means that there is no predictable time relationship among the various instruction sequences. One sequence may execute a portion of its instructions only to be prematurely interrupted so that some portion of another sequence may execute. The actual point of transition between the two sequences is not predictable. If there is data that both sequences must access, then the program's freedom to switch from one instruction sequence to another must somehow be restricted so that the access becomes *synchronized*.

Conventional desktop application programs are usually designed as a single thread of code. Only the interrupt-service routines (ISRs) execute asynchronously with respect to the application. Although shared memory is used to buffer data between the ISRs and the operating system, we rely on the latter to synchronize the access. Within the application program, all data is allocated, initialized, used, and released by a single thread of code. Data used in this manner is said to be *private* to the thread.

Embedded software, however, is I/O-intensive and often multithreaded with many requirements and opportunities (intentional or otherwise) for shared memory. Shared memory is essential in order to allow inter-thread or inter-task communication and coordination, so we cannot simply eliminate its use.

Besides its propensity for data corruption, shared memory also increases program complexity. Threads are easier to design, understand, and debug when they are designed to be as independent of other threads as possible. Each occurrence of shared memory establishes one more relationship between threads, thus reducing their independence.

12.1 RECOGNIZING SHARED OBJECTS

Whether an object's data *can* be shared is determined neither by its scope nor by its memory allocation method, but only by *how* the object is used. There are three mechanisms that can allow an object's data to become shared.

12.1.1 Shared Global Data

A global object referenced by name from within the source code of multiple threads is the easiest kind of shared memory to recognize. You should always try to minimize the number of global objects anyway, whether your program is multithreaded or not, because global objects create linkages between functions and thus increase program complexity.

12.1.2 Shared Private Data

If one thread gives the address of one of its private objects to another thread, then that object can be accessed by both threads and is no longer private. Neither changing the object's scope nor changing its memory allocation method can eliminate this form of shared memory.

12.1.3 Shared Functions

A shared function is one that is called by more than one thread; any function called by a shared function is also a shared function. Any static object referenced within a shared function is thus a form of shared memory. It does not matter if the object's scope is global or local. Since there is only a single instance of the object, its content is inherently shared by all threads that call a function that references it.

Most programmers do not expect objects that are local to a function to be shared memory. However, if those objects are statically allocated and the function is called from more than one thread (either directly or indirectly), sharing will occur and can be extremely difficult to recognize. Do not forget that library functions are more likely to be used in multiple threads. Any functions called from more than one thread should be considered shared functions, and so it becomes critical to be sure that they do not manipulate any static objects.

12.2   REENTRANT FUNCTIONS

In multithreaded software, several different threads may be executing concurrently. In some systems, the context switch from one thread to another can thus occur at almost any time. If a context switch occurs in the middle of a shared function, then that function might be reentered (much like recursive functions) even though no recursive functions exist.

As illustrated in Figure 12-1, thread A might be in the middle of executing the strstr library function only to be preempted by thread B. It is then possible that the thread B may also call (and perhaps return from) strstr before thread A is resumed.

In multithreaded programs, functions called from more than one thread must use separate *thread-specific* instances of any data that should not be shared with other threads. This happens automatically when only automatic or dynamic allocation is used within the function and creates a class of *reentrant* functions that are inherently *thread-safe* because every entry to the function creates new instances of its objects. Static objects, however, can never be thread-specific, since they have only a single instance.

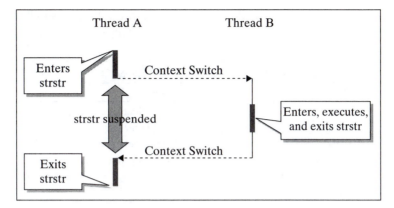

FIGURE 12-1   Preemptive context switching requiring reentrancy.

If one of the parameters passed to a reentrant function happens to be a pointer, then a situation is created that *allows* (but does not force) the function to modify an external shared object. This does not mean that the function is no longer reentrant; rather, it is simply a problem with the *manner* in which the function has been used, and we must examine the call to correct any problem.

12.3 READ-ONLY DATA

Not all shared data affect the complexity of multithreaded programs in the same way. Data corruption occurs when shared data is modified. If the shared data is read but never written, then no data corruption can occur. A table of constants would be used in this manner and is considered an example of *read-only* data.

It is always difficult to anticipate how the use of an object may change as a program matures. Program modifications may one day add code that modifies data that was once read only. For example, configuration data that was once hard-coded into a program may one day be loaded from a file during program initialization.

At a minimum, you should add a comment to any shared read-only data so that you will remember that it can be ignored when trying to locate the cause of a shared data problem. But a better way is to syntactically protect the data against modification by declaring the object with the type qualifier "const."

12.3.1 Type Qualifier "const"

The keyword const is used to declare that an object's value may not be modified by the program—that is, that its value is "read only." This provides a bit of defensive programming since the compiler will then report any attempt to directly modify the object as a syntax violation. The declaration statement that creates a const object must include an initial value, since no subsequent attempt to set its value is allowed.

As compared to defining a macro to represent a constant value, note that a const declaration makes the data type explicit:

```
#define AGE 35         /* "AGE" is merely text to be replaced    */
const int age = 35;    /* "age" is a signed int with value 35    */
```

The const keyword allows a number of interesting possibilities when used in the declaration of a pointer, as suggested by the examples shown in Table 12-1.

TABLE 12-1   Sample Use of the const Type Qualifier

Declaration	Interpretation
int total;	"total" is a (modifiable) int.
const int year = 1999;	"year" is a read-only int.
const int *p;	"p" is a (modifiable) pointer that points to a read-only int.
int * const p = &total;	"p" is a read-only pointer that points to a (modifiable) int.
const int * const p = &year;	"p" is a read-only pointer that points to a read-only int.

Note that attaching the const attribute to an object does not mean that its value cannot be modified—it is simply a syntactic restriction enforced only during compilation. It still remains possible to circumvent this restriction during program execution.

12.4   CODING PRACTICES TO AVOID

Static objects are most commonly problematic when they are *modified* within shared functions. However, there are two good reasons why it is always a good idea to try to avoid modifying static objects in *any* function—even in those that are called by only a single thread:

1. First, you cannot determine whether a function is shared simply by checking whether it is called by name in more than one thread. Finding calls in multiple threads is a sufficient, but not necessary, condition of sharing. That is because when a shared function calls another function, the second function is implicitly shared as well.

2. Second, we all strive to be productive programmers, and thus try to avoid "reinventing the wheel" by reusing existing code as much as we can. But this sometimes means that an unshared function previously used in only one thread may one day be used in multiple threads.

We cannot eliminate the problems of static objects by not using them. Sometimes they are just plain necessary. But by avoiding certain coding practices, we can eliminate the most common problems. The following are two typical examples of functions that modify local static objects and should be avoided.

12.4.1 Functions That Keep Internal State in Local Static Objects

Figure 12-2 illustrates a typical use of the strtok function. In the first call, a pointer to a sentence is passed as the first parameter to strtok; subsequent calls pass a null pointer instead. With a little thought, you will soon realize that a copy of the initial pointer must be held inside strtok and then updated in subsequent calls, to keep track of the current position within the sentence. To preserve the value of this pointer from one

```
                char *strtok(char *str1, char *str2) ;
```

The strtok function locates tokens (i.e., substrings) within the string str1. The string str2 defines a set of one or more characters that act as token separators. The following example separates the words of a sentence and prints each word on a line by itself:

```
char *sentence = " ... any English sentence ... " ;
char *word ;

for (word = sentence; word = strtok(word, " ,;.?!"); word = NULL)
   {
   printf("%s\n", word) ;
   }
```

FIGURE 12-2   Typical usage of the strtok library function.

invocation of strtok to the next, the pointer must use static allocation, and this means that only a single copy of the pointer exists. But this will cause obvious problems when more than one thread tries to use this function!

We now know that library function strtok keeps track of local *state* information that is used the next time it is called. A sample source-code version of strtok is given in Figure 12-3, showing the use of a static local variable called state to hold this information.

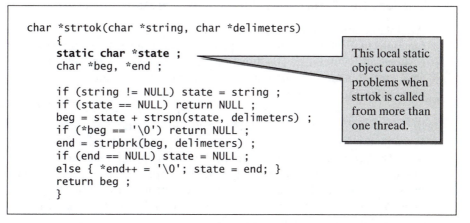

FIGURE 12-3   Library function strtok with problematic local static object.

A thread-safe (reentrant) version of strtok (called strtok_r) solves the problem by replacing the local static pointer by a thread-specific object created by the caller and accessed by the function via a parameter as shown in Figure 12-4.

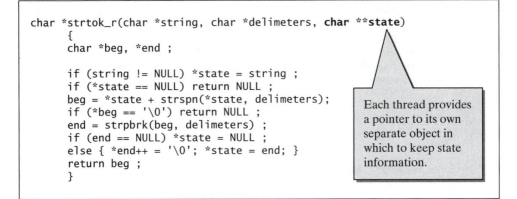

```
char *strtok_r(char *string, char *delimeters, char **state)
    {
    char *beg, *end ;

    if (string != NULL) *state = string ;
    if (*state == NULL) return NULL ;
    beg = *state + strspn(*state, delimeters);
    if (*beg == '\0') return NULL ;
    end = strpbrk(beg, delimeters) ;
    if (end == NULL) *state = NULL ;
    else { *end++ = '\0'; *state = end; }
    return beg ;
    }
```

Each thread provides a pointer to its own separate object in which to keep state information.

FIGURE 12-4   Library function strtok_r replaces local static by a third parameter.

Another example of a library function with similar problems caused by keeping a local static object is the random number generator, rand. A sequence of calls to rand produces a sequence of pseudo-random numbers. A companion function srand initializes the sequence using a starting "seed" value; for any one seed, the sequence of numbers produced by rand is deterministic and thus repeatable. However, if multiple threads call rand (or srand), the sequence returned within any one thread will no longer be deterministic. This may not be acceptable in certain situations.

12.4.2 Functions That Return the Address of a Local Static Object

Another coding practice that causes problems in multithreaded programs is the use of functions that return the address of a local static object. An example of such a function is shown in Figure 12-5. This function combines a string and an integer to form a 12-character filename. The filename is prepared in a local static buffer whose address is returned as the value of the function.

Suppose we call this function to prepare a filename to be used in a subsequent file creation. Then, if a second thread calls the same function before we have a chance to create the file, our filename will have been modified.

The problem, of course, is that there is only a single buffer shared by all threads; the solution is to have each thread provide its own separate buffer. In general, there are two ways to accomplish this: (1) let the thread provide the buffer by passing its address as an extra parameter to the function, as shown in Figure 12-6, or (2) allocate the buffer from the heap, as shown in Figure 12-7.

Allocating from the heap eliminates adding a new function parameter but requires that the programmer release the space by an explicit call to library function free when the filename is no longer needed. Having the caller provide the buffer is faster, since we do not have to search for heap space, and it guarantees that the function will not fail when insufficient heap space is available.

```
char *Make_Filename(char *name, int version)
    {
    static char fname_bfr[13] ;

    sprintf(fname_bfr, "%.8s.%03d", name, version) ;
    return fname_bfr ;
    }
```

FIGURE 12-5   Example of a function that returns the address of a local static object.

```
char *Make_Filename(char *name, int version, char *fname_bfr)
    {
    sprintf(fname_bfr, "%.8s.%03d", name, version) ;
    return fname_bfr ;
    }
```

FIGURE 12-6   Function modified to let the caller provide the thread-specific buffer.

```
char *Make_Filename(char *name, int version)
    {
    char *fname_bfr = (char *) malloc(13) ;
    if (fname_bfr == NULL) return NULL ;
    sprintf(fname_bfr, "%.8s.%03d", name, version) ;
    return fname_bfr ;
    }
```

FIGURE 12-7   Function modified to allocate a thread-specific buffer from the heap.

The standard C library contains several functions that return the address of a local static object. These functions include ctime, asctime, localtime, gmtime, getenv, strerror, and tmpnam. Some C compilers provide special versions of these functions that have been modified for use in multithreaded programs. The modified versions usually have a name that appends "r" (for reentrant) onto the end of the original name, as in ctime_r.

12.5 ACCESSING SHARED MEMORY

Let us suppose we have a program that contains shared memory, and that we have decided that it cannot be avoided. For example, a queue to buffer data from the ISR of an input device is shared memory, even if the program is not multithreaded. So how exactly can the queue data structure get corrupted? And how do we synchronize access to the queue so that it is protected?

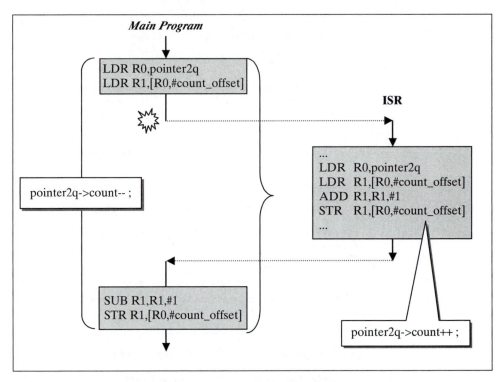

FIGURE 12-8 Corruption of data in shared memory.

Consider the code shown in Figure 12-8. On the left is a sequence of instructions in the main program that has removed an item from a queue and is now decrementing its count. On the right is the ISR that enters data into the queue and then increments its count. If the ISR interrupts the main program in the middle of the instruction sequence that decrements the count, then the ISR's incremented count will be overwritten when it returns to the main program, and the program will not know that a new item has been added to the queue.

For example, suppose that the initial count of items in the queue is 10. When the main program removes an item from the queue, it starts to decrement the count. It loads the old count (10) into register R1 to begin the decrement sequence but is suddenly interrupted by the ISR before it can go any further. All of the registers (including R1) of the main program are saved on the stack upon entry to the ISR. Then the ISR inserts a new item into the queue and increments the queue count from 10 to 11, restores the registers of the main program (including the value of 10 that was in R1), and returns. The main program resumes where it left off, decrements R1 to R9, and then stores that into count, thus overwriting the value of 11 that was put there by the ISR. Note that there was one queue insertion and one deletion, so the queue count should still be 10 when we are done. But because of the shared memory conflict, the count was left at 9!

12.5.1 The Effect of Processor Architecture

The previous example usually applies only to load/store architectures like that of the ARM processor. Other processors often have increment and decrement instructions that can update the count in a single instruction instead of a sequence as shown. Since interrupts occur only *between* instructions, the decrement of the count would then complete before the interrupt was recognized. However, if the count is kept in a 32-bit integer (such as the timer tick count in the IBM-PC) and if the processor registers are only 8 or 16 bits wide, then more than one instruction would be required to increment or decrement the count. In general, any multi-instruction increment or decrement sequence would have to be protected against interruption. Thus you would have to disable interrupts before the increment or decrement operation, and reenable them after, as shown in Figure 12-9.

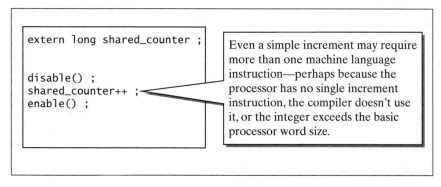

```
extern long shared_counter ;


disable() ;
shared_counter++ ;
enable() ;
```

Even a simple increment may require more than one machine language instruction—perhaps because the processor has no single increment instruction, the compiler doesn't use it, or the integer exceeds the basic processor word size.

FIGURE 12-9   Even simple operations in C must be protected against interruption.

As we have just seen, interrupts can occur not only between two lines of C code, but also between any two machine instructions. As shown in Table 12-2, even the simplest line of C code can produce more than one machine instruction, especially when it involves operands whose sizes exceed the capabilities of single instructions. For 16-bit processors this includes longs, pointers, any floating-point data, and most structures. For 8-bit processors we have to also consider all of the 16-bit operands, such as shorts. Rather than worrying about these differences, it is a good programming practice to just protect access to *any* shared memory—regardless of size. But life is clearly simpler with a 32-bit processor!

ISRs are not the only example of code sequences that execute asynchronously. Preemptive real-time kernels are common in embedded software, and they use ISRs as trigger points to context switch from one thread to another in a multithreaded application. When an interrupt occurs, the ISR may return to a thread other than the one that was interrupted. Since an interrupt can occur at any point during the execution of a thread, all threads are asynchronous with respect to all other threads. As a result, we must worry about objects shared between threads, even if those objects are not accessed by any ISR.

TABLE 12–2   When simple C statements become Critical Sections

Architecture	Data Type	Operand Size	8-bit CPU	16-bit CPU	32-bit CPU
1. "x = 0" in ANY architecture, or **2. "x++" in a non-Load/Store architecture** (a processor in which a single instruction such as ADD can modify memory using read-modify-write. E.g., CISC processors, such as Intel x86.)	char	8 bits			
	short int	16 bits	*		
	long int, or any pointer	32 bits	×	*	
	long long int	64 bits	×	×	×
"x++" in a Load/Store Architecture (a processor in which only Load and Store instructions can access memory. E.g., RISC processors, such as ARM and MIPS.)	Data Type and CPU word size are irrelevant; <u>any</u> read-modify-write update of an object in memory requires executing a sequence of instructions. If the object is accessed by multiple threads, then each access becomes a critical section.				

*The table assumes that a single instruction can store a memory operand no larger than the word size of the processor. However, some processors have instructions that can store a double-length operand (e.g., STRD).

12.5.2 Read-Only and Write-Only Access

Even if you only want to read the current value of a shared object and are not modifying it, you must still protect the read. On a 16-bit processor, if you simply copy the value of a shared 32-bit long, an interrupt might occur between the copying of the least significant 16 bits and that of the most significant 16 bits. If the interrupt causes the value in the long to be modified, then one half of the copied value will be from before the change and the other half from after. One way to protect against this kind of data corruption when the value is used in several places in a code sequence is to disable interrupts, make a local (private) copy, reenable interrupts, and then use the local copy. This technique is shown in Figure 12-10.

```
extern long shared_variable ;
long private_copy ;

/* make a copy with interrupts disabled */

disable() ;
private_copy = shared_variable ;
enable() ;

/* subsequent code can use "private_copy"   */
/* without fear of data corruption.         */
```

FIGURE 12-10   Protecting read-only access to a shared memory object.

12.5.3 Type Qualifier "volatile"

The keyword volatile may be attached as a qualifier on the declaration of any object in C to indicate that its value may be asynchronously modified by mechanisms other than the code in which the declaration appears, such as a change in the status port of a memory-mapped I/O device, or modification of data in memory by direct memory access or an interrupt routine.[1] However, adding the qualifier to their declaration does not eliminate the problems of critical sections discussed earlier.

The keyword is useful because it disables certain compiler optimizations that would otherwise cause the code to fail. For example, the code in Figure 12-11 is intended to access a 64-bit shared variable without disabling interrupts, disabling task switching, or using a mutex. This strategy can actually work in certain situations, such as accessing a shared count value that is updated infrequently relative to the speed of the loop.

```
unit64_t get_Shared(void)
      {
      extern unit64_t shared ;
      unit64_t validated ;

      do validated = shared ;                   /* 1st access */
      while (validated != shared ) ;            /* 2nd access */

      return validated ;
      }
```

FIGURE 12-11   Code to illustrate need for using the volatile qualifier.

However, instead of reading the shared variable out of memory twice as intended, an optimizing compiler is likely to notice that the function never modifies shared, that validated is simply a copy of shared, and thus eliminate the loop altogether, as shown in the middle column of Figure 12-12. As shown in the right-hand column, adding the keyword volatile to the declaration of the shared variable corrects these problems by preventing these optimizations from being applied.

As a precaution, *every* declaration of a shared memory object should use the volatile qualifier. It also suggests defining a macro:

```
#define  SHARED_MEMORY  volatile
```

that helps to document shared objects in a more obvious manner:

```
extern SHARED_MEMORY  long  shared;
```

---

[1] In a preemptive kernel, interrupts can trigger a task switch to another thread, which may modify shared memory.

Un-Optimized	Optimized without volatile	Optimized with volatile
```get_shared:` ```PUSH {R$,R5}` ```L1: ADR R2,shared` ```LORD R4,R5,[R2]` ```MOV R0,R4` ```MOV R1,R5` ```ADR R2,shared` ```LORD R4,R5,[R2]` ```CMP R1,R5` ```BNE L1` ```CMP R0,R4` ```BNE L1` ```POP {R4,R5}` ```BNE L1` ```POP {R4,R5}` ```BX LR```	```get_shared:` ```ADR R2,shared` ```LORD R0,R1,[R2]` ```BX LR` An optimizing compiler has eliminated both the second read of shared from memory, as well as the entire loop!	```get_shared:` ```PUSH {R4,R5}` ```ADR R2,shared` ```L1: LORD R0,R1,[R2]` ```LORD R4,R5,[R2]` ```CMP R1,R5` ```BNE L1` ```CMP R0,R4` ```BNE L1` ```POP {R4,R5}` ```BX LR```

FIGURE 12-12 Assembly code generated by a compiler.

The volatile keyword may also be used in the declaration of a pointer—not because the pointer itself is volatile, but rather because the data it points to is volatile, as in the following:

```
volatile long *pv; /* pointer to shared data */
```

Since the volatile object pointed to by pv is usually at a fixed memory location, it is quite common to make pv a constant pointer, as in the following:

```
volatile long * const pv = <initial-value>;
```

Although perhaps counterintuitive, it is occasionally appropriate to use both volatile and const to describe the object itself:

```
const volatile long * const pv = <initial-value>;
```

The above use of the const and volatile qualifiers has the following effect on code *within the scope of identifier pv*:

1. The first const prevents modification of the object *pv in the source code where it is declared.
2. The volatile qualifier tells the optimizer that the object *pv may be modified by mechanisms outside the scope of identifier pv.
3. The second const disallows any modification of pointer pv.

PROBLEMS

1. TRUE/FALSE:

(a) Data corruption due to shared memory can occur only in multithreaded programs.

(b) Data corruption due to shared memory can occur only in preemptive multithreaded programs.

(c) Shared functions are only those that are called by name from more than one thread.

(d) Functions that modify local static objects are never thread-safe.

(e) Functions that do not modify local static objects are inherently thread-safe.

(f) Recursive functions are inherently reentrant.

(g) Adding the type qualifier "const" to the declaration of a variable prevents it from being modified during program execution.

(h) Adding the type qualifier "volatile" to the declaration of a shared object tells the compiler that another thread may change its value so that the compiler will generate code to protect against data corruption.

2. Which of the following combinations requires additional coding to protect access to shared data? (Circle all that apply.)

(a) An ISR and a thread in a non-preemptive system

(b) An ISR and a thread in a preemptive system

(c) Two threads in a non-preemptive system

(d) Two threads in a preemptive system

(e) Two ISRs

3. Which of the following kinds of memory objects can become shared, even if its address is not explicitly given to another thread? (Circle all that apply.)

(a) Data declared outside all functions

(b) Static memory declared within a function

(c) Automatic memory declared within a function

(d) Dynamic memory allocated from the heap

(e) Function parameters

4. Which of the following types of data are considered thread-specific? (Circle all that apply).

(a) Data declared outside all functions

(b) Static memory declared within a function

(c) Automatic memory declared within a function

(d) Dynamic memory allocated from the heap

(e) Function parameters

5. For which combinations of the following data types and CPU word size is the assignment statement "x = 0;" (where "x" is a shared object) a critical section that must be protected against the possibility of data corruption?

```
Data types: int8_t, int16_t, int32_t, int64_t
CPU word size: 8 bits, 16 bits, 32 bits
```

6. For which combinations of the following data types and CPU word size is the assignment statement "x++;" (where "x" is a shared object) a critical section that must be protected against the possibility of data corruption? (Assume the processor uses a load/store architecture.)

```
Data types: int8_t, int16_t, int32_t, int64_t
CPU word size: 8 bits, 16 bits, 32 bits
```

7. The function shown below causes run-time errors when called by more than one thread in a multithreaded application. Explain the cause of the problem, and then modify the function to correct the problem without changing the function's parameter list or its return value.

```
int ExtractWords(char *sentence, char *words[])
{
char *word;
int count;
count = 0;
word = sentence;
for (;;)
        {
        word = strtok(word, ",;.?!");
        if (!word) break;
        words[count++] = word;
        word = NULL;
        }
return count;
}
```

8. Which of the following functions are thread-safe?
   (a) `int f1(int select)`
   ```
        {
        static const int a[] = {-2, -1, 0, +1, +2} ;
        ...
        return a[select] ;
        }
   ```

   (b) `char *f2(char *b)`
   ```
        {
        static char a[100] ;
        strcpy(a, b) ;
        return a ;
        }
   ```

   (c) `long long int f3(void)`
   ```
        {
        static long long int x = 0 ;
        return ++x ;
        }
   ```

   (d) `unsigned f4(unsigned a, unsigned b)`
   ```
        {
        if (a == 0) return 0 ;
        if (a == 1) return b ;
        return f4(a - 1, b) ;
        }
   ```

9. The original strtok function shown in Figure 12-3 is not thread-safe. Design a thread-safe version that protects each of its critical sections by disabling interrupts only where absolutely necessary.

10. Design a thread-safe version of the following function without adding code to protect its critical sections.

```
double AvgSoFar(double value)
{
static double total = 0.0 ;
static int count = 0 ;
return (total += value) / ++count ;
}
```

C H A P T E R   1 3

System Initialization

Desktop application programmers never have to worry about *system* initialization. The vast majority of application programs are loaded and executed by some sort of operating system that has already initialized the system during the boot process to provide an appropriate run-time environment. Embedded applications, however, almost always start from a power-off condition. When power is applied, the processor has no stack, no heap, no interrupt system, and no timer. In addition, the I/O devices have to be initialized and the initial values of variables must be copied from ROM to RAM.

Much of what has to be done to get up and running is hardware specific. That is, it varies according to the type of CPU, the amount and type of memory, and the kind of I/O devices that are attached. It can also be software-specific, in the sense that each compiler and/or real-time kernel may impose its own peculiar requirements regarding how memory should be organized, how the interrupt system should be configured, and the preferred rate of timer ticks.

This chapter cannot possibly cover every possible variation of how initialization can or should be done; it *does* cover how it might be done for programs written in C using IAR Systems Embedded Workbench and compiled to run on the Texas Instruments LM3S811—a microcontroller (MCU) based on the ARM Cortex-M3 processor. Beyond that, this chapter will illustrate how some of the I/O devices (including the interrupt controller and programmable timer) would be programmed.

The order of events in which initialization proceeds is not necessarily the same as that presented here. In general, however, CPU initialization is usually first, and enabling of the interrupt system is usually last.

13.1 MEMORY LAYOUT

A good starting point for designing initialization code is to consider what the compiler expects. Most applications partition memory into five regions: program code (called "text"), initialized statics (called "data"), uninitialized statics (called "bss"), the stack, and the heap. Although the relative positions of these regions may vary, the initial vector table and code must be located in nonvolatile memory (such as flash EPROM) with the vector table positioned at address 0 and everything else in read/write memory (RAM) (Figure 13-1).

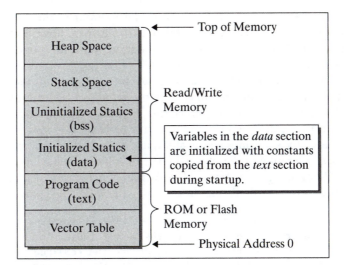

FIGURE 13-1   Memory organization for an embedded C program.

13.2 THE CPU AND VECTOR TABLE

When power is first applied, the ARM Cortex-M3 processor automatically loads the stack pointer (R13) from address 0 (the first vector table entry) and the program counter (R15) from address 4 (the second vector table entry). Then execution begins. Thus the initial vector table and the code that it points to must be kept in nonvolatile memory that will not lose its content when power is removed.

The stack may be declared as an array of 32-bit unsigned longs. Since the first push will be stored at the address given by SP-4, SP should be initialized to the address of the 32-bit word located just after the last entry in the array. Thus if the array is declared as [1]:

```
static unsigned long pulStack[128] @ ".noinit" ;
```

then the initial value for SP may be specified as &stack[128]. To avoid having two places where the size of the stack (128) is specified, the same initial value may be specified as:

```
((unsigned long) &pulStack[0]) + sizeof(pulStack)
```

or simplified as:

```
(unsigned long) pulStack + sizeof(pulStack)
```

---

[1] The unusual text at the end of the line starting with the "at" sign (@) is used in IAR's Embedded Workbench to tell the compiler that this variable should not be included among the statics that are initialized by the startup code executed just before entering function main as discussed in Section 13.3.2.

The value loaded into the program counter is the entry point address of a *startup* function whose responsibility is to perform any additional initialization as needed and then to branch to the entry point of function main to start the application.

There are two other entries in the vector table that must have initial values before execution begins. Since nonmaskable interrupts and hard faults cannot be disabled, handlers for these two exceptions must already exist and their entry point addresses stored as the next two entries in the vector table at addresses 8 and 12, respectively. All other interrupts are initially disabled and all interrupt priorities are at their default values. At a minimum therefore, the vector table must have its first four entries populated. When using IAR Embedded Workbench, the vector table can be created in C and forced to be located at address 0 using the following code:

```
//**********************************************************************************
// A union that describes the entries of the vector table. The union is needed
// since the first entry is the stack pointer and the remainder are function pointers.
//**********************************************************************************
typedef union
        {
        void (*pfnHandler)(void);
        unsigned long ulPtr;
        } uVectorEntry;


//**********************************************************************************
// The vector table. Note that the proper constructs must be placed on
// this to ensure that it ends up at physical address 0x0000.0000.
//**********************************************************************************
__root const uVectorEntry __vector_table[] @ ".intvec" =
        {
        {.ulPtr = (unsigned long) pulStack + sizeof(pulStack)}, // Initial SP
        __iar_program_start,                                    // Initial PC
        NmiSR,                                                  // The NMI handler
        FaultISR,                                               // The hard fault handler
        ...
```

The declaration of the table uses a few C language extensions that are supported by the IAR Embedded Workbench compiler:

1. The text "__root" that appears at the beginning of the declaration prevents the linker from removing the variable even though the identifier "__vector_table" is never referenced by name anywhere else in the program.
2. The text **@ ".intvec"** causes the linker to locate the vector table starting at address 0.
3. The first entry in the table uses a C99 feature called a *designated initializer*. It is an expression enclosed in curly braces; the ".ulPtr =" text at the beginning of the expression tells the compiler that this value is to be assigned to the union member named ulPtr.

The first stack push stores a value into address SP-4, thus the expression "(unsigned long) pulStack + sizeof(pulStack)" yields the address of the 32-bit word located immediately above the stack.

13.3 C RUN-TIME ENVIRONMENT

Once the processor is up and running but *before* execution enters function main, the startup function must initialize the content of the initialized statics (data) and uninitialized statics (bss) that are located in read/write memory.

13.3.1 Copying Initial Values from Nonvolatile Memory into the Data Region

All static variables (which implicitly include all global variables) must be initialized by the startup function. Those statics whose initial values were specified in their declaration reside as a single contiguous group in the "data" region; the constants that are their initial values reside as a corresponding but separate contiguous group in the text region of nonvolatile memory. Before entering function main, the startup function must copy these constants into their respective destinations in the data region of read/ write memory. The startup function used by programs created with the IAR Embedded Workbench IDE looks like the following[2]:

```
unsigned long *pulSrc, *pulDest, *pulEnd;

//
// Copy the data segment initializers from flash to SRAM.
//
pulSrc = __segment_begin("DATA_ID") ;
pulDest = __segment_begin("DATA_I") ;
pulEnd = __segment_end("DATA_I") ;
while(pulDest < pulEnd)
    {
    *pulDest++ = *pulSrc++;
    }
```

In addition to initializing the data section by copying from nonvolatile memory, it may also be desirable on some MCUs to copy the program code to read/write memory because the access time for nonvolatile memory is often somewhat slower than that for read/write memory.

13.3.2 Zeroing Uninitialized Statics

There is a convention in C that uninitialized statics in the bss region of memory are filled with zeroes during startup. This region includes all static objects that were declared without specifying an initial value. Since some programs contain code that depends on this

---

[2] "__segment_begin()" and "__segment_end()" are used in IAR's Embedded Workbench to provide the address of the first byte and byte after, respectively, of the segment specified by the argument; "DATA_ID" refers to the constants in nonvolatile memory that are the initial values of the initialized statics (data); "DATA_I" refers to the segment in read/write memory where the initialized statics reside.

feature, it is a necessary part of initializing the C run-time environment. Programs created with the IAR Embedded Workbench IDE include the following code to do this[3]:

```
unsigned long *pulDest, *pulEnd;


//
// Zero fill the bss segment.
//
pulDest = __segment_begin("DATA_Z");
pulEnd = __segment_end("DATA_Z");
while(pulDest < pulEnd)
    {
    *pulDest++ = 0;
    }
```

13.3.3 Setting Up a Heap

The heap is traditionally implemented as a linked list of dynamic memory blocks. Normally, the list should initially contain a single free block corresponding to the entire heap space. When memory is to be allocated, the list is searched to find a block large enough to satisfy the request. The search may use a first-fit or best-fit algorithm. If no block large enough is found, failure is indicated by returning a NULL pointer to the requestor. Otherwise, the selected block is split into two blocks, one that is allocated and given to the requestor and another that holds the remaining free space.

The code that manages the heap is provided as a set of library routines. Either they will be part of the regular C run-time library, or you may replace them with your own.

It is possible in many embedded applications to avoid using dynamic memory entirely and thus save the code space required to manage the heap. Having a heap, however, is usually convenient and sometimes required by the real-time kernel for the data structures that are needed to create a thread, queue, semaphore, or mutex. In many cases this may be the only use of the heap with no need to provide a function to release allocated blocks. This not only completely eliminates the possibility of heap fragmentation, but also reduces the size of the code considerably since there is no need to recombine adjacent free blocks when memory is released.

Embedded applications that must be able to occasionally release heap space must be designed to avoid heap fragmentation. A common strategy is to round up the size of each request so that all allocated blocks are of the same size, or to create wrapper functions that divide the heap into a set of allocation pools, each with a fixed block size. Although blocks may be released, these techniques do prevent fragmentation, and also eliminate the need to recombine adjacent free blocks, thus simplifying and improving the speed of the code.

For these reasons, you may find that there is more than one version of the heap library,[4] or that it may be compiled with different configuration options.

---

[3] "DATA_Z" refers to the segment in read/write memory where the uninitialized statics reside.

[4] The FreeRTOS kernel includes source code for three different sets of heap functions. As described above, one eliminates the function that releases memory, a second provides this function but does not combine adjacent free blocks, and the third is simply a wrapper for the standard C run-time library functions malloc and free.

13.4 SYSTEM TIMER

Almost any embedded application will require some sort of system timer. Timers are used to measure elapsed time, to keep track of the actual time of day and date, to schedule threads, and for other purposes. Timers are so common in embedded applications that almost every MCU includes the timer hardware on the same chip.

The Cortex-M3 includes a "SysTick" timer. It is a counter that can be programmed to an initial value called the "reload value." The counter counts down by one on each cycle of the CPU clock. When it reaches zero, it triggers a SysTick interrupt and automatically reloads the counter to start the next countdown sequence. Multithreaded systems use the SysTick counter to provide a periodic interrupt and program the counter's reload value to create interrupts at a rate that is typically 1,000 interrupts/sec.

Since the CPU clock can be programmed to operate at different rates, the reload value is a function of the CPU clock rate:

```
#define TICK_RATE_HZ    1000        // 1000 interrupts/sec (1 kHz)
#define CPU_CLOCK_HZ    6000000     // default core clock is 6 MHz
#define SYST_RVR        0xE000E014 // Adrs of SysTick Reload Value Register

*((uint32_t *) SYST_RVR) = ( CPU_CLOCK_HZ / TICK_RATE_HZ ) - 1  ;
```

Once the reload value has been set, the next step is to configure the SysTick Control and Status Register to tell the counter which clock source to use, to enable SysTick interrupts, and to turn on the counter.

```
#define SYST_CSR        0xE000E010 // Adrs of SysTick Control & Status Registers
#define SYSTICK_CLK     0x00000004 // Use core clock to drive SysTick counter
#define SYSTICK_INT     0x00000002 // Enable SysTick interrupt generation
#define SYSTICK_ENABLE 0x00000001 // Enables the SysTick counter

*((uint32_t *) SYST_CSR) = SYSTICK_CLK | SYSTICK_INT | SYSTICK_ENABLE ;
```

We also need to configure the relevant register in the nested vector interrupt controller (NVIC) to set the interrupt priority level of the SysTick interrupt:

```
#define NVIC_SHPR         0xE000ED18 // Adrs of System Handler Priority Registers
#define SYSTICK_EXC_NMBR 15         // Exception number of SysTick interrupt
#define SYSTICK_PRIORITY 250        // Typically a low priority (high number)

((uint8_t *) NVIC_SHPR)[SYSTICK_EXC_NMBR - 4] = SYSTICK_PRIORITY ;
```

The handler for SysTick interrupts typically increments a variable that keeps track of the number of SysTick interrupts that have occurred. If they are programmed to occur 1,000 times/sec, then the counter will record the number of milliseconds (0.001 sec) that have elapsed.

13.5 OTHER PERIPHERAL DEVICES

Interrupt handlers for Cortex-M3 may be written as normal C functions. Besides the SysTick handler, you may need to write a handler for a device that inputs or outputs data. For an input device, the handler normally reads the data from the device and enters it into an associated queue. An interrupt from an output device signals the completion of the previous output command, thus its handler would normally check an output queue to see if there is more data to be sent to the device. If more output data is available, it would be removed from the queue and sent.

Installing a handler is simply a matter of storing its entry point address at the appropriate position in the vector table. Some of the vector table entry positions are predefined by the Cortex-M3 architecture, while others depend on what peripheral devices are available in a specific implementation and would have to be found in documentation for the MCU.

There are several good source code examples available that show how to initialize a particular peripheral device, and how to implement an interrupt handler for it. These examples are found in the laboratory assignments on the Companion Website at www.pearsonhighered.com/lewis and in the source code of the Stellaris Peripheral Driver Library and the FreeRTOS real-time kernel used by those assignments.

Answers to Selected Problems

CHAPTER 1

Problem 9.	(c) 32 bits
Problem 10.	(a) C
Problem 11.	(d) None of these

CHAPTER 2

Problem 3a.	−115
Problem 4a.	45
Problem 5b.	5DC
Problem 6a.	.1110
Problem 7c.	13.34
Problem 8a.	1111 1010 . 1100 1110
Problem 10.	10011100
Problem 12c.	0111.1111
Problem 20a.	10101010, overflow
Problem 26.	0
Problem 31.	False

CHAPTER 3

Problem 1.	Shift right by 3 bits
Problem 3.	000000.000001
Problem 7.	Power of 2
Problem 8.	Most significant 32 bits

CHAPTER 4

Problem 1a.	False
Problem 1i.	False
Problem 2a.	1
Problem 3a.	255
Problem 5c.	00FF
Problem 11c.	−6
Problem 11i.	1

Problem 11l.	1
Problem 11m.	−1
Problem 11q.	13
Problem 13e.	11110000
Problem 13f.	00000000
Problem 14b.	0
Problem 16d.	x = x << (n + 2)
Problem 17a.	abcd1fgh
Problem 22.	A63F

CHAPTER 5

Problem 2.	(b) CPU
Problem 3c.	32
Problem 4f.	Execute Phase
Problem 6.	Execute Phase
Problem 11d.	1
Problem 13.	(b) The most significant byte
Problem 16.	(b) Big-endian numbering
Problem 17.	(a) From least to most significant bit, starting at 0
Problem 18a.	101
Problem 21.	(c) A 3-operand instruction format
Problem 23.	3
Problem 27.	(b) The address of the memory location

CHAPTER 6

Problem 1.	12344	
Problem 5b.	2	
Problem 7a.	LDR	R0,=100
	STR	R0,u32
Problem 7l.	LDR	R0,=-1
	STRD	R0,R0,s64

Problem 7o.	LDR	R0,u32
	LDR	R1,=0
	STRD	R0,R1,u64
Problem 8a.	LDR	R0,s64
	LDRB	R1,s8
	ADD	R0,R0,R1
	STR	R0,s32
Problem 8e.	LDR	R0,pp16
	LDR	R0,[R0]
	LDR	R1,=0
	STR	R1,[R0,#2]

CHAPTER 7

Problem 2a.	LDR	R0,x
	LDR	R1,y
	CMP	R0,R1
	BGE	Else
	LDR	R0,=6
	STR	R0,z
	B	EndIf
Else:	LDR	R0,x
	STR	R0,z
EndIf:		
Problem 5b.	LDR	R0,x
	CMN	R0,#10
	BLE	EndIf
	CMP	R0,#10
	BLT	L1
EndIf:		
Problem 6b.	LDRB	R0,c
	BL	f2
Problem 6e.	LDR	R0,=100
	ADR	R1,n32
	BL	foo
	STRD	R0,R1,n64

CHAPTER 8

Problem 1.	(c) DMA
Problem 4.	(c) Maximum memory bandwidth
Problem 6a.	1
Problem 9.	(a), (b), and (c)
Problem 12.	(a) A hard-coded constant built into the CPU
Problem 14.	(b) Tail-chaining
Problem 15.	(c) Late arrival processing

CHAPTER 9

Problem 1.	(a) Disabling interrupts
Problem 4.	(c) If floating-point operations are used in more than one thread
Problem 6.	(a) Only by an explicit call to a kernel function
Problem 8.	(b) Preemptive kernel
Problem 12.	(b) Non-preemptive (cooperative)
Problem 15.	1

CHAPTER 10

Problem 1.	(b) The low-priority thread
Problem 5.	(a) The priority inheritance protocol
Problem 11c.	The minimum number of threads is 2; the minimum number of shared resources is 2.
Problem 13.	(a) Priority ceiling protocol
Problem 16.	(d) Are triggered by events that occur most frequently

CHAPTER 11

Problem 2. int *AddressOfCopy(int value)
```
{
    static int copy ;
    copy = value ;
    return&copy ;
}
```

Problem 3a. Automatic, register, dynamic, alloca, VSAs

Problem 3h. Dynamic

Problem 3m. None of these

Problem 7. 1st printf: 1
2nd printf: 1
3rd printf: 1
4th printf: 2

Problem 12. static int s2 = s1 + 1 ;
if (r1 == 0) return &r1 ;

CHAPTER 12

Problem 1g. False

Problem 4. (c), (d), and (e)

Problem 8. (a) and (d)

Index